GENERAL EQUILIBRIUM THEORY

GENERAL EQUILIBRIUM THEORY

An Introduction

ROSS M. STARR

University of California, San Diego

CAMBRIDGE
UNIVERSITY PRESS

PUBLISHED BY THE PRESS SYNDICATE OF THE UNIVERSITY OF CAMBRIDGE
The Pitt Building, Trumpington Street, Cambridge CB2 1RP, United Kingdom

CAMBRIDGE UNIVERSITY PRESS
The Edinburgh Building, Cambridge CB2 2RU, United Kingdom
40 West 20th Street, New York, NY 10011-4211, USA
10 Stamford Road, Oakleigh, Melbourne 3166, Australia

First published 1997

Printed in the United States of America

Typeset in Times Roman

Library of Congress Cataloging-in-Publication Data
Starr, Ross M.
General equilibrium theory : an introduction / Ross M. Starr.
p.   cm.
Includes bibliographical references (p.   ).
ISBN 0 521 56414 X. – ISBN 0 521 56473 5 (pbk.)
1. Equilibrium (Economics)   2. Economics, Mathematical.
I. Title.
HB145.SB   1997
330′.01′51 – dc20   96-43842
                                              CIP

*A catalog record for this book is available from
the British Library*

ISBN 0 521 56414 X hardback
ISBN 0 521 56473 5 paperback

To Susan

Contents

List of illustrations   *page* xi
Foreword   xiii
Preface   xix
Table of notation   xxi

A   Getting started   **1**
1   Concept and history of general equilibrium theory   3
 1.1   Partial and general equilibrium: Development of the field   3
 1.2   An elementary general equilibrium model – The Robinson
   Crusoe economy   9
 1.3   The Edgeworth box   20
 1.4   A first approach: Existence of general equilibrium in an
   economy with an excess demand function   31
 1.5   Bibliographic note   38
   Exercises   38
2   Mathematics   41
 2.1   Set theory   41
 2.2   Quasi-orderings   44
 2.3   Functions   45
 2.4 R^N: Real N-dimensional Euclidean space   46
 2.5   Continuous functions   53
 2.6   Convexity   55
 2.7   Brouwer Fixed-Point Theorem   57
 2.8   Separation theorems   63
 2.9   Bibliographic Note   65
   Exercises   66
3   Prices and commodities   69
 3.1   The market, commodities, and prices   69
 3.2   Bibliographic note   70
   Exercise   70

B An economy with bounded production technology, supply and demand functions   **71**

4 Production with bounded firm technology   73
   4.1 Firms and production technology   73
   4.2 The form of production technology   74
   4.3 Strictly convex production technology   75
   4.4 Attainable production plans   78
   4.5 Bibliographic note   79
        Exercises   79
5 Households   80
   5.1 The structure of household consumption sets and preferences 80
   5.2 Representation of $\succsim_i$: Construction of a continuous utility function   84
   5.3 Choice and boundedness of budget sets, $\tilde{B}^i(p)$ 87
   5.4 Demand behavior under strict convexity   90
   5.5 Bibliographic note   92
        Exercises   93
6 A market economy   96
   6.1 Firms, profits, and household income   96
   6.2 Excess demand and Walras' Law   97
   6.3 Bibliographic note   99
        Exercises   99
7 General equilibrium of the market economy with an excess demand function   100
   7.1 Existence of equilibrium   100
   7.2 Bibliographic note   104
        Exercises   104
C An economy with unbounded production technology, supply and demand functions   **109**

8 Theory of production: The unbounded technology case   111
   8.1 Unbounded production technology   111
   8.2 Boundedness of the attainable set   112
   8.3 An artificially bounded supply function   115
   8.4 Bibliographic note   118
        Exercises   119
9 Households: The unbounded technology case   120
   9.1 Households   120
   9.2 Choice in an unbounded budget set   120
   9.3 Demand behavior under strict convexity   122
   9.4 Bibliographic note   125
        Exercise   125

10	A market economy: The unbounded technology case	126
	10.1 Firms and households	126
	10.2 Profits	126
	10.3 Household income	127
	10.4 Excess demand and Walras' Law	127
	10.5 Bibliographic note	129
	Exercises	129
11	General equilibrium of the market economy: The unbounded technology case	131
	11.1 General equilibrium	131
	11.2 An artificially restricted economy	132
	11.3 General equilibrium of the unrestricted economy	133
	11.4 The Uzawa Equivalence Theorem	135
	11.5 Bibliographic note	138
	Exercises	138
D	**Welfare economics**	**141**
12	Pareto efficiency and competitive equilibrium	143
	12.1 Pareto efficiency	143
	12.2 First Fundamental Theorem of Welfare Economics	144
	12.3 Second Fundamental Theorem of Welfare Economics	146
	12.4 Bibliographic note	151
	Exercises	151
E	**Bargaining and equilibrium: The core**	**155**
13	The core of a market economy	157
	13.1 Bargaining and competition	157
	13.2 The core of a pure exchange economy	158
	13.3 The competitive equilibrium allocation is in the core	160
	13.4 Bibliographic note	161
	Exercise	161
14	Convergence of the core of a large economy	162
	14.1 Replication; a large economy	162
	14.2 Equal treatment	163
	14.3 Core convergence in a large economy	165
	14.4 Interpreting the core convergence result	168
	14.5 Bibliographic note	169
	Exercises	170
F	**The scope of markets**	**175**
15	Time and uncertainty: Futures markets	177
	15.1 Introduction	177
	15.2 Time: Futures markets	179
	15.3 Uncertainty – Arrow-Debreu contingent commodity markets	185

	15.4	Uncertainty – Arrow securities markets	190
	15.5	Conclusion – the missing markets	193
	15.6	Bibliographic note	194
		Exercises	194
G	**An economy with supply and demand correspondences**		**197**
16	Mathematics: Analysis of point to set mappings		201
	16.1	Correspondences	201
	16.2	Upper hemicontinuity (also known as upper semicontinuity)	201
	16.3	Lower hemicontinuity (also known as lower semicontinuity)	204
	16.4	Continuous correspondence	206
	16.5	Cartesian product of correspondences	207
	16.6	Optimization subject to constraint: Composition of correspondences; the Maximum Theorem	207
	16.7	Kakutani Fixed-Point Theorem	209
	16.8	Bibliographic note	213
		Exercises	213
17	General equilibrium of the market economy with an excess demand correspondence		215
	17.1	General equilibrium with set-valued supply and demand	215
	17.2	Production with a (weakly) convex production technology	216
	17.3	Households	220
	17.4	The market economy	226
	17.5	The artificially restricted economy	229
	17.6	Existence of competitive equilibrium	230
	17.7	Bibliographic note	232
		Exercises	232
H	**Conclusion**		**235**
18	Summary and conclusion		237
	18.1	Overview and summary	237
	18.2	Bibliographic note	238
		Exercises	238
	Bibliography		241
	Index		247

List of illustrations

1.1	The Robinson Crusoe economy: efficient allocation.	*page* 11
1.2	The Robinson Crusoe economy: equilibrium and disequilibrium.	15
1.3	The Edgeworth box.	21
1.4	The Edgeworth box: bargaining and allocation.	23
1.5	The Edgeworth box: efficient allocation and the contract curve.	26
1.6	The Edgeworth box: disequilibrium.	28
1.7	The Edgeworth box: general equilibrium.	28
1.8	A two-good economy: general equilibrium in production and distribution.	30
2.1	A vector in $\mathbf{R}^2$.	47
2.2	Vector addition.	48
2.3	Convex and nonconvex sets.	56
2.4	The Brouwer Fixed-Point Theorem in $\mathbf{R}$.	57
2.5	An admissibly labeled simplicial subdivision of a simplex.	59
2.6	Sperner's Lemma for $N = 1$.	60
2.7	Bounding and separating hyperplanes for convex sets.	65
4.1	$\mathcal{Y}^j$: Technology set of firm j.	74
4.2	Convex and nonconvex technology sets.	76
5.1	Lexicographic preferences.	83
5.2	Constructing the utility function.	86
7.1	Mapping from P into P.	102
8.1	Bounding firm j's production technology.	116
9.1	Household i's budget sets and demand functions.	124
11.1	The Uzawa Equivalence Theorem.	137
12.1	Supporting an efficient allocation (Theorem 12.2).	147
14.1	Core convergence (Theorem 14.2).	167
14.2	Nonconvex preferences (Exercise 14.5).	172
15.1	Uncertain states of the world: An event tree.	185
G.1	Linear production technology and its supply correspondence.	198
G.2	Preferences for perfect substitutes and the demand correspondence.	199
G.3	Equilibrium in a market with supply and demand correspondences.	200
16.1	A typical correspondence, $\varphi(x) = \{y \mid x - 1 \le y \le x + 1\}$.	202
16.2	Example 16.1 – An upper hemicontinuous correspondence.	203

16.3   Example 16.2 – A correspondence that is not upper hemicontinuous at 0.   204

16.4   Example 16.3 – A lower hemicontinuous correspondence.   205

16.5   Example 16.5 – A continuous correspondence.   206

16.6   The Maximum Problem.   208

16.7   An upper hemicontinuous mapping from an interval (1-simplex) into itself without a fixed point.   210

16.8   An upper hemicontinuous convex-valued mapping from an interval (1-simplex) into itself with a fixed point.   210

16.9   Lemma 16.2 – Approximating an upper hemicontinuous convex-valued correspondence by a continuous function.   211

16.10 Example 16.7 – Applying the Kakutani Fixed-Point Theorem.   213

17.1   Example 17.1 – An upper hemicontinuous, convex-valued supply correspondence.   217

17.2   Example 17.2 – an upper hemicontinuous supply correspondence that is not convex-valued.   218

17.3   Theorem 17.2 – continuity of the budget set showing the construction of y^v.   223

Foreword

The foundations of modern economic general equilibrium theory are contained in a surprisingly short list of references. For primary sources, it is sufficient to master Arrow and Debreu (1954), Arrow (1951), Arrow (1953), and Debreu and Scarf (1963). An even shorter list is comprehensive; Debreu (1959) and Debreu and Scarf (1963) cover the topic admirably. Why should anyone write (or read!) a secondary source, a textbook? Because, unfortunately, this body of material is extremely difficult for most students to read and comprehend. Professor Hahn described Debreu's (1959) book as "very short, but it may well take as long to read as many works three times as long. This is not due to faulty exposition but to the demands rigorous analysis makes on the reader. It is to be hoped that no one will be put off by this, for the ... return ... is very high indeed..." [Hahn (1961)]. Unfortunately, in teaching economic theory we find that many capable students are indeed put off by the mathematical abstraction of the works above. What theorists regard as elegantly terse expression, students may find inaccessible formality. The focus of this textbook is to overcome this barrier and to make this body of work accessible to a wider audience of advanced undergraduates and graduate students in economics.

This book presents the theory of general economic equilibrium incrementally, from elementary to more sophisticated treatments. Chapter 1 presents a nontechnical introduction to the Robinson Crusoe and Edgeworth box models of general equilibrium and Pareto efficiency using differential calculus (the only portion of the book in which calculus is used). Chapter 1 includes a brief introduction to the use of the Brouwer Fixed-Point Theorem to prove the existence of general equilibrium. Chapter 2 presents a summary of the mathematics used throughout the rest of the book: analysis and convexity in $\mathbf{R}^N$, separation theorems, and the Brouwer Fixed-Point Theorem (including a combinatorial proof of the Brouwer Theorem on the simplex). Although it is not a substitute for a course in real analysis, Chapter 2 does provide a useful summary and presents the mathematical issues important to economic theory that are sometimes omitted from a real analysis course.

Like all scientific theories, the theory of general economic equilibrium is a family of "if–then" statements: "If the world looks like this family of assumptions, then here's what the outcome will be." The unifying view of firms and households throughout microeconomic theory is to characterize their behavior as maximization of a criterion function (profit or utility) subject to constraint.

A technical issue that persistently arises is the possibility that those maxima may not exist if constraint sets are unbounded (a budget constraint where some prices are nil or a technology constraint where outputs are limited only by available inputs). When the price of a desirable good is zero, there may be no well-defined value for the demand function at those prices, since the quantity demanded will be arbitrarily large. Nevertheless, it is important that we be able to deal with free goods (zero prices). The classic means of dealing with this issue [Arrow and Debreu (1954)] is to recognize that attainable outputs of the economy are bounded. It is then possible to impose *the modeler's* bounds on individual firms' supplies and households' demands (bounds slightly larger than the bounds naturally arising from the limited production possibilities of the real economy). The economy with modeler-bounded individual opportunities has well-defined maxima for firms and households.[1] In equilibrium, the bounds are not binding constraints. The bounds can be deleted and the equilibrium prices of the bounded economy are equilibrium prices of the original economy described without the modeler's bound on individual firm and household behavior.

Part B presents the special case in which technology really is bounded. Here the bounds are not exogenously imposed by the modeler but are supposed to represent the underlying technology. Chapter 4 introduces most of the theory of the firm used throughout the book. Chapter 5 introduces most of the theory of the household (consumer), including derivation of a continuous utility function from the household preference ordering. Chapters 6 and 7 develop Walras' Law and the existence of general equilibrium.

Part C generalizes the results of Part B to the case of unbounded technology. We prove in Chapter 8 that the set of attainable outputs is bounded. In Chapters 8 and 9 we introduce the modeler's bound on the opportunity sets of firms and households – a bound tight enough that maximizing behavior is well defined,

---

[1] This approach to solving the problem of ill-defined maxima appears completely wrong-headed! The concept of decentralized market allocation using the price system is that *prices* (not the economic modeler) should communicate scarcity and resource constraints to firms and households. Here is the strategy of proof: Find a general equilibrium in the model of the economy where firms and households are subject to the *modeler's* bounds. In equilibrium, the bounds are not binding constraints. The bounds can be deleted and the equilibrium prices of the bounded economy are equilibrium prices of the economy described without the modeler's bound on individual firm and household behavior.

but loose enough that all attainable outputs are (strictly) included in their opportunity sets. In Chapter 10 we develop the Walras' Law. In Chapter 11 we prove the existence of general equilibrium in the artificially bounded economy created in Chapters 8 and 9. That economy is an example of the bounded model of Part B, so the existence of general equilibrium in the artificially bounded economy is merely an application of the existence theorem of Chapter 7 (using the mathematician's trick of reducing the current problem to one previously solved). But an equilibrium is necessarily attainable; the constraint that firm and household behavior lie in the bounded set is not binding in equilibrium. The artificial constraint of modeler-bounded opportunity sets can be removed, and the prices and allocations constitute a general equilibrium for the unconstrained economy. That is the existence of general equilibrium result of Chapter 11.

Part D, Chapter 12, presents the classic fundamental theorems of welfare economics, which describe the relationship of general equilibrium to efficient allocation. Part E presents the theory of the core of a market economy, the modern counterpart to the Edgeworth box. This includes, in Chapter 14, proof of the classic result that in a large economy individual economic agents have no significant bargaining power, so that a competitive price-taking allocation is sustainable. Part F introduces futures markets over time and uncertainty.

Throughout Chapters 3 through 11, we use strict convexity of tastes and technology to ensure point-valued demands and supplies. That treatment excludes the set-valued supply and demand behavior that can arise from perfect substitutes in consumption or from linear production technologies. In Part G we generalize those results to the case of set-valued demands and supplies. Chapter 16 introduces the mathematics of correspondences: point to set mappings. Particularly important in this setting are the continuity concepts and the Kakutani Fixed-Point Theorem. Chapter 17 presents the economic model of firms, households, the market economy, and general equilibrium with (upper hemi-)continuous, convex, set-valued supply and demand.

The careful reader will note that the outline above includes four developments of demand, supply, excess demand, and existence of general equilibrium. Repetition aids comprehension, but isn't that overdoing it? For advanced undergraduates in economics, typically the answer is "no." They generally benefit from seeing the ideas developed in a simple and then a more complex context. For advanced graduate students in economic theory, the answer is probably "yes." These students will want to choose to avoid some repetition to achieve the most complete and general treatment of these classic issues.

How should the reader/student make use of this material without wasting time and attention?

A typical one-semester advanced undergraduate course in mathematical general equilibrium theory would include Chapters 1 through 7 and Chapter 12. A two-semester course would cover the whole book in order, with the possible omission of Chapters 16 and 17. A several-week segment on general equilibrium in the graduate core microeconomic theory course would include Chapters 4–7 and 12–15. A one-semester graduate introduction to general equilibrium theory would include Chapters 2–5, a choice of Chapters 8–11 *or* 16 and 17, and Chapters 12–15.

What portions of the book can be omitted without loss of continuity? Which parts are essential?

Chapter 1 introduces Robinson Crusoe and the Edgeworth box. Chapter 1 is intended to introduce the concepts of general equilibrium and Pareto efficiency in a simple tractable context. The well-prepared student can skip this material without loss of continuity.

Proofs are provided for most of the mathematical results in the two pure mathematics chapters (2 and 16). The proofs are there because mathematical theory necessarily involves the understanding and development of mathematical results. Nevertheless, the student can – without loss of continuity – skip the proofs in these chapters; only an understanding of the definitions and results is essential. Conversely, the student unfamiliar with real analysis will want to supplement the material in Chapter 2 with a sound text in real analysis such as Bartle (1976), Bartle and Sherbert (1992), or Rudin (1976).

Chapters 4 and 5 which introduce the firm and the household, cannot easily be omitted.

Chapters 6 and 7 present Walras' Law and equilibrium in the market economy with bounded technology. The substance of these chapters is repeated in Chapters 10 and 11 in the setting of an economy with unbounded production technology. The student who loathes repetition may wish to skip Chapters 6 and 7 and go on to Chapters 8–11 (for the point-valued case) or to Chapters 16 and 17 (for the most general and difficult, set-valued, case).

The student who has completed Part B can, without loss of continuity, skip Part C (Chapters 8 to 11). The treatment in Part C, however, significantly generalizes that of Part B.

Welfare economics – the relationship of equilibrium to efficiency – is a cornerstone of microeconomic theory that recurs throughout the book. Most readers will want to complete Chapter 12.

Parts E, F, and G are virtually independent of one another. They can be read in any order or combination.

Notation

Vectors, coordinates. Most variables treated in this book are vectors in $\mathbf{R}^N$, real N-dimensional space. For $x \in \mathbf{R}^N$, we will typically denote the coordinates of x by subscripts. Thus,

$$x = (x_1, x_2, x_3, \ldots, x_{N-1}, x_N).$$

We will generally designate ownership or affiliation by superscripts (with rare exceptions). Thus, x^h will be household h's consumption vector and y^j will be firm j's production vector.

Vector inequalities. For two N-dimensional vectors, x and $y \in \mathbf{R}^N$, inequalities can be read in the following ways: $x \geq y$ means that for all $k = 1, 2, \ldots, N$, $x_k \geq y_k$; the weak inequality holds coordinatewise. $x \gg y$ means that for all $k = 1, 2, \ldots, N$, $x_k > y_k$; a strict inequality holds coordinatewise.

Preface

In June of 1993 a remarkable birthday party took place at CORE (Center for Operations Research and Econometrics) of the Université Catholique de Louvain in Louvain-la-neuve, Belgium. The gathering celebrated the fortieth anniversary of one of the great achievements of modern economic theory: the mathematical theory of general economic equilibrium. For several days and nights, hundreds of professors, researchers, and students from around the world presented papers, discussions, and reminiscences of the specialty they had pursued for years. At the center of the celebration were the modern founders of the field: Professors Kenneth Arrow (Nobel laureate), Gerard Debreu (Nobel laureate), and Lionel McKenzie.

This book presents the cause of that celebration, the field of mathematical general equilibrium theory. The approach of the field is revolutionary: It fundamentally changes your way of thinking. Once you see things this way, it is hard to conceive of them otherwise.

This book reflects the experience of students at Yale University, University of California at Davis, University of California at San Diego, and the Economics Training Center of the People's University of China (Renda) in Beijing. They deserve my thanks for their patience, the stimulus they provided for this book, and their contributions to it. A number of students and colleagues have reviewed portions of the manuscript. I owe thanks to Manfred Nermuth for critical advice and to Nelson Altamirano, Elena Bisagni, Peter Reinhard Hansen, Dong Heon Kim, Bernhard Lamel, Martin Meurers, Elena Pesavento, and Heather Rose who helped by catching typographical and technical errors. Cameron Odgers discovered more substantial oversights. Remaining errors are my responsibility. Illustrations were prepared by Nic Paget-Clarke.

It is a pleasure to acknowledge two very special debts. My wife Susan has lived with this book as long as I have; she is an unfailing source of strength. My friend and mentor Kenneth Arrow is the intellectual father of generations of students; it is an honor to be counted among them. This volume is intended to further communicate some of his contributions.

Ross M. Starr
La Jolla, California
June 1996

Table of notation

∀   "for all"

\#   denotes number of elements in a set

∃   "there exists"

∋   "such that," or "includes as an element"

<   "less than"

=   "equals"

>   "greater than"

≤   "less than or equal to," applies coordinatewise to vectors

$\succsim$ quasi-order symbol

$\succsim_i$ preferred or indifferent by household i's preferences

$\precsim_i$ inferior or indifferent by household i's preferences

$\succ_i$ strictly preferred by household i's preferences

$\prec_i$ strictly inferior by household i's preferences

∞   infinity, without bound

→   approaches as a limit

≥   "greater than or equal to," applies coordinatewise to vectors

∂   partial derivative

·, ·   space holder for argument of a function

·   raised dot, denotes product or scalar product

×   denotes Cartesian product (when placed between the names of two sets)

≠   is not equal to

≡   is identically (or by definition) equal to

$|, \|$ denotes length measure, written as $|x|$ or $\|x\|$

∩   set intersection

Δ   capital Greek delta, denotes closed ball of radius C (space of possible excess demands, Chapter 17)

∪   set union

⊄   is not a subset of

φ   empty set, null set

Φ	capital Greek phi, denotes price and quantity adjustment correspondence from the set $\Delta \times P$ into itself (Chapter 17)
Γ^i	set of preferred net trades for households of type i (Chapter 14)
Γ	convex hull over all household types i of the sets Γ^i, aggregate average preferred net trade set (Chapter 14)
$\subset, \subseteq$	set inclusion, subset
$\in$	set inclusion, is an element of
$\notin$	is not an element of
ν	Greek nu, running index on sequences
Π	capital Greek pi, denotes multiple product
$\pi^j(p)$	profits of firm j at prices p based on production technology Y^j (Y^j may be unbounded)
$\tilde{\pi}^j(p)$	profits of firm j at prices p based on (bounded) production technology $\mathcal{Y}^j$ or $\tilde{Y}^j$
ρ	price adjustment mapping from Δ to P (Chapter 17)
$\Leftrightarrow$	"if and only if," denotes a necessary and sufficient condition
$\sum$	capital Greek sigma, denotes repeated summation
$\{\}$	braces or curly brackets, denote a set or an algebraic quantity
$[\,]$	bracket, denotes algebraic quantity
$(\,)$	parentheses, denotes algebraic quantity
$+$	plus sign, denotes scalar, vector, or set addition
$-$	minus sign, denotes scalar, vector, or set subtraction
$A^i(x)$	upper contour set, set of points in X^i preferred or indifferent to x
$B^i(p)$	budget set of household i at prices p
$\tilde{B}^i(p)$	bounded budget set of household i at prices p
c	large positive real number, chosen to exceed the Euclidean length of any attainable production or consumption bundle, upper bound on length of elements in $\tilde{Y}^j$, $\tilde{B}^i(p)$
C	very large positive real number, upper bound on length of elements in Δ, strict upper bound on Euclidean length of excess demands in $\tilde{Z}(p)$
$D^i(p)$	demand function (or correspondence – Chapter 17) of household i evaluated at p
$\tilde{D}^i(p)$	bounded demand function (or correspondence – Chapter 17) of household i at p
$f(\,)$	typical functional notation
F	set of firms (finite)
$G^i(x)$	lower contour set, set of elements of X^i inferior or indifferent to x under i's preferences
h, i	representative households, elements of H
H	set of households (finite)
j	representative firm, element of F

k	representative commodity, $k = 1, 2, \ldots, N$
$M^i(p)$	value of budget of household i at prices p in an economy with technology sets Y^j
$\tilde{M}^i(p)$	value of budget of household i at prices p in an economy with technology sets $\mathcal{Y}^j$ or $\tilde{Y}^j$
N	number of commodities, finite positive integer
n	running index on a sequence or commodities, $n = 1, 2, 3, \ldots$
p	price vector
P	price space, unit simplex in $\mathbf{R}^N$
q	running index on individuals in a replica economy (Chapter 14)
Q	number of replications in a replica economy (Chapter 14)
$\mathbf{R}$	set of real numbers
$\mathbf{R}^N$	real N-dimensional Euclidean space
$\mathbf{R}^N_+$	nonnegative quadrant (orthant) of $\mathbf{R}^N$
$\mathbf{R}^N_-$	nonpositive quadrant (orthant) of $\mathbf{R}^N$
S	N-simplex
S, T	representative sets
$S^j(p)$	supply function (or correspondence – Chapter 17) of firm j based on technology set Y^j
$\tilde{S}^j(p)$	supply function (or correspondence – Chapter 17) of firm j based on (bounded) technology set $\mathcal{Y}^j$ or $\tilde{Y}^j$
$u^i(\ )$	household i's utility function
x	representative commodity bundle
X^i	household i's possible consumption set
X	aggregate possible consumption set, sum of sets X^i
$\mathcal{Y}^j$	firm j's production technology in a model of bounded firm technology sets (Chapters 4 to 7)
$\mathcal{Y}$	aggregate (sum of individual firm sets) technology set in a model of bounded firm technology sets (Chapters 4 to 7)
Y^j	firm j's technology set (may be unbounded; Chapters 8–11 and 17)
Y	aggregate (possibly unbounded) technology set, sum of Y^js
$\tilde{Y}^j$	firm j's artificially bounded technology set; intersection of Y^j with a closed ball of radius c (Chapters 8–11 and 17)
$\tilde{Y}$	aggregate artificially bounded technology set; sum of $\tilde{Y}^j$s (Chapters 8–11 and 17)
$Z(p)$	excess demand function (or correspondence – Chapter 17) of an unbounded economy (Chapters 8–11 and 17)
$\tilde{Z}(p)$	excess demand function (or correspondence – Chapter 17) of an economy subject to exogenous or artificial bounds on demand and supply functions and correspondences

Part A

Getting started

Two elegantly simple and insightful models of general equilibrium (simultaneous price-guided clearing of several goods markets) are simple enough to introduce in elementary classes and rich enough to provide insights in advanced treatments. These are

- the Robinson Crusoe model, which emphasizes the interaction of the consumption and production sides of the economy and
- the Edgeworth box, which investigates bargaining and equilibrium in the exchange of commodities among consumers.

We present these models in Chapter 1. In addition, the chapter includes a sample proof of existence of market general equilibrium, describing the structure of demand and supply functions needed to establish that prices can adjust so that markets can clear.

Chapter 2 presents an introduction to real analysis, the mathematics needed to pursue the mathematical general equilibrium theory. Two topics that are particularly prominent in the general equilibrium theory get special emphasis: the Brouwer Fixed-Point Theorem and separation theorems for convex sets. We present a combinatorial proof of the Brouwer Theorem, a proof that requires patience and attention more than mathematical sophistication. In addition, we present statements and proofs of the bounding and separating hyperplane theorems, theorems that are essential in the study of welfare economics (Chapter 12) and the core of an economy (Chapters 13 and 14).

1

Concept and history of general equilibrium theory

1.1 Partial and general equilibrium: Development of the field

The typical student's first exposure to an economic model consists of crossing supply and demand curves on the blackboard. They lead to a surprisingly definite result. Market prices are determined where the curves cross, at prices characterized by supply equaling demand. This is not merely a mathematical equality, but a stationary position of a dynamic process – the price and quantity adjustments of the market. This is, of course, partial equilibrium, the adjustment of prices so supply equals demand in a single market; the role of other markets and prices are summarized by the qualification, "other things being equal."

The conditions for finding a partial equilibrium are painfully simple. It is just that the supply and demand curves should cross, on the axis if nowhere else. Let p_k be the market price of good k, $S_k(p_k)$ be the supply function, and $D_k(p_k)$ the demand function. Equilibrium occurs at a price p_k^0 where

$$S_k(p_k^0) \geq D_k(p_k^0), \quad \text{with } p_k^0 \geq 0,$$

and

$$p_k^0 = 0 \quad \text{if } S_k(p_k^0) > D_k(p_k^0).$$

That is, supply equals demand in equilibrium, with the exception of free goods, that may be in excess supply at an equilibrium price of zero. The notation here indicates that the market for good k is considered in isolation – only the price of good k is entering into the supply and demand for good k. This practice of isolating the market for each good separately is known as *partial* equilibrium analysis. The notion of isolating the market for good k is summarized by the phrase, "other things being equal," indicating that prices for all other goods are held fixed while considering the market for good k. The partial equilibrium is a powerfully simple technique, allowing us a successful first pass at issues of equilibrium, efficiency, and comparative statics.

3

What's wrong with partial equilibrium? An example may help; let's try the automobile market in 1974. As the 1973 model year ended in August, sales and price projections for U.S. automobile manufacturers in 1974 looked sound and solid. Estimating the demand curves and cost functions for cars in the United States led inescapably to the conclusion of continued profitability and ample sales. In fact, the 1974 model year was the worst in decades for U.S. auto makers and initiated the period of the great decline in their market share as smaller imports, particularly from Japan, sold to consistently larger portions of the U.S. market. What went wrong? Had demand or cost been incorrectly estimated? No, the estimates were sound – as far as they went. But they ignored what they could not foresee: dramatic changes in *other* markets and their effects on the demand for cars. In the course of 1974 gasoline prices quadrupled. Demand for cars, particularly large fuel-hungry Detroit cars, dried up. The gasoline market trashed auto sales in 1974. Interactions across markets are essential to forecasting and understanding economic activity.

When we need to inquire more deeply into the interactions between markets, we relax the assumption of other things being equal and then look at multiple markets simultaneously. Because there are distinctive interactions across markets (e.g., between the price of gasoline and the demand for automobiles), it is important that the equilibrium concept include interactive simultaneous determination of equilibrium prices across markets. The concept can then represent a solution concept for the economy as a whole and not merely for a single market that is artificially isolated. That is the concept of *general* economic equilibrium. General equilibrium for the economy consists of an array of prices for each good, where simultaneously supply equals demand for each good. The prices of cars and of gasoline both adjust so that demand and supply of cars and of gasoline are each equated. This is *general* equilibrium in the sense that it deals with all markets simultaneously and their interactions, rather than a single market in isolation.

Our most elementary model of general equilibrium, developed below, considers the market equilibrium for a Robinson Crusoe (one-person) economy. We investigate this example not because we actually expect a one-person economy to actively use a price system, but because an economy so simple lets us easily analyze its efficient allocations and see directly the workings of the price system in all markets simultaneously. We will go over the Robinson Crusoe model in the next section. The balance of this book is designed to present the next step – a full mathematical model of the economy and its equilibrium price and allocation determination for all markets simultaneously.

General equilibrium analysis has proved essential in modern economics in describing the efficiency and stability of the market mechanism, in macroeconomic analysis, and in providing the logical foundations of economic analysis. One of the essential notions is the view that decentralized market mechanisms promote efficient allocation, a concept investigated in the simple models of Sections 1.2 and 1.3 and more fully in Chapter 12. General equilibrium theory provides the basis for major innovations in modern economic theory and for the full mathematically rigorous confirmation of long-held traditional views in economics.

The economy is in general equilibrium when prices have fully adjusted so that supply equals demand in all markets. Let the goods be $i = 1, \ldots, N$. The demand and supply for good i will depend on the price of good i and on many other prices, so we denote them $D_i(p_1, p_2, \ldots, p_N)$ and $S_i(p_1, \ldots, p_N)$. Prices $p_1^0, p_2^0, \ldots, p_N^0$ are said to constitute general equilibrium prices if simultaneously each market is in equilibrium at the stated prices. That is, for all $i = 1, \ldots, N$,

$$D_i(p_1^0, p_2^0, \ldots, p_N^0) \leq S_i(p_1^0, \ldots, p_N^0), \quad p_i^0 \geq 0,$$

and

$$p_i^0 = 0 \quad \text{for goods } i \text{ such that } D_i(p_1^0, \ldots, p_N^0) < S_i(p_1^0, \ldots, p_N^0).$$

The distinction between general equilibrium and the definition of partial equilibrium presented above is formally in the arguments of the functions D_i and S_i. All prices enter the supply and demand functions for good i, not merely the price of i. That's what makes this a *general* equilibrium. General equilibrium theory consists in studying these equilibria. In the process we will develop fundamental abstract models of the economy and an axiomatic method of analyzing them.

Why are economists interested in general equilibrium? The reason it is called equilibrium is that we expect there are forces in the economy, supply and demand, driving the system to this array of allocations and prices. That's where we expect the economy to end up or to move toward. Equilibrium is the descriptive and predictive principle for the market economist. Furthermore, the desirable efficiency properties of a market economy depend on the economy being in general equilibrium – or moving in that direction. The traditional major questions on equilibrium include:

- existence – the study of conditions under which there is a solution to the equations characterizing market clearing;
- uniqueness – whether there is only one family of prices that clears markets or there are multiple (or infinite) solutions to the market clearing problem;
- stability – whether a price formation mechanism that raises prices of goods in excess demand and reduces those in excess supply will converge to market clearing prices;
- efficiency – welfare economics, the effectiveness of the resource utilization implied at the equilibrium allocation; and

- bargaining – the relation of strategic bargaining solutions to passive price-taking equilibrium.

The treatment in this book, like that of the field, will concentrate on existence, efficiency, and bargaining in characterizing equilibrium.

A market economy poses a tricky puzzle. It is a complex interactive interdependent system subject to intelligent human control, but without central direction. How can this anarchic system operate consistently – let alone successfully? Nevertheless, the notion of decentralized independent decision making is of long standing in market economics. The notion of decentralization is powerful for two reasons. First, the complex interactions of a large and varied economy may be very hard to compute and control correctly in a centralized fashion. Efficient administration may require many separate foci of decision making. Second, decentralization means providing incentives to individual firms and households to operate in a fashion that promotes efficient resource allocation. This represents the long-standing view in market economics that it is important to harness the self-interest of economic agents to promote economically efficient allocation. The general equilibrium model provides a setting where the resultant allocation for the economy as a whole can be evaluated.

1.1.1 The role of mathematics

Throughout the past century, economic theory and applications have become increasingly mathematical. The area of general equilibrium theory, necessarily abstract, has led in that movement, using the relatively abstract mathematical techniques of real analysis. The mathematics of N-dimensional space has turned out to be very suitable for modeling the interactions of N different markets for N goods produced by $\#F$ firms and consumed by $\#H$ households.

General equilibrium theory has been a particular leader in emphasizing the axiomatic method, stating assumptions clearly and definitely in mathematical form and deriving conclusions from them, making it explicitly an "if–then" exercise. The reason behind this development is twofold. Economics is an area where reason and intuition, and assumptions and conclusions, tend to become confused and mix unpredictably. This must be particularly true in an area where we are trying to look at the whole economy at once, rather than at a single market. A disciplinary approach that emphasizes the logical development of ideas, clearly distinguishing between assumptions and conclusions, is then most appropriate. The second related rationale is the structure of economic knowledge. Much of what we know of the economy is based on simple, sometimes naive, intuition about individual economic units – firms and households. There is often broad agreement on the first principles governing their behavior, even when there is disagreement regarding conclusions and policy. This leads to a bottom-up approach stressing the construction of a model of the economy as a whole from agreed principles on firm and household behavior.

1.1.2 History of general equilibrium theory

Classical economists had a strong, if imprecise, notion of equilibrium. It represented the conditions that the economy centered on over time and returned to after a disturbance. The best-known statement of how equilibrium is achieved is more a sample of poetry than of logic: Adam Smith's notion of an "invisible hand" guiding the market participants and the allocation mechanism. Nineteenth century economists, including Ricardo, Mill, Marx, and Jevons all recognized a notion of stable equilibrium tendencies in the economy and the importance of the interaction among markets (general equilibrium) without formalizing these notions mathematically.

The supply and demand diagram generally presented for partial equilibrium analysis is known as *Marshallian*, after the treatment of Alfred Marshall (1890) who popularized it in the English speaking literature. Nevertheless, priority in the concept, its articulation, and mathematical presentation goes to Augustin Cournot (1838). To the extent modern presentation fails to give full credit to Cournot, it probably reflects that he presented his ideas in two forms inaccessible to many readers: mathematics and French.

Cournot and other nineteenth century writers clearly understood that partial equilibrium analysis presented a special case and that multiple market interactions were the appropriate generalization. They did not, however, formulate a full general equilibrium model. That exercise was first successfully undertaken by Leon Walras, a French economist at the School of Lausanne, Switzerland. His elegant comprehensive treatment appeared as *Elements of Pure Economics (Elements d'Economie Politique Pure)* in 1874. Walras set the problem and principal research agenda for all of twentieth century mathematical general equilibrium theory. The Walrasian model represented the first full recognition of the general equilibrium concept in the literature. It clearly stated that for N commodities, there are N equations, $S_i(p_1, p_2, \ldots, p_N) = D_i(p_1, p_2, \ldots, p_N)$, in the N unknowns p_i. Walras' approach to proving existence consisted in counting equations and unknowns to assure us that they were equal in number. If the equations were linear, independent, and otherwise unrestricted, this would constitute a sufficient condition for existence of a solution. The equation-counting approach is now regarded as inadequate inasmuch as the equations will typically be nonlinear and there are additional constraints on the system (in particular, nonnegativity requirements on quantities) so that equation counting will not typically ensure the existence of a solution.

F. Y. Edgeworth[1] presented the field with new concepts in bargaining and new tools to analyze them in *Mathematical Psychics* (1881). The modern elaboration of this inquiry takes place in Debreu and Scarf (1963) and is presented here in Chapters 13 and 14.

The modern period in general equilibrium theory starts amid the intellectual ferment and political instability of Vienna in the 1930s. The biweekly mathematics seminar chaired by the mathematician Karl Menger (son of the economist Carl Menger) included both the unemployed Hungarian Jewish mathematician Abraham Wald and Karl Schlesinger, a wealthy Viennese banker and gifted amateur economist. (Wald is often described inaccurately as Rumanian, reflecting changes in the borders of the adjacent countries.) In order to support Wald (who, in that period, was unemployable at the University of Vienna because he was Jewish) Menger arranged a private position for him with Schlesinger. Schlesinger introduced Wald to the problem of existence of general economic equilibrium. Wald presented mathematical proofs of existence of general equilibrium in a variety of models, each representing a special case of a general equilibrium system [see Wald (1934–35, 1936, 1951)]. With the deterioration of the political situation on the continent, most of the seminar members subsequently emigrated to England and the United States, tragically with the exception of Schlesinger who apparently committed suicide during the Nazi *Anschluss*.

In the early 1950s, three American authors, Kenneth Arrow, Gerard Debreu,[2] and Lionel McKenzie, entered the field. They worked at first separately and independently; then Arrow and Debreu worked in collaboration. The papers of Arrow and Debreu (1954) and McKenzie (1954) were presented to the 1952 meeting of the Econometric Society. They shared the same essential modeling insight: A fixed-point theorem would lead to general proofs of existence of equilibrium. Additional contributions to the field in this period include Arrow (1951) restating the essential ideas of welfare economics in the language of general equilibrium theory and Arrow (1953) extending the notions of commodity to include allocation under uncertainty. The body of work was then summarized by Debreu (1959).

It is a commonplace in intermediate microeconomics that competitive price-taking behavior is most appropriate to a setting where there is a large number of buyers and sellers. The next major step in the progress of the general equilibrium theory is the elaboration of the Edgeworth bargaining model, culminating in the

---

[1] Edgeworth was by profession a barrister (a lawyer specializing in advocacy in court). Considering the prominence and significance of his research in economic theory, he was also a superb leading economic theorist.

[2] Debreu was then a French national doing research with the Cowles Commission for Research in Economics at the University of Chicago. As a leading French mathematical economist, he had won a fellowship to study there, based on the flip of a coin (administered by Maurice Allais). The other (equally well qualified) contender for the fellowship was Dr. Marcel Boiteux, subsequently a leader in French economics and chief economist for Electricité de France.

contribution of Debreu and Scarf (1963). They demonstrated Edgeworth's notion of equivalence, in a large economy, of price-taking equilibrium and the outcome of multilateral group and individual bargaining. The role of large numbers in a competitive economy was confirmed mathematically. Arrow and Debreu received Nobel prizes in economics for their research in general equilibrium theory in 1972 and 1983, respectively. The class of general equilibrium economic models presented in this book is often called the Arrow-Debreu model.

The theory of general economic equilibrium remains an active, productive, demanding specialty of economic theory today. Each of the issues discussed above has gone through rich elaboration over the past several decades. Further research proceeds on allocation under uncertainty, general equilibrium models in industrial organization, monetary economics, and macroeconomics. Nevertheless, presenting the model as it was achieved in the mid 1960s allows a clear coherent and intuitive presentation with mathematics at the level of analysis in $\mathbf{R}^N$. This is essentially the treatment presented in most advanced textbooks in economic theory. The presentation of general equilibrium theory in this book is based on the model of Arrow and Debreu (1954). The treatment of allocative efficiency (welfare economics) is based on Arrow (1951). The notion of time reflects Hicks (1939). The treatment of uncertainty is based on Debreu (1959) and Arrow (1953). The treatment of bargaining and the core of a market economy is based on Debreu and Scarf (1963).

1.2 An elementary general equilibrium model – The Robinson Crusoe economy

The simplest general economic equilibrium system we can consider consists of a single household, usually named Robinson Crusoe. This one-person economy has many of the usual problems of any economy: production and consumption choices. The simple structure of the economy allows us fully to model a single centralized family of efficient allocation decisions. We can then, somewhat artificially, decompose the one-person economy into separate production and consumption sectors interacting through a market mechanism. This is a common classroom exercise, designed to illustrate the concepts of efficient allocation, general equilibrium, and decentralization through a market mechanism. In the one-person economy it is particularly easy to present the concept of efficient allocation. Since there is only one agent, there is a unique maximand (the utility function of the lone household/person/agent). The efficiency concept is simply to maximize Robinson's utility subject to the available resources and technology. Problems of distribution among individuals (regarding both considerations of efficiency and fairness) do not arise because there is only one household.

The exercise we perform in the Robinson Crusoe model is to solve two apparently quite separate problems and then show that they are nearly identical. First we will solve for an efficient allocation in the Robinson Crusoe economy. That is, we find a production and consumption plan that maximizes Robinson's utility subject to the constraints of available resources and technology. This maximization will result in a distinctive family of equations characterizing the efficient allocation.

Then we restate the problem of characterizing a competitive economy on Robinson's island with a single firm, a single owner (Robinson) of the firm, a single consumer (Robinson) buying from the firm, and a single worker (Robinson again) employed by the firm. We assume that the firm, worker, and household all act as price-takers (despite the small number of agents). That is, they treat prices parametrically, as variables that they have to deal with but cannot affect. The notion of price-taking is a representation of the competitive model; buyers and sellers are thought to lack the bargaining power to individually affect prices, and they do not form cartels to do so. This notion of individual strategic powerlessness is appropriate in a large economy, but is not a correct representation of Robinson's personal situation. Nevertheless, using the price-taking assumption here lets us investigate the character of the price-taking equilibrium in a tractable simple model.

Robinson Crusoe is endowed with 168 man-hours per week. On his island there is only one production activity, harvesting oysters from an oyster bed, and only one input to this production activity, Robinson's labor. This simple specification allows us to keep the exposition in two dimensions. Robinson faces a production function for the output of oysters

$$q = F(L), \tag{1.1}$$

where F is concave, L is the input of labor, and q is the output of oysters. On the consumption side, denote Robinson's consumption of oysters by c and his consumption of leisure by R. Available leisure is determined by

$$R = 168 - L, \tag{1.2}$$

and his utility function is $u(c, R)$. To assure that a well-defined maximum is located at an interior tangency we assume that u and F are concave and sufficiently steep near the boundary. That is, we assume

$$F'(\cdot) > 0, \, F''(\cdot) < 0, \, \frac{\partial u}{\partial R} > 0, \, \frac{\partial u}{\partial c} > 0, \, \frac{\partial^2 u}{\partial R^2} < 0, \, \frac{\partial^2 u}{\partial c^2} < 0, \, \frac{\partial^2 u}{\partial R \partial c} > 0,$$

and that $F'(0) = +\infty$.

At first we'll treat Robinson, quite sensibly, as a single individual with a single problem, getting the most from his situation. Our job then is to find a choice of L and q consistent with the initial resource endowment of 168 hours per week and available technology, $F(\cdot)$, that will maximize $u(c, R)$, where $c = F(L) = q$, subject to the resource constraint $R = 168 - L$. Since this is a single problem summarizing all of the resource allocation decisions of this small economy, we will call this the *centralized* allocation mechanism. The next step (to be taken later) will be to break the problem down into two distinct parts, the consumption decision (which we characterize as made by a household) and the production decision (which we characterize as made by a firm). That constitutes the *decentralized* problem.

1.2.1 Centralized allocation

A diagrammatic treatment of the problem is presented in Figure 1.1. The horizontal scale (abscissa) represents the labor/leisure opportunities and the vertical scale (ordinate) represents the production level of oysters. Labor runs right to left; leisure runs left to right. The curve HSMD is the production frontier representing the possible technically efficient mixes available of leisure and oyster production.

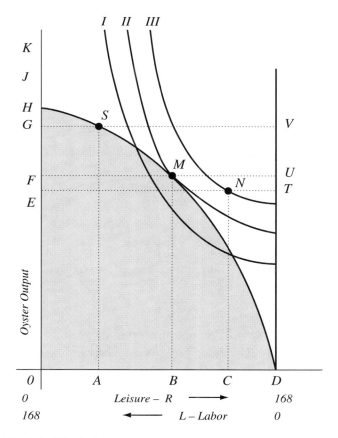

Fig. 1.1. The Robinson Crusoe economy: efficient allocation.

We derive it simply by evaluating the production function $F(\cdot)$ at varying levels of L. The curves I, II, and III are some of Robinson's indifference curves, level surfaces of $u(\cdot, \cdot)$. The efficient allocation is at the point M where the production frontier reaches the highest level it can achieve on Robinson's indifference map. This is the point where utility is maximized subject to resource endowment and production technology. Note that this is a point of tangency of the indifference curve and the production frontier, indicating that they have the same slope at the efficient point. The indifference curve and production frontier having the same slope at the optimum means that the trade-off in production between leisure and oysters is the same as the trade-off in consumption. The optimum is characterized as a position where the number of oysters that the technology requires to be sacrificed to achieve an additional hour of leisure is the same as the number of oysters willingly sacrificed in Robinson's preferences for an additional hour of leisure. Having treated the problem diagrammatically, now let's solve the same problem analytically.

Robinson seeks to maximize u subject to (1.1) and (1.2). Assuming an interior solution, we can use calculus to characterize this maximum. We can restate the problem as a maximization in one variable, the allocation of labor L between oyster production and leisure:

$$u(c, R) = u(F(L), 168 - L). \tag{1.3}$$

We now seek to choose L to maximize u:

$$\max_{L} u(F(L), 168 - L). \tag{1.4}$$

The first-order condition for an extremum then is

$$\frac{d}{dL} u(F(L), 168 - L) = 0. \tag{1.5}$$

That is,

$$u_c F' - u_R = 0, \tag{1.6}$$

where u_c and u_R denote partial derivatives. Hence, we have

$$\frac{u_R}{u_c} = -\frac{dq}{dR} = F'. \tag{1.7}$$

Equations (1.5), (1.6), and (1.7) represent conditions evaluated at the optimizing allocation, fulfilling (1.4). This family of properties is familiar from the geometric treatment; it says that the slopes of the indifference curve and of the production function are the same at the maximizing allocation. We will describe this allocation as *Pareto efficient* (after the economist Vilfredo Pareto). This term means two things: that the allocation makes technically efficient use of productive resources (labor) to produce output (that the input-output combination is on the production frontier) and that the mix of outputs (oysters and leisure) is the best possible in terms of achieving household utility. Equation (1.7), which shows the equality of slopes of the production function and the indifference curve, is the principal characterization of an efficient allocation.[3] The left-hand side of this expression, u_R/u_c, is the trade-off between consumption of oysters and leisure at the efficient allocation – the marginal rate of substitution of leisure for oysters, $MRS_{R,c}$. The right-hand side is the marginal product of labor in oyster harvesting. Since labor and leisure are converted into one another at the constant rate of one for one, the marginal product of labor in oyster harvesting is also the trade-off between leisure and oysters on the production side – the rate of product transformation (marginal rate of transformation). Therefore, at the utility maximum subject to technology and resource constraints,

$$MRS_{R,c} = RPT_{R,q},$$

where *MRS* is marginal rate of substitution in consumption and *RPT* is rate of product transformation (also known as marginal rate of transformation *MRT*). The equality of these marginal rates (and the implicit requirement that the allocation be on the production frontier) is the principal characterization of a Pareto efficient allocation of resources in the Robinson Crusoe model.

1.2.2 Decentralized allocation

Now we would like to take this simple economy and see if we can achieve its allocation decision using a market mechanism rather than the optimization above. Of course, we don't really expect a shipwrecked oyster harvester to set up a market, but this is so simple an economy that it lets us see directly the working of the market mechanism.

Oyster harvesting, the production activity, then takes place in a firm that hires labor (Robinson's) and sells oysters. Its profits go to its owner (Robinson). As a household, Robinson gets income from two sources: the profits he receives as owner of the firm and his wage income from the labor he sells to the firm. There are two markets to deal with, the labor market and the oyster market. Fix the price of oysters at unity (one); this is known as letting oysters act as numeraire. The wage rate w is expressed in oysters per man-hour. Profits of the oyster harvesting firm then are

$$\Pi = F(L) - wL = q - wL, \tag{1.8}$$

where q is oyster supply and L is labor demanded.

---

[3] The conditions in (1.7) are known as first-order necessary conditions for an interior maximum. Combined with the concavity properties assumed for $F(\cdot)$ and $u(\cdot)$ (second-order conditions) they ensure a utility maximum subject to constraint.

Robinson is the sole owner of the oyster harvester, so he includes profits of the oyster firm as part of his income. A simplifying convention is to treat Robinson's labor income as the value of all of his labor. This amounts to the (awkward) usage that he sells all of his labor on the market and then buys most of it back as leisure. This convention is harmless and simplifies the exposition. Robinson's income Y can be treated as the value of his labor endowment plus his profits Π:

$$Y = w \cdot 168 + \Pi. \tag{1.9}$$

As a consumer, Robinson spends Y on the purchase of oysters c and on the (re)purchase of leisure R, giving the budget constraint

$$Y = wR + c. \tag{1.10}$$

As a household, Robinson is a price-taker; he regards w parametrically (as a fixed value that he cannot affect by bargaining). As the passive owner of the oyster harvesting firm, he is also a profit-taker; he treats Π parametrically.

Figure 1.2 illustrates the price and allocation problem in the Robinson Crusoe market economy. This is the same as Figure 1.1 with the addition of a budget and profit line. The horizontal axis represents the allocation of endowment between leisure R, left to right, and labor L, right to left. The vertical axis represents oyster output q and oyster consumption c. The curve HSMD represents $q = F(L)$: the oyster output as a function of labor expended. The firm recognizes that its profits can be expressed as

$$\Pi = q - wL, \tag{1.11}$$

a line of slope $-w$ in L-q space. The line is known as an isoprofit line; each point represents a mix of q and L consistent with a given level of profit. Lines of this form can be visualized as a parallel family in q-L space. As a profit maximizer, the firm tries to achieve the highest profit possible consistent with available technology; thus, we can think of it choosing to produce at the point (q, L) that is on the highest isoprofit line (i.e., has the highest profit level) consistent with production technology (i.e., on the production function). At wage rate w, the firm chooses the highest isoprofit line

$$\Pi^0 = q - wL = F(L) - wL \tag{1.12}$$

consistent with the production frontier defined by $q = F(L)$. Using calculus to maximize Π subject to given w, we find at the maximum Π^0, q^0, L^0 that

$$\frac{d\Pi}{dL} = F' - w = 0, \quad \text{and so} \quad F'(L^0) = w, \tag{1.13}$$

which is the familiar condition that the wage rate equal the marginal product of labor. In summary, we consider the firm here as a price-taker in the output (oyster)

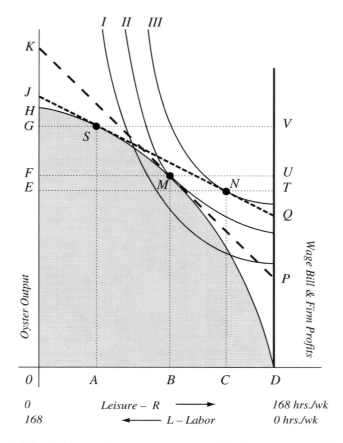

Fig. 1.2. The Robinson Crusoe economy: equilibrium and disequilibrium.

and input (labor) markets. Given those prices (unity for oysters, w for labor) the firm chooses labor input at a level L^0 that maximizes profits given the firm's technology characterized by the production function $F(L)$. Based on the information the firm receives from the market (wage rate w, output price 1), it replies to the market with a demand for labor in the amount L^0 and an offer of oysters in the quantity q^0. Further, it sends a dividend notice to shareholders of profits in the amount Π^0.

The consumer then faces the budget constraint

$$wR + c = Y = \Pi^0 + 168w. \tag{1.14}$$

The household treats the right-hand side of this equation parametrically – as fixed and given. The left-hand side includes the decision variables R and c that the household can choose to maximize utility. The household faces the problem:

Choose c, R to maximize $u(c, R)$ subject to $wR + c = Y$. (1.15)

We have then that $R = (Y - c)/w$. We can restate the household's problem as choosing c (and implicitly choosing R) to

$$\text{maximize} \quad u\left(c, \frac{Y - c}{w}\right) \tag{1.16}$$

without additional constraint (assuming an interior solution). We have then

$$\frac{du}{dc} = \frac{\partial u}{\partial c} - \frac{1}{w}\frac{\partial u}{\partial R} = 0 \tag{1.17}$$

as the characterization of the optimizing mix of c and R. But this means

$$\frac{\dfrac{\partial u}{\partial R}}{\dfrac{\partial u}{\partial c}} = w. \tag{1.18}$$

That is, the necessary condition for optimizing utility is that the marginal rate of substitution of leisure for oysters should be the wage rate. The household acts in this market as a price-taker and a profit-taker. Given the wage rate w, oyster price 1, and the profits received Π^0, the household knows its income and chooses leisure R and oyster purchases c to maximize $u(c, R)$ subject to budget constraint. Based on w, 1, and Π^0, communicated by the market, the household responds with c and R.

For each wage rate w, we can show that the household budget constraint and the firm's chosen isoprofit line coincide. Equation (1.8) at maximum profit Π^0 describes the line of slope $-w$ through $(L, q) = (0, \Pi^0)$. Equation (1.9) at $\Pi = \Pi^0$ combined with (1.10) gives

$$wR + c = 168w + \Pi^0 \tag{1.19}$$

or

$$c = w(168 - R) + \Pi^0, \tag{1.20}$$

which is the equation of the line with slope $-w$ through $(R, q) = (168, \Pi^0)$. Since $R = 168 - L$, this is the same line as derived by (1.8). This means that Robinson the consumer can afford to buy the oysters produced by the harvesting firm at any prevailing wage. Equations (1.19) and (1.20) are accounting identities, but are very useful. They say that the value of firm output at market prices is paid to factors of production (Robinson's labor) and to the firm's owners (Robinson) as profit. Hence, Robinson's income is precisely sufficient to buy the firm's output (plus repurchase his endowment). This is not an equilibrium condition; it holds at any allocation merely from the description of the economy. This follows from the requirement that the household budget include the firm profits. This means that any change in wage rate shows up in two offsetting places in the household budget constraint so that – at any wage rate – the budget is adequate to purchase the production of the firm.

The market is in equilibrium if supply equals demand in the two markets, oysters and labor/leisure. The supply of oysters and the demand for labor is determined by the firm choosing a level of output q and input L to maximize Π subject to given w. Demand for oysters and the demand for leisure is determined by the household choosing c and R to maximize $u(\cdot, \cdot)$ subject to the budget constraint (1.14). It is the job of the wage rate w to adjust so that supply and demand are equated in the two markets. In reality, the oysters consumed in the economy cannot exceed those produced by the firm, and the firm's labor input cannot exceed the labor provided by the household. The firm and household allocations are necessarily interdependent. But their decisions are taken separately. It is the job of prices, the wage rate w, to provide incentives so that the separate independent decisions are nevertheless consistent. The equilibrium choice of wage rate w allows us to *decentralize* (treat separately and independently) the firm and household decisions. In a large economy, with many firms, households, and goods, decentralization of the allocation process strengthens the allocation mechanism by reducing the immense complexity of an interdependent system to many smaller simpler optimizations.

We have already argued that the budget and chosen isoprofit line coincide. An equilibrium in the market will be characterized by a wage rate w so that $c = q$ and $L = 168 - R$. When that happens, the separate household and firm decisions will be consistent with one another, the markets will clear, and equilibrium will be determined. In Figure 1.2, point M represents the equilibrium allocation. The wage rate w^0, chosen so that $-w^0$ is the slope of the budget/isoprofit line KMP, is the equilibrium wage rate. At M, the separate supply and demand decisions coincide. Though taken independently, they are consistent with one another. They have been successfully coordinated by the adjustment of prevailing prices, w, equating supply and demand. Further, we can see that the allocation M is Pareto efficient, since it occurs on the highest indifference curve that intersects the production function, that is, the highest technically feasible indifference curve. We have the following equilibrium quantities, which can be found on the diagram:

KMP = equilibrium budget/isoprofit line,
OF = equilibrium oyster output/demand,
OB = equilibrium leisure demand,
DB = equilibrium labor demand,
UP = equilibrium wage bill, and
PD = equilibrium profit.

The idea of equilibrium becomes clearer when we consider the corresponding disequilibrium. Suppose we have not found an equilibrium wage rate, and we would like to try out the wage w' as a candidate. In Figure 1.2, let JSNQ represent the budget/isoprofit line at wage rate w'. Then we have

OG = planned supply of oysters,
OE = planned demand for oysters,
EG = excess supply of oysters,
DA = planned demand for labor,
DC = planned supply of labor,
AC = excess demand for labor,
DQ = planned profit of firm,
VQ = planned wage bill of firm, and
TQ = planned labor income of household.

Because supply and demand in the two markets differ, this is a disequilibrium. Since there is an excess demand for labor, we expect the wage rate to increase to allow the labor market (and the oyster market) to clear.

We can now establish a classic result, Walras' Law.[4] It says that at any prevailing prices (in or out of equilibrium) the value – at those prices – of the outstanding excess demands and supplies sums to zero. From (1.8), (1.9), and (1.10), we have

$$Y = w \cdot 168 + \Pi = 168w + q - wL = wR + c. \tag{1.21}$$

Subtracting the right-hand side expression from the center we have

$$0 = w[(168 - L) - R] + (q - c), \tag{1.22}$$

where w is the wage rate in oysters per hour, L is labor demanded, R is leisure demanded, $q = F(L)$ is oyster supply, and c is oyster demand. This is Walras' Law. Note the decentralization of the decision process here: The firm chooses L and q; the household chooses c and R. Only in equilibrium will the separate decisions be consistent with one another. Consistency requires $q = c$ and $R = 168 - L$. Nevertheless, the separate decisions are linked through the budget constraint (1.21), allowing us to infer the Walras' Law (1.22). There are a few points to note about (1.22). It is not an equilibrium condition, since it is true both in and out of equilibrium. It does summarize two observations: (1) that household income is sufficient to purchase total economic output and (2) that in an economy of scarcity, all income will be spent. One implication of Walras' Law is that in an economy with N goods ($N = 2$ in this example), whenever there is market equilibrium for $N - 1$ goods, the Nth market clears as well.

We can now prove analytically the existence of a market clearing wage rate in the Robinson Crusoe model. To do so we will use a standard theorem in real analysis, the Intermediate Value Theorem:

---

[4] Named for the French economist (at the school of Lausanne, Switzerland), Leon Walras.

Intermediate Value Theorem Let $[a, b]$ be a closed interval in $\mathbf{R}$ and f a contin-uous real-valued function on $[a, b]$ so that $f(a) < f(b)$. Then for any real c so that $f(a) < c < f(b)$ there is $x \in [a, b]$ so that $f(x) = c$.

In order to apply the intermediate value theorem we will assume some properties about the supply and demand behavior coming from the maximization of $u(\cdot, \cdot)$ subject to (1.14) and the maximization of Π subject to given F and w. We need continuity and some properties of excess demand and supply at extreme values of w. The lowest possible value of w is 0.

We make the following assumptions:

(1) For $w = 0$, we have $R = 168$; that is, no labor is voluntarily supplied when the wage rate is nil. Supposing $F' > 0$, then at $w = 0$, labor will be demanded and so $L > 0$.

(2) For a sufficiently large w, call it $\overline{w}$, we have $L \to 0$, but $R \ll 168$. That is, for a high enough wage rate, very little labor will be demanded but substantial amounts of labor will be willingly supplied.

(3) Labor and leisure demand and oyster supply and demand are continuous func-tions of w and Y.

Definition *Market equilibrium. Market equilibrium consists of a wage rate w^0 such that at w^0, $q = c$ and $L = 168 - R$, where q and L are determined by firm profit maximizing decisions and c and R are determined by household utility max-imization.*

We can now use the Intermediate Value Theorem to show that there exists an equilibrium wage rate w^0. Denote leisure demand at w by $R(w)$ and labor demand at w, by $L(w)$. Then under the assumptions above we have:

(a) $R(w)$ and $L(w)$ are continuous.
(b) For $w = 0$, $R(0) = 168$ and $L(0) > 0$.
(c) For w large $(w = \overline{w})$, $R(\overline{w}) < 168$ and $L(\overline{w}) \to 0$.

Denote the excess demand for labor/leisure as $Z_R(w) = R(w) + L(w) - 168$. We have $Z_R(0) > 0$ and $Z_R(\overline{w}) < 0$, where $Z_R(w)$ is continuous. By the Intermediate Value Theorem, we can find w^0; $\overline{w} > w^0 > 0$ so that $Z_R(w^0) = 0$. Walras' Law then implies that at w^0, $q = c$. This establishes w^0 as the general equilibrium wage rate.

This is a major result. We have established the existence of a general competitive equilibrium in the Robinson Crusoe model. The principal assumptions used are continuity of demand and supply behavior and the limiting behavior of demand and supply at extreme values of w. The Walras Law is essential, embodying the assumption that the budget constraint (1.19) is fulfilled as an equality. Now that we have established the existence of the competitive equilibrium in this model, we would like to show that the equilibrium is Pareto efficient.

To demonstrate Pareto efficiency, first we characterize trade-offs between goods in consumption and production in equilibrium. Profit maximization for equilibrium wage rate w^0 requires $w^0 = F'(L^0)$. Utility maximization subject to budget constraint requires (at market-clearing w^0 corresponding to leisure demand R^0)

$$\frac{u_R(c^0, R^0)}{u_c(c^0, R^0)} = w^0, \tag{1.23}$$

where R^0 and c^0 are utility optimizing leisure and consumption levels subject to budget constraint. However, at market-clearing $R^0 = 168 - L^0$ and $c^0 = F(L^0)$. By (1.13), $F'(L^0) = w^0$. Hence,

$$F' = \frac{u_R}{u_c}, \tag{1.24}$$

which is the first-order condition for Pareto efficiency established above. Therefore, the equilibrium allocation in the Robinson Crusoe economy is Pareto efficient. This is a distinctive and powerful result. It says that we can find an efficient allocation through a decentralized market process using only the price mechanism as a coordinating device. Prices, in this case the wage rate w, adjust to equate the demand and supply sides of the market. Robinson's single problem – getting the highest utility from available production opportunities – can be decomposed and decentralized as two related problems: profit maximization for the firm and utility maximization subject to budget constraint for the household.

1.3 The Edgeworth box

The Robinson Crusoe model in Section 1.2 describes the price system of a simple economy as a means of making efficient decentralized choices. That model focuses on the relationship of the production side of the market to the consumption side. The market in equilibrium allocates resources between competing productive uses so as to efficiently satisfy consumer demands and to utilize the available production technology. It is a model of the decentralized market arranging the allocation of resources in production to satisfy households. Another aspect of efficient allocation is to arrange efficient allocation of goods among consumers. It does us no good to produce an efficient mix of outputs if they are subsequently misallocated among consumers.

The modeling technique we will use for this allocation decision is the brilliant and brilliantly simple device due to F. Y. Edgeworth, known as the Edgeworth box.

Suppose we have fixed positive quantities of two goods, X and Y, and two house-holds, 1 and 2. We would like to know how to allocate the fixed supplies of X and Y between the two households. Three allocation schemes will be developed: efficient allocation, a bilateral bargaining allocation, and a market equilibrium al-location. We will demonstrate the following classic results: Bargaining and market equilibrium lead to efficient allocations, and the market equilibrium allocation is among the bargaining allocations.

To get started, household 1 is endowed with $\overline{X}^1$ of good X and $\overline{Y}^1$ of good Y. It has utility function $U^1(X^1, Y^1)$, where X^1 is 1's consumption of good X and Y^1 is 1's consumption of good Y. Household 2 is endowed with $\overline{X}^2$ of good X and $\overline{Y}^2$ of good Y. Its utility function is $U^2(X^2, Y^2)$, where X^2 is 2's consumption of good X and Y^2 is 2's consumption of good Y. The problem facing households 1 and 2 is how to divide the endowment of goods X and Y between them. The resource constraint says that $X^1 + X^2 = \overline{X}^1 + \overline{X}^2 \equiv \overline{X}$ and $Y^1 + Y^2 = \overline{Y}^1 + \overline{Y}^2 \equiv \overline{Y}$. Within these limits, how will 1 and 2 divide $\overline{X}$ and $\overline{Y}$ between them?

The first part of Edgeworth's contribution to this problem provides us with a compelling geometric representation, depicted in Figure 1.3. Form a rectangle with horizontal side of length $\overline{X}$ and vertical side of length $\overline{Y}$. If we cleverly label

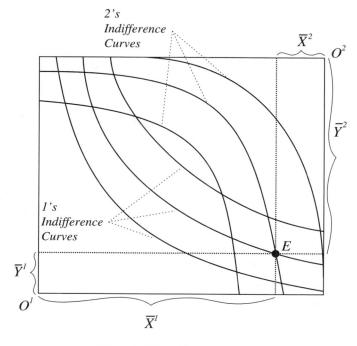

Fig. 1.3. The Edgeworth box.

this rectangle, we can represent any allocation of X and Y between 1 and 2 by a point in the box. Let the lower left corner of the box represent the origin in a quadrant representing 1's consumption and the upper right corner represent the origin in a quadrant showing 2's consumption. Any point in the box can then represent a division of $\overline{X}$ and $\overline{Y}$ between 1 and 2. Choose a point in the box and draw a line from it perpendicular to the horizontal sides and another to the vertical sides. The perpendiculars divide their sides in two. The distance from 1's origin to the intersection of the perpendicular with the horizontal side represents 1's consumption of X; the distance from 1's origin to the intersection with the perpendicular on the vertical side represents 1's consumption of Y. The distance from 2's origin to the intersection of the perpendicular with the horizontal side represents 2's consumption of X; the distance from 2's origin to the intersection with the perpendicular on the vertical side represents 2's consumption of Y. Each point in the box represents a choice of X^1 and X^2, Y^1 and Y^2 so that $X^1 + X^2 = \overline{X}^1 + \overline{X}^2 \equiv \overline{X}$ and $Y^1 + Y^2 = \overline{Y}^1 + \overline{Y}^2 \equiv \overline{Y}$. Household 1's consumption increases as the allocation point moves in a northeast direction; 2's increases as the allocation point moves in a southwest direction.

Now we need to represent 1's and 2's preferences. Starting from 1's origin we can portray 1's indifference curves (level surfaces of the utility function U^1) on its consumption space. We give the indifference curves their usual convex to the origin shape representing convex preferences (diminishing marginal rate of substitution) or equivalently a (quasi-) concave utility function. We can do the same for 2, though this representation will look a bit strange since we are depicting 2's situation upside down from the usual orientation. These arrays of indifference curves are shown in Figure 1.3. Increasing satisfaction levels for 1 are indicated to the northeast, whereas for 2 they are to the southwest. Each point in the box represents an allocation of the fixed totals of X and Y between households 1 and 2. Again, movements of the allocation northeast in the box improve 1's satisfaction and movements southwest improve 2's.

Recall that an indifference curve represents a family of possible consumption plans that have the same utility. They are equally satisfactory in utility terms. The slope of an indifference curve represents the rate at which the household will willingly give up one good in exchange for the other without loss of utility. The slope (or its absolute value) is the household's $MRS_{X,Y}$, the marginal rate of substitution of X for Y.

Now let's take a closer look at possible reallocations (Figure 1.4). Our starting point is the endowment, $(\overline{X}^1, \overline{Y}^1)$, $(\overline{X}^2, \overline{Y}^2)$, which we denote E (for endowment). Starting from the endowment, movements northwest into the lens-shaped area bounded by the indifference curves I^1 and I^2 improve the utility levels of both 1 and 2. Movement in this direction means that household 1 gives up X, which he values very little at $(\overline{X}^1, \overline{Y}^1)$, in exchange for Y, which he values quite highly.

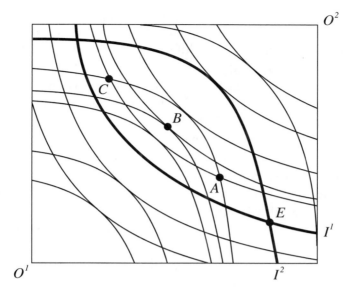

Fig. 1.4. The Edgeworth box: bargaining and allocation.

Obviously, household 2 makes the opposite exchange for the opposite reason. Both are made better off by moving to what each regards as a more desirable balance between X and Y. The slope of 1's indifference curve at point E represents the rate at which household 1 is willing to exchange good Y for good X at that point. That 1's and 2's slopes differ (their indifference curves intersect at E rather than coincide) means that their respective rates of exchange differ. That means that there's room for a deal; there is a possible mutually advantageous trade for 1 and 2. Consider the path of possible trades depicted in Figure 1.4. From the endowment point E, we consider a sequence of moves to the northwest to positions A, B, and C. Starting from E, we note that the indifference curves for 1 and 2 intersect. Their slopes differ. Households 1 and 2 have different $MRS_{X,Y}$ values. Their marginal valuations of the two goods differ. Consequently, a mutually advantageous deal can be made. Suppose 1 and 2 meet to trade. They agree to trade from the endowment point E to A. Why do they agree? The move to A moves both 1 and 2 to higher indifference curves on their respective indifference maps. They are both made better off.

The move to A does not, however, completely exhaust the possibilities for mutually advantageous trades. At A, 1's and 2's indifference curves still intersect, indicating differing personal rates of exchange (marginal rate of substitution, *MRS*) of X for Y. There is still room for a deal. Once again 1 and 2 get together to discuss a possible trade. They agree to trade to B. The move to B makes both better off again. Point B's geometry is distinctive. It's a point of tangency for 1's and 2's respective indifference curves. The slopes of the curves coincide. That means that the rate at which 1 will willingly trade X for Y is the same as the rate at which 2 will willingly trade. Their indifference curves no longer intersect; they are tangent at point B. Continuing from B, can 1 and 2 still find room for a mutually advantageous deal? How about continuing in the same direction to C? That move makes them both worse off. Along this path, it looks like B is the best they can do. Point B is a bargaining solution to the bilateral allocation problem.

Point B has a distinctive property that we would like to formalize. The allocation B is said to be efficient or *Pareto* efficient. We will say an allocation is Pareto efficient if all of the opportunities for mutually desirable reallocations have been fully used. The allocation is Pareto efficient if there is no available reallocation that can improve the utility level of one household while not reducing the utility of any household. Positions E, A, and C are Pareto inefficient. Mutually desirable reallocations are available from them. Point B is Pareto efficient. From B there are no further mutually beneficial reallocations available. Further moves to the northeast would make 1 better off and to the southwest would make 2 better off, but there are no further moves that can make both better off. Although this may sound discouraging, it is actually good news. It means that, at B, households 1 and 2 have made very effective use of their endowment of X and Y. Pareto efficiency of an allocation is a desirable property. It indicates that the resources are being effectively used; they are not being wasted. Pareto efficiency is one of the defining properties of the bilateral bargaining solution. The other defining property is individual rationality. Households 1 and 2 will agree to move to B only if they are each made better off (or no worse off) by the move from E to B. So B must lie on 1's indifference map above I^1 and on 2's indifference map above I^2.

As the discussion above suggests, tangency of 1's and 2's indifference curves is the geometric characterization of the Pareto efficient allocations. We should be able to prove that mathematically as well. We defined a Pareto efficient allocation by the property that there are no further available mutually advantageous reallocations. One way of formalizing this statement mathematically is to say that a Pareto efficient allocation (X^{o1}, Y^{o1}), (X^{o2}, Y^{o2}) is characterized as maximizing $U^1(X^1, Y^1)$ subject to $U^2(X^2, Y^2) = U^2(X^{o2}, Y^{o2}) \equiv U^{o2}$ and subject to the resource constraints

$$X^1 + X^2 = \overline{X}^1 + \overline{X}^2 \equiv \overline{X}$$

and

$$Y^1 + Y^2 = \overline{Y}^1 + \overline{Y}^2 \equiv \overline{Y}.$$

We can restate the material balance constraints to simplify the problem:

$$X^2 = \overline{X} - X^1$$
$$Y^2 = \overline{Y} - Y^1.$$

The convenient way to solve this problem is to use the technique of Lagrange. We form the expression, L, known as the Lagrangian:

$$L \equiv U^1(X^1, Y^1) + \lambda[U^2(\overline{X} - X^1, \overline{Y} - Y^1) - U^{o2}].$$

To solve the maximization problem subject to constraint we now solve the unconstrained problem of maximizing L with regard to the choice of X^1, Y^1, and λ (speaking more precisely, we are solving for a saddle point). We have

$$\frac{\partial L}{\partial X^1} = \frac{\partial U^1}{\partial X^1} - \lambda \frac{\partial U^2}{\partial X^2} = 0,$$

$$\frac{\partial L}{\partial Y^1} = \frac{\partial U^1}{\partial Y^1} - \lambda \frac{\partial U^2}{\partial Y^2} = 0,$$

$$\frac{\partial L}{\partial \lambda} = U^2(X^2, Y^2) - U^{o2} = 0.$$

This gives us the condition

$$\frac{\dfrac{\partial U^1}{\partial X^1}}{\dfrac{\partial U^1}{\partial Y^1}} = \frac{\dfrac{\partial U^2}{\partial X^2}}{\dfrac{\partial U^2}{\partial Y^2}}$$

or, equivalently,

$$\frac{\partial Y^1}{\partial X^1}\bigg|_{U^1 = \text{constant}} = \frac{\partial Y^2}{\partial X^2}\bigg|_{U^2 = \text{constant}}.$$

The problem we solved is to characterize a Pareto efficient allocation in the Edgeworth box. The concluding equation says that the mathematical characterization of efficiency is that the slope of 2's indifference curve at an efficient allocation will equal the slope of 1's indifference curve. The slope of the indifference curve is the rate of exchange at which the trader will willingly trade Y for X without loss of utility. Efficient allocations are characterized by all households experiencing the same $MRS_{X,Y}$, the same trade-off between the goods.

This result then gives us a clear geometric characterization of the efficient allocations in the Edgeworth box. They occur at those points where the slopes of 1's and 2's indifference curves coincide, the points of tangency of the two curves. The set of these points then is the set of Pareto efficient allocations in the box. Those Pareto efficient points lying in the lens-shaped area between the two indifference curves through the initial endowment point are particularly important. They are the individually rational Pareto efficient points, the points that voluntary bargaining from the endowment to efficient allocation should achieve. This set is sufficiently important that it has its own name; it is known as the *contract curve*. The rationale

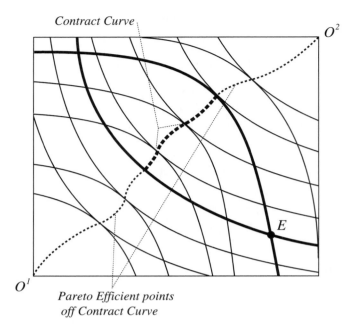

Fig. 1.5. The Edgeworth box: efficient allocation and the contract curve.

behind this name is that as 1 and 2 trade, voluntary trading to mutually improving allocations will lead to a position on the contract curve. The Pareto efficient set and the contract curve are illustrated in Figure 1.5.

Though direct bargaining among individuals may appear a sensible allocative procedure when there are only two persons, it would be cumbersome in a large economy. The alternative is a market price system. How would the price system work in this simple example? The solution concept here is the competitive equilibrium: Prices adjust so that supply equals demand in all markets. Let p^x be the price of x and p^y be the price of y. Each household will choose its most desirable mix of X and Y to consume subject to budget constraint. Household 1's problem is:

$$\text{Choose} \quad X^1, Y^1 \quad \text{to maximize} \quad U^1(X^1, Y^1)$$
$$\text{subject to} \quad p^x X^1 + p^y Y^1 = p^x \overline{X}^1 + p^y \overline{Y}^1 = B^1 \tag{B1}$$

Expression (B1) states 1's budget constraint: the value at prevailing prices of 1's purchases is limited by the value at those prices of household 1's endowment. The budget constraint is a straight line passing through the endowment point $(\overline{X}^1, \overline{Y}^1)$ with slope $-(p^x/p^y)$.

To characterize the solution to 1's utility optimization subject to budget constraint, we can restate it as:

$$\text{Choose} \quad X^1 \quad \text{to maximize} \quad U^1\left(X^1, \frac{B^1}{p^y} - \frac{p^x}{p^y}X^1\right).$$

To characterize the solution, set dU^1/dX^1 equal to 0. We have

$$\frac{dU^1}{dX^1} = \frac{\partial U^1}{\partial X^1} - \frac{p^x}{p^y}\frac{\partial U^1}{\partial Y^1} = 0.$$

Therefore, at the utility optimum subject to budget constraint we have

$$\frac{\dfrac{\partial U^1}{\partial X^1}}{\dfrac{\partial U^1}{\partial Y^1}} = \frac{p^x}{p^y}.$$

Household 2 faces the same utility optimization problem with the superscript 2 replacing the 1's above. Hence 2's utility optimizing demands for X and Y, denoted X^2 and Y^2, will be characterized by

$$\frac{\dfrac{\partial U^2}{\partial X^2}}{\dfrac{\partial U^2}{\partial Y^2}} = \frac{p^x}{p^y}.$$

The Walrasian auctioneer receives the demands of 1 and 2 and adjusts prices so that supply and demand for X and for Y are equated. The auctioneer adjusts prices to equilibrium prices p^{*x} and p^{*y} so that

$$X^{*1} + X^{*2} = \overline{X}^1 + \overline{X}^2 \equiv \overline{X}$$

and

$$Y^{*1} + Y^{*2} = \overline{Y}^1 + \overline{Y}^2 \equiv \overline{Y},$$

where the asterisks denote individually optimizing chosen values. That is, X^{*1} and Y^{*1} are 1's utility maximizing mix of X and Y at prices p^{*x} and p^{*y} and similarly for X^{*2} and Y^{*2}. Most importantly, these choices clear the market.

Since the endowment point in the Edgeworth box represents the endowments of both households (viewed in mirror image), the households face a common budget line (although the value of their respective budgets will of course differ). Figure 1.6 presents the problem facing the Walrasian auctioneer: disequilibrium prices. Out of equilibrium, the demands of the households add up to an excess of one of the goods and leave a surplus of the other. It is the auctioneer's job to adjust prices to bring them into balance. Of course, we don't really believe in an auctioneer representing

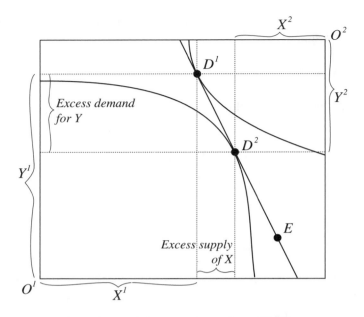

Fig. 1.6. The Edgeworth box: disequilibrium.

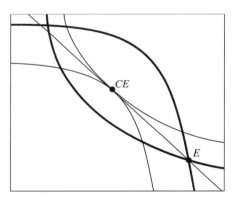

Fig. 1.7. The Edgeworth box: general equilibrium.

the price formation mechanism of the economy; this fictional construct serves to mimic the decentralized price formation process of the competitive market. We suppose that this price formation mechanism leads to a market-clearing equilibrium allocation. Figure 1.7 presents the market equilibrium of the Edgeworth box. The separate decisions of 1 and 2 lead them to the same point, the competitive equilibrium allocation, denoted CE in the figure.

Note the geometry of CE in Figure 1.7. Household 1's and 2's indifference curves through CE are each tangent to the budget line (indicating utility maximization subject to budget constraint) at CE and tangent to each other. We have

$$-\left.\frac{\partial Y^1}{\partial X^1}\right|_{U^1=U^{1*}} = \frac{\dfrac{\partial U^1}{\partial X^1}}{\dfrac{\partial U^1}{\partial Y^1}} = \frac{p^x}{p^y} = \frac{\dfrac{\partial U^2}{\partial X^2}}{\dfrac{\partial U^2}{\partial Y^2}} = -\left.\frac{\partial Y^2}{\partial X^2}\right|_{U^2=U^{2*}}$$

(where the asterisk denotes optimizing levels). This expression tells us that, at the competitive equilibrium, households 1 and 2 have been separately guided by prices – the same prices facing both households – to adjust their consumption so that the rates at which they willingly trade good Y for good X, $-(\partial Y^1/\partial X^1)$, $-(\partial Y^2/\partial X^2)$, are equated to one another. They are each separately set equal to the (same) prevailing price ratio by utility maximization. This means that the necessary conditions for a Pareto efficient allocation are fulfilled at CE.

That's the bottom line. The set of Pareto efficient allocations in the Edgeworth box is the set of tangencies of household 1's and 2's indifference curves. The contract curve is the subset of Pareto efficient allocations bounded by the indifference curves through the endowment point, that is, the individually rational (i.e., individually preferable to endowment) efficient points. Bargaining will get 1 and 2 to the contract curve through a succession of mutually beneficial trades. The price system will also get the traders to the contract curve, to a Pareto efficient allocation. The competitive equilibrium allocation is on the contract curve. The competitive market equilibrium is Pareto efficient. Both Edgeworth box bargaining and the competitive market equilibrium get us to a Pareto efficient allocation. What is there especially to recommend the price system? Why do economists so extol the virtues of markets and prices? The answer lies in the comparative simplicity of the price system and its adaptability to large economies. Edgeworth box style bilateral bargaining makes sense for a small number of isolated individuals. That same kind of bargaining would be completely unmanageable in a large economy. A price system can expand to a large economy with little increase in complexity. The reason for the adaptability of the price system is that it allows each economic unit (each household) to perform most of the necessary decision making separately. In contrast, the bargaining that proceeds in the Edgeworth box means that all traders enter interactively in deciding the quantity of each good going to each household. The price system *decentralizes* the allocation decision.

We should take one further step with the Edgeworth box and bring the production decision and the interpersonal allocation decision together. The Robinson Crusoe model showed us how the price system can give an efficient allocation of productive resources to produce a mix of outputs that best satisfies consumer demands – a Pareto efficient allocation of resources. We learned from that exercise that equating the consumer's *MRS* to the production sector's *RPT* was a necessary condition for an

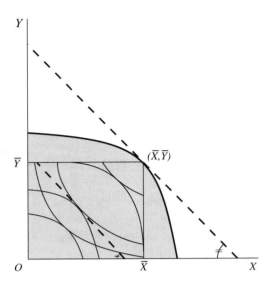

Fig. 1.8. A two-good economy: general equilibrium in production and distribution.

efficient allocation, a condition that is fulfilled in competitive equilibrium since the *MRS* and *RPT* are each separately equated to the price ratio in firm and household optimizations. We learned above that efficient interpersonal allocation requires that all households' *MRS*s be equated to one another. That happens everywhere on the contract curve. In particular, it is achieved in competitive equilibrium because each household's *MRS* is separately equated to the price ratio.

The Robinson Crusoe model treated the consumption/production interaction with only one household. We can now combine the Robinson Crusoe production decision with the Edgeworth box consumption allocation to portray the production/ interpersonal allocation decision at one shot. The joint equilibrium of production and interpersonal allocation is depicted in Figure 1.8. For each price ratio, the production sector chooses the profit-maximizing output mix. The Edgeworth box then depicts the allocation of these outputs among households. The budget line in the box shows how households react to prevailing prices. The figure shows the production decision as profit maximization subject to prevailing prices, technology, and resources, just as in the Robinson Crusoe model. The slopes of the isoprofit line and of the budget line are identical. The consumption allocation decision takes the output produced (the decision made according to profit maximization) and allocates it between the households using the price system as in the Edgeworth box model. In a price equilibrium the decisions of households and the production sector will coincide: Combined household consumptions at prevailing prices will equal output of the production sector. The defining properties of the equilibrium are:

- Production and consumption plans are each separately optimized at the prevailing prices – the same prices facing all firms and households.
- Markets clear; supply equals demand. There is a single consistent point chosen in the Edgeworth box. The dimensions of the box are set to reflect precisely the production decision. Consumption decisions are consistent with one another and with the output produced, precisely exhausting available goods.

The allocation is Pareto efficient. The defining properties of Pareto efficiency are:

- The production sector is technically efficient; each firm is producing maximal output from its inputs and there is no reallocation of inputs among firms that would result in a higher output of some goods without a reduction in output of others. (In the Robinson Crusoe example above, with a single firm and a single input, we do not see the full complexity of production efficiency.)
- The *MRS*, the tradeoff in consumption between goods, is the same for all households. This is ensured by the competitive equilibrium since in equilibrium each household sets its *MRS* equal to the common price ratio. Equating *MRS*s results in locating the consumption plan at a point on the contract curve.
- The *MRS* equals the *RPT*: The tradeoff in output choice is the same on both the production and consumption sides. This property holds in competitive equilibrium since both the firm and the households face the same equilibrium prices. It shows up in the figure as two lines having *the same slope equal to the price ratio*. The budget line in the Edgeworth box and the isoprofit line tangent to the production choice have the same slope equal to the price ratio (times -1).

In a general economic equilibrium the price system communicates sufficient information to allow producers and consumers to coordinate their separate production and consumption decisions. Prices adjust to bring supply and demand into balance. Because all firms and households face the same prices, they are all exposed to the same trade-offs in production and consumption that lead to a Pareto efficient allocation.

1.4 A first approach: Existence of general equilibrium in an economy with an excess demand function

Economists think in terms of prices adjusting in the market for a good so that supply equals demand for that good – a market equilibrium. General equilibrium theory focuses on finding market equilibrium prices for all goods at once. Since there are distinctive interactions across markets (for example, between the price of gasoline and the demand for automobiles) it is important that the equilibrium concept include the simultaneous joint determination of equilibrium prices. The concept can then represent a solution concept for the economy as a whole and not merely for a single market that is artificially isolated. General equilibrium for the economy consists of an array of prices for all goods, where simultaneously supply equals demand for each good. The prices of cars and of gasoline both adjust so that demand and supply of cars and of gasoline are each equated.

Let there be a finite number N of goods in the economy. Then a typical array of prices could be represented by an N-dimensional vector such as

$$p = (p_1, p_2, p_3, \ldots, p_{N-1}, p_N) = (3, 1, 5, \ldots, 0.5, 10).$$

The first coordinate represents the price of the first good, the second the price of the second good, and so forth until the Nth coordinate represents the price of the Nth good. This expression says that the price of good 1 is three times the price of good 2, that of good 3 is five times the price of good 2, ten times that of good $N - 1$, and half that of good N.

We simplify the problem by considering an economy without taking account of money or financial institutions. For example, there would be no difference in this model between a situation where the wage rate is $1 per hour and a car costs $1000 and another where the wage rate is $15 and the same car costs $15,000. Only *relative prices* (price ratios) matter here, not monetary prices. This is an assumption common in microeconomic modeling in which the financial structure is ignored.

Since only the relative prices matter, and not their numerical values, we can choose to represent the array of prices in whatever numerical values are most convenient. We will do this by confining the price vectors to a particularly convenient set known as the *unit simplex*. The unit simplex comprises a set of N-dimensional vectors fulfilling a simple restriction: Each coordinate of the vectors is nonnegative, and together the N coordinates sum up to 1. We think of a point in the simplex as representing an array of prices for the economy. There is no loss of generality in this formulation. Any possible combination of (nonnegative) relative prices can be represented in this way. To convince yourself of this, simply take any vector of nonnegative prices you wish. Take the reciprocal of the sum of the coordinates (that is, 1 divided by the sum) and multiply each term in the vector by this fraction. The result is a vector in the unit simplex reflecting the same relative prices as the original price vector. Hence, without loss of generality we can confine attention to a price space characterized as the unit simplex.

Formally, our price space, the unit simplex in $\mathbf{R}^N$, is

$$P = \left\{ p \mid p \in R^N, \, p_i \geq 0, \, i = 1, \ldots, N, \, \sum_{i=1}^{N} p_i = 1 \right\}. \tag{1.25}$$

The unit simplex is a (generalized) triangle in N-space. For $N = 2$, it is a line segment running from (1,0) to (0,1); for $N = 3$, it is the triangle with angles (vertices) at (1,0,0), (0,1,0), and (0,0,1); for $N = 4$, it is a tetrahedron (a three-sided pyramid with triangular sides and base) with vertices at (1,0,0,0), (0,1,0,0), (0,0,1,0), and (0,0,0,1); and so forth in higher dimensions.

A household's demand for consumption or a firm's supply plans are represented as an N-dimensional vector. Each of the commodities is represented by a coordinate. We will suppose there is a finite set of households whose names are in the set H. For each household $h \in H$, we define a demand function, $D^h(p)$, as a function of the prevailing prices $p \in P$, that is, $D^h : P \to \mathbf{R}^N$. There is a finite set of firms whose names are in the set F, each with a supply function $S^j(p)$, which also takes its values in real N-dimensional Euclidean space: $S^j : P \to \mathbf{R}^N$. The economy has an initial endowment of resources $r \in \mathbf{R}^N$ that is also supplied to the economy.

We combine the individual demand and supply functions to get a market excess demand function representing unfulfilled demands (as positive coordinates) and unneeded supplies (as negative coordinates). The market excess demand function is defined as

$$Z(p) = \sum_{h \in H} D^h(p) - \sum_{j \in F} S^j(p) - r, \qquad (1.26)$$

$$Z : P \to \mathbf{R}^N \qquad (1.27)$$

Each coordinate of the N-dimensional vector p represents the price of the good corresponding to the coordinate. p is $(p_1, p_2, p_3, \ldots, p_N)$, where p_k is the price of good k. $Z(p)$ is an N-dimensional vector, each coordinate representing the excess demand (or supply if the coordinate has a negative value) of the good represented. $Z(p)$ is $(Z_1(p), Z_2(p), Z_3(p), \ldots, Z_N(p))$, where $Z_k(p)$ is the excess demand for good k. When $Z_k(p)$, the excess demand for good k, is negative, we will say that good k is in excess supply. We will assume the following properties on $Z(p)$:

Walras' Law:

$$For\ all \quad p \in P,\ p \cdot Z(p) = \sum_{i=1}^{N} p_i \cdot Z_i(p) = 0. \qquad (1.28)$$

The economic basis for Walras' Law involves the assumption of scarcity and the structure of household budget constraints.

Continuity:

$$Z(p)\ is\ a\ continuous\ function.$$

That is, small changes in p result in small changes in $Z(p)$.

Continuity of $Z(p)$ reflects continuous behavior of household and firm demand and supply as prices change. It includes the economic assumptions of diminishing marginal rate of substitution *(MRS)* for households and diminishing marginal product of inputs for firms.

We assume in this chapter that $Z(p)$ is well defined and fulfills Walras' Law and Continuity. Nevertheless, among the principal tasks pursued in the rest of this book is developing models and the mathematical structure needed to deal with the many situations in which $Z(p)$ is not well defined[5] and to prove the Walras' Law and continuity as results of more elementary assumptions. In Chapters 4 through 11 we will use a formal axiomatic method: describing the economy as a mathematical model, stating economic assumptions in formal mathematical form, and finally deriving results like Walras' Law and Continuity and the existence of market equilibrium (below) as the logical result of these more elementary assumptions.

The economy is said to be in equilibrium if prices in all markets adjust so that for each good, supply equals demand. When supply equals demand, the excess demand is zero. The exception to this is that some goods may be free and in excess supply in equilibrium.[6] Hence, we characterize equilibrium by the property that for each good i, the excess demand for that good is zero (or in the case of free goods, the excess demand may be negative – an excess supply – and the price is zero).

Definition $p^0 \in P$ *is said to be an equilibrium price vector if* $Z(p^0) \leq 0$ *(0 is the zero vector; the inequality applies coordinatewise) with* $p_i^0 = 0$ *for i such that* $Z_i(p^0) < 0$. *That is,* p^0 *is an equilibrium price vector if supply equals demand in all markets (with possible excess supply of free goods).*

We will now state and prove the major result of this introduction, that under the assumptions introduced above, Walras' Law and Continuity, there is an equilibrium in the economy. To do this we will need one additional piece of mathematical structure, the Brouwer Fixed-Point Theorem:

Theorem 1.1 (Brouwer Fixed-Point Theorem) *Let* $f(\cdot)$ *be a continuous function,* $f : P \to P$. *Then there is* $x^* \in P$ *so that* $f(x^*) = x^*$.

The Brouwer Fixed-Point Theorem is a powerful mathematical result. We will use it again in later chapters. It takes advantage of the distinctive structure of the simplex. It says that if we have a continuous function that maps points of the simplex back into the simplex (i.e., it maps the simplex into itself) then there exists some point on the simplex that is left unchanged in the process. The unchanged

---

[5] For example, when the price of a desirable good is zero, there may be no well-defined value for the demand function at those prices (since the quantity demanded will be arbitrarily large). Nevertheless, it is important that we be able to deal with free goods (zero prices).

[6] Of course, a price of zero is hard to distinguish from no price at all. Goods that are free may not even be thought of as property. Examples of free goods include rainwater, air, or access to the oceans for sailing.

point is the fixed point. We can now use this powerful mathematical result to prove a powerful economic result – the existence of general economic equilibrium.

Theorem 1.2[7] *Let Walras' Law and Continuity be fulfilled. Then there is* $p^* \in P$ *so that* p^* *is an equilibrium.*

Proof The proof of the theorem is the mathematical analysis of an economic story. We suppose prices to be set by an auctioneer. He calls out one price vector p, and the market responds with an excess demand vector $Z(p)$. Some goods will be in excess supply at p, whereas others will be in excess demand. The auctioneer then does the obvious. He raises the price of the goods in excess demand and reduces the price of the goods in excess supply, but not too much of either change can be made: Prices must be kept on the simplex. How should he be sure to keep prices on the simplex? First, the prices have to stay nonnegative. When he reduces a price, he should be sure not to reduce it below zero. When he raises prices, he should be sure that the new resulting price vector stays on the simplex. How? By adjusting the new prices so that they sum up to one. Moreover, we would like to use the Brouwer Fixed-Point Theorem on the price adjustment process; so the auctioneer should make price adjustment a continuous function from the simplex into itself. This leads us to the following price adjustment function T, which represents how the auctioneer manages prices.

Let $T : P \rightarrow P$, where $T(p) = (T_1(p), T_2(p), \ldots, T_i(p), \ldots, T_N(p))$. $T_i(p)$ is the adjusted price of good i, adjusted by the auctioneer trying to bring supply and demand into balance. The adjustment process of the ith price can be represented as $T_i(p)$, defined as follows:

$$T_i(p) \equiv \frac{\max[0,\, p_i + Z_i(p)]}{\displaystyle\sum_{n=1}^{N} \max[0,\, p_n + Z_n(p)]}. \tag{1.29}$$

The function T is a price adjustment function. It raises the relative price of goods in excess demand and reduces the price of goods in excess supply while keeping the price vector on the simplex. The expression $p_i + Z_i(p)$ represents the idea that prices of goods in excess demand should be raised and those in excess supply should be reduced. The operator $\max[0, \cdot]$ represents the idea that adjusted prices should be nonnegative. The fractional form of T reminds us that after each price is adjusted individually, they are then readjusted proportionally to stay on the simplex. In order for T to be well defined, we must show that the denominator is nonzero, that is,

$$\sum_{n=1}^{N} \max[0,\, p_n + Z_n(p)] \neq 0. \tag{1.30}$$

---

[7] Acknowledgement and thanks to John Roemer for help in simplifying the proof.

We omit the formal demonstration of (1.30), noting only that it follows from Walras' Law. For the sum in the denominator to be zero or negative, all goods would have to be in excess supply simultaneously, which is contrary to our notions of scarcity and – it turns out – to Walras' Law as well. Recall that $Z(\cdot)$ is a continuous function. The operations of max[ ], sum, and division by a nonzero continuous function maintain continuity. Hence, $T(p)$ is a continuous function from the simplex into itself.

By the Brouwer Fixed-Point Theorem there is $p^* \in P$ so that $T(p^*) = p^*$. Because $T(\cdot)$ is the auctioneer's price adjustment function, this means that p^* is a price at which the auctioneer stops adjusting. His price adjustment rule says that once he has found p^* the adjustment process stops.

Now we have to show that the auctioneer's decision to stop adjusting the price is really the right thing to do. That is, we'd like to show that p^* is not just the stopping point of the price adjustment process, but that it actually does represent general equilibrium prices for the economy. We therefore must show that at p^*, all markets clear with the possible exception of a few with free goods in oversupply.

Since $T(p^*) = p^*$, for each good k, $T_k(p^*) = p_k^*$. That is, for all $k = 1, \ldots, N$,

$$p_k^* = \frac{\max[0, p_k^* + Z_k(p^*)]}{\sum_{n=1}^{N} \max[0, p_n^* + Z_n(p^*)]}. \tag{1.31}$$

Looking at the numerator in this expression, we can see that the equation will be fulfilled either by

$$p_k^* = 0 \quad \text{(Case 1)} \tag{1.32}$$

or by

$$p_k^* = \frac{p_k^* + Z_k(p^*)}{\sum_{n=1}^{N} \max[0, p_n^* + Z_n(p^*)]} > 0 \quad \text{(Case 2).} \tag{1.33}$$

CASE 1 $p_k^* = 0 = \max[0, p_k^* + Z_k(p^*)]$. Hence, $0 \geq p_k^* + Z_k(p^*) = Z_k(p^*)$ and $Z_k(p^*) \leq 0$. This is the case of free goods with market clearing or excess supply in equilibrium.

CASE 2 To avoid repeated messy notation, let

$$\lambda = \frac{1}{\sum_{n=1}^{N} \max[0, p_n^* + Z_n(p^*)]} \tag{1.34}$$

so that $T_k(p^*) = \lambda(p_k^* + Z_k(p^*))$. Since p^* is the fixed point of T we have $p_k^* = \lambda(p_k^* + Z_k(p^*)) > 0$. This expression is true for all k with $p_k^* > 0$, and

λ is the same for all k. Let's perform some algebra on this expression. We first combine terms in p_k^*:

$$(1 - \lambda)p_k^* = \lambda Z_k(p^*), \tag{1.35}$$

then multiply through by $Z_k(p^*)$ to get

$$(1 - \lambda)p_k^* Z_k(p^*) = \lambda(Z_k(p^*))^2, \tag{1.36}$$

and now sum over all k in Case 2, obtaining

$$(1 - \lambda) \sum_{k \in \text{Case 2}} p_k^* Z_k(p^*) = \lambda \sum_{k \in \text{Case 2}} (Z_k(p^*))^2. \tag{1.37}$$

Walras' Law says

$$0 = \sum_{k=1}^{N} p_k^* Z_k(p^*) = \sum_{k \in \text{Case 1}} p_k^* Z_k(p^*) + \sum_{k \in \text{Case2}} p_k^* Z_k(p^*). \tag{1.38}$$

But for $k \in$ Case 1, $p_k^* Z_k(p^*) = 0$, and so

$$0 = \sum_{k \in \text{Case 1}} p_k^* Z_k(p^*). \tag{1.39}$$

Therefore,

$$\sum_{k \in \text{Case 2}} p_k^* Z_k(p^*) = 0. \tag{1.40}$$

Hence, from (1.13) we have

$$0 = (1 - \lambda) \cdot \sum_{k \in \text{Case 2}} p_k^* Z_k(p^*) = \lambda \cdot \sum_{k \in \text{Case 2}} (Z_k(p^*))^2. \tag{1.41}$$

Using Walras' Law, we established that the left-hand side equals 0, but the right-hand side can be zero only if $Z_k(p^*) = 0$ for all k such that $p_k^* > 0$ (k in Case 2). Thus, p^* is an equilibrium. This concludes the proof. QED

The demonstration here is striking; it displays the essential economic and mathematical elements of the proof of the existence of general equilibrium. These are the use of a fixed-point theorem, of Walras' Law, and of the continuity of excess demand. If the economy fulfills continuity and Walras' Law, then we expect it to have a general equilibrium. The mathematics that assures us of this result will be a fixed-point theorem. Most of the rest of this book is devoted to developing, from more fundamental economic and mathematical concepts, the tools and properties demonstrated here.

1.5 Bibliographic note

An excellent history of economic thought, including the formulation of the Edgeworth box and the general equilibrium theory of Walras, is available in Blaug (1968). Walras' original – and still highly readable – exposition of the general equilibrium system is in Walras (1874). Weintraub (1983) describes the modern history of general equilibrium theory. Arrow (1989) provides a detailed discussion of the Viennese period. Arrow (1968) and Arrow and Hahn (1971) provide an analytic treatment of the history of thought. For an excellent treatment of the Robinson Crusoe economy, see Cornwall (1979). The Edgeworth box was originally developed in Edgeworth (1881) and is fully expounded in Newman (1965).

Exercises

Exercises 1.1–1.3 deal with the Robinson Crusoe economy described as follows: Robinson Crusoe is endowed with 168 man-hours per week. There is a production function for the output of oysters

$$q = F(L), \tag{1.42}$$

where L is labor applied to oyster harvesting. Robinson's leisure, R, is determined by

$$R = 168 - L. \tag{1.43}$$

His utility function is $u(c, R)$, where c is Robinson's consumption of oysters.

Let production be organized in a firm, and let consumption and labor supply decisions occur in the household. Let oysters act as numeraire (monetary unit), with their price fixed at unity. The wage rate w is expressed in oysters per man-hour. Planned profits of the oyster harvesting firm then are

$$\Pi = F(L^d) - wL^d = q^s - wL^d, \tag{1.44}$$

where q^s is oyster supply and L^d is labor demanded. Robinson is the sole owner of the oyster harvester. His income Y may most easily be thought of as the value of his labor endowment plus his profits:

$$Y = w \cdot 168 + \Pi. \tag{1.45}$$

He spends his income Y on the (re)purchase of leisure R and on the purchase of oysters c, giving the budget constraint

$$Y = wR + c. \tag{1.46}$$

As a household, Robinson is a price-taker; he regards w parametrically. He is also a profit-taker; he treats Π parametrically. Given his income from (1.45) and his budget constraint (1.46), he chooses c and R to maximize $u(c, R)$ subject to (1.46). At wage rate w, the firm chooses the production plan giving the highest profit

$$\Pi^0 = F(L^d) - wL^d$$

consistent with the production function. The consumer then faces the budget constraint $wR + c = Y = \Pi^0 + 168w$. Each budget-isoprofit line has slope $-w$. Walras' Law results from subtracting the right-hand side of this expression from the left. It can be stated as

$$0 = w(R + L^d - 168) + (c - q^s), \tag{W}$$

where w is the wage rate in oysters per man-hour, L^d is labor demanded, R is leisure demanded, $q^s = F(L^d)$ is oyster supply, and c is oyster demand.

1.1 Define fully a general competitive equilibrium. What does equilibrium require for w? What is required of c, R, q, and L? Clearly describe firm behavior, household behavior, and market-clearing conditions.

1.2 Suppose w is set at a disequilibrium level. Then $L^d + R \neq 168$ and $q^s \neq c$.
(a) Does the Walras' Law (W) hold at the disequilibrium w? Why or why not?
(b) At the disequilibrium wage rate w, the firm's plans for its profits cannot be fulfilled. Does this affect the household budget at w?
(c) Suppose at the disequilibrium wage rate w, $L^d > 168 - R$. How would you expect w to adjust?

1.3 Suppose the economy achieves a wage rate w^o that gives the economy a general competitive equilibrium, as defined in Exercise 1.1.
(a) Show that the equilibrium allocation is identical to the solution of the problem: Choose c and R to maximize $u(c, R)$, where $c = q$, subject to (1.42) and (1.43).
(b) What can you then conclude about the allocative efficiency of the market mechanism?
(c) The comparison in part (a) is sometimes described as comparing centralized and decentralized allocation mechanisms. Explain this interpretation.

1.4 Consider a simple Robinson Crusoe economy. There is an initial endowment of one day of endowed time, T, per day of calendar time. There is no leisure. Time can be used to produce guavas, x, or oysters, y. Let T^X denote the time devoted to guavas and T^Y denote the time devoted to oysters (the superscripts denote distribution, not raising to a power; they are not exponents). The production function of guavas is

$$x = \sqrt{T^X}, \tag{1}$$

and that of oysters is

$$y = \sqrt{T^Y}.$$ (2)

The resource constraint is characterized as

$$T^X + T^Y = 1.$$ (3)

We can summarize these relations as

$$x^2 + y^2 = 1 \quad x \geq 0, y \geq 0$$ (4)

or

$$y = (1 - x^2)^{1/2}, \quad x \geq 0, y \geq 0.$$ (5)

Preferences are characterized by the utility function

$$U(x, y) = x \cdot y.$$ (6)

Find the Pareto efficient allocation for this economy. Explain your method. (You may find it convenient to solve for x, y that maximize U^2 instead of U.)

What are equilibrium prices that will support the efficient allocation as an equilibrium? (You can set one price arbitrarily at unity as numeraire.) Demonstrate your result.

1.5   Consider the following example of supply and demand relations between two markets. There are two goods, denoted 1 and 2, with prices p_1 and p_2, supply functions $S_1(p_1, p_2)$ and $S_2(p_1, p_2)$, and demand functions $D_1(p_1, p_2)$ and $D_2(p_1, p_2)$. These are specified by the expressions

$$S_1(p_1, p_2) = 3p_1; \qquad D_1(p_1, p_2) = 8 - 4p_2 - p_1; \qquad p_2 \leq 2$$

and

$$S_2(p_1, p_2) = 5p_2; \qquad D_2(p_1, p_2) = 24 - 6p_1 - p_2; \qquad p_1 \leq 4.$$

The market for good 1 is said to be in equilibrium at prices (p_1^0, p_2^0) where $S_1(p_1^0, p_2^0) = D_1(p_1^0, p_2^0)$. The market for good 2 is said to be in equilibrium at prices (p_1', p_2') where $S_2(p_1', p_2') = D_2(p_1', p_2')$. Demonstrate that each market has an equilibrium when the other's price is fixed. Show that, nevertheless, no pair of prices exists for the two markets at which they are both in equilibrium. Does this supply-demand system provide a counterexample to Theorem 1.2, the existence of general equilibrium prices?

2

Mathematics

This chapter presents a survey of all of the mathematical topics used in Chapters 3 through 15 – the mathematics needed to describe an economy with continuous supply and demand functions.[1] Many of the topics treated here are part of the usual content of an introductory course on analysis in $\mathbf{R}^N$: sets, limits, convergence, open and closed sets, and continuous functions. In addition, there are topics that often are not prominent in the course on real analysis that turn out to be central to mathematical economics: convexity, separation theorems, and fixed-point theorems. This chapter assumes the student is familiar with the notation and concepts of analytic geometry. It is not a substitute for a course in real analysis (to which the student is strongly recommended).

2.1 Set theory

Let us review some basic elements of set theory.

Logical inference In mathematical logic the word *implies* means "leads to the logical inference that" and can be represented by the symbol of the double shaft arrow, $\Rightarrow$.

Definition of a set *We think of a set as a group or collection, defined by the items in the collection. A typical set might consist of all UCSD freshmen, all surfers in southern California (there is obviously some overlap here), or of the positive integers between 1 and 10. We might call a set by another name, such as a collection, a family, a class, an aggregate, or an ensemble. We use the notation of a pair of*

---

[1] In Part G, we generalize this treatment to include set-valued supplies and demands (as might arise for a firm with a linear production technology or a household with perfect substitution in its preferences). Chapter 16 (in Part G) presents the concepts and techniques treating the point to set mappings used in Chapter 17.

braces, { }, to denote a set. We can use a description of elements of the set to define the set. Thus, the entity denoted {x | x has property P} is the set of all things with property P (whatever that is). The set of positive integers between 1 and 10 can be expressed then as {1, 2, . . . , 9, 10} or, equivalently, as {x | x is an integer, $1 \leq x \leq 10$}.

Elements of a set The elements of a set are the things in the collection. If x is an element of the set A, we write $x \in A$. If, on the contrary, x is not an element of A, we write $x \notin A$. We distinguish between an element of the set A and the set itself. Thus, x and the set consisting of x are distinct. $x \neq \{x\}$ but $x \in \{x\}$. We use ϕ to denote the empty set ($\equiv$ null set), the set with no elements.

Subsets We are interested in set inclusion. If A and B are sets and every element of A is an element of B then we say that A is a subset of B. We denote this relationship as $A \subset B$ or $A \subseteq B$ (less commonly $B \supset A$). We will use the inclusion symbols, $\subset$ and $\subseteq$, interchangeably to denote the subset relationship. Every nonempty set has at least two subsets, itself and the empty set ($A \subset A$ and $\phi \subset A$).

Set equality If the same elements comprise two sets, A and B, then the sets are said to be equal. If the sets A and B have precisely the same elements, they are equal and we write $A = B$. For sets A and B, $A = B$ if and only if $x \in A$ implies $x \in B$ and $y \in B$ implies $y \in A$. From this definition of set equality and the definition of subsets above, it follows that $A = B$ if and only if $A \subset B$ and $B \subset A$.

Set union We may wish to combine the elements of two or more distinct sets into a combined set known as the *union* of the original sets. The operation union is denoted $\cup$. The union of the sets A and B is denoted $A \cup B$. $A \cup B = \{x \mid x \in A$ or $x \in B\}$ (the mathematician's use of "or" includes "or both"). We can take the union over a family of sets (e.g., $\cup_{j=1}^{50} A_j$).

Set intersection We sometimes wish to consider the set of those elements that are common to two distinct sets. This is known as the intersection of the two sets, denoted by the symbol $\cap$. Formally, the intersection of the sets A and B is $A \cap B = \{x \mid x \in A$ and $x \in B\}$. If A and B have no elements in common then their intersection is the null set, ϕ, and A and B are said to be disjoint. More formally, if $A \cap B = \phi$ we say that A and B are disjoint. Just as we can take multiple unions, so we can take multiple intersections, asking what are the elements in common to a large family of sets, for example, $\cap_{i=1}^{N} A_i$.

We now have enough structure on set operations to demonstrate some relations among them.

Theorem 2.1 *Let A, B, and C be sets, then*

(a) $A \cap A = A$, $A \cup A = A$ *(idempotency)*
(b) $A \cap B = B \cap A$, $A \cup B = B \cup A$ *(commutativity)*
(c) $A \cap (B \cap C) = (A \cap B) \cap C$ *(associativity)*
     $A \cup (B \cup C) = (A \cup B) \cup C$
(d) $A \cap (B \cup C) = (A \cap B) \cup (A \cap C)$ *(distributivity)*
     $A \cup (B \cap C) = (A \cup B) \cap (A \cup C)$

Proof Exercise 2.3.

Complementation (set subtraction) We are sometimes interested in identifying those elements of one set, A, that are not elements of a second set, B. This set is known as A minus B or the complement of B in A. The operation of complementation is denoted by the backslash symbol, $\setminus$. Formally, $A \setminus B = \{x \mid x \in A, x \notin B\}$. If A is understood, without explicitly specifying it, we may unambiguously refer to $A \setminus B$ as "B complement." This will occur, for example, if A is the whole space; in that case B complement consists of the elements of the whole space not included in B.

Cartesian product It is sometimes very useful to be able to discuss the set of combinations of elements, one from each of two or more sets, while retaining the identity of the original sets. For two sets, we do this by forming the set of *ordered pairs* whose first element is from the first of the sets and whose second element is from the other. This is known as Cartesian multiplication and its result is a Cartesian product. We denote the operation of taking a Cartesian product by a multiplication symbol, $\times$, and denote an ordered pair by the symbol $(\cdot, \cdot)$. Thus, the Cartesian product of sets A and B is denoted $A \times B = \{(x, y) \mid x \in A, y \in B\}$.

The order of elements in the ordered pair (x, y) is essential. If $x \neq y$, then $(x, y) \neq (y, x)$.

Example 2.1 Let $A = B = [0, 1] = \{x \mid x$ is a real number, $0 \leq x \leq 1\}$, then $A \times B$ is the unit square.

Example 2.2 Let A be the set of all given names and B the set of all surnames. Then $A \times B$ is the set of all possible first and last name combinations, and a typical element of $A \times B$, (a, b), is a possible entry in the list of individual names.

We can take multiple products, for example, $\Pi_{i=1}^{K} A_i = A_1 \times A_2 \times \ldots \times A_K$. The Cartesian product is used most commonly in this book to describe the set of possible commodity bundles: the set of possible consumption and production plans. We will typically say there are N possible commodities. We describe the quantity of a particular commodity then by a real number, that is, by a positive or negative rational number, irrational number, or integer. We denote the set of real numbers by $\mathbf{R}$. A possible commodity combination, a mix of the N different goods, can thus be described by listing the quantity of each of the N different goods in the combination. The amount of any single good will be denoted by an element of $\mathbf{R}$. Hence the amounts in a combination of the N goods can be denoted by an element of $\mathbf{R}^N$, an N-dimensional vector, which is an element of the N-fold Cartesian product of $\mathbf{R}$ with itself. $\mathbf{R}^N = \mathbf{R} \times \mathbf{R} \times \mathbf{R} \times \ldots \times \mathbf{R}$, where the product is taken N times.

The order of elements in the ordered N-tuple $(x, y, \ldots)$ is essential. If $x \neq y$, then $(x, y, \ldots) \neq (y, x, \ldots)$.

2.2 Quasi-orderings

As we develop our ideas about the theory of the household or the consumer we will want to have a systematic notion of tastes or preferences. This is sometimes summarized in a utility function, but traditionally in general equilibrium theory we try to start from a more fundamental notion of tastes, represented as a simple ordering of household preferences. A theory of the utility function is then derived from this primitive notion of the preference ordering. We then search for a mathematical structure for a theory of preferences. There is actually a well-developed theory of orderings. We will outline elements of it now.

By a *binary relation* we mean some characteristic that ties together two things, for example:

a is the brother of b,
c is to the left of d,
e is bigger than f,
g is preferred to h,
i is equal to j.

We can denote a binary relation by some sign between the characters; for example, $a\beta b$ could represent "a is the brother of b." In defining a relation, we must also define the domain on which it is defined.

A number of other definitions that will be helpful are presented next.

Reflexivity Let R denote a relation on S. The relation R is said to be reflexive if for all $x \in S$, xRx. The relation is reflexive if all elements in the domain of the relation bear that relation to themselves. For example, the equality relation $(=)$ is reflexive.

Transitivity The binary relation R is said to be transitive if xRy and yRz implies xRz. For example, the equality relation is transitive, as is the greater than relation $(>)$ on the set of real numbers $\mathbf{R}$.

Quasi-orderings A binary relation that is reflexive and transitive is called a pre-order or quasi-order. We can use any convenient notation to denote a quasi-ordering. The generic quasi-ordering symbol is $\succsim$. A typical quasi-ordering is the greater than or equal to relation, $\geq$, on the set of real numbers $\mathbf{R}$.

Complete relations The relation R on S is said to be *complete* if for every $x, y \in S, xRy$ or yRx, or both. The relation is complete on S if it is defined in one direction or the other (or both) for all pairs of elements of S. The relation R is complete if it is well defined on every pair of elements in S.

Upper bound of a quasi-ordering Let S be quasi-ordered by $\succsim$. Let $X \subset S$. If there is $y \in S$ such that for each $x \in X$, $y \succsim x$, then y is said to be an upper bound for X. Let $Y = \{y \mid y \succsim x \text{ for all } x \in X\}$. If there is $y' \in Y$ so that $y \succsim y'$ for all $y \in Y$, then y' is said to be X's least upper bound.

    Note: It is a property of the real numbers $\mathbf{R}$ quasi-ordered by $\geq$ that whenever $X \subset \mathbf{R}$ has an upper bound, X has a least upper bound.

Upper contour set of $\succsim$ Let S be quasi-ordered by $\succsim$. Starting from a point $y \in S$, we can describe the set of points superior to y under $\succsim$, y's upper contour set: $A(y) = \{x \mid x \in S, x \succsim y\}$.

    Similarly, we can describe y's lower contour set under $\succsim$, the set of values inferior to y under $\succsim$: $G(y) = \{x \mid x \in S, y \succsim x\}$.

    In the case where $\succsim$ is a preference ordering, we are familiar with representing the ordering by it's indifference curves. The indifference curve through y would be represented as $\{x \mid x \in S, x \succsim y \text{ and } y \succsim x\} = A(y) \cap G(y)$.

2.3 Functions

We typically think of mathematical functions as a relationship between one class of values and another. For example, the temperature function might give the temperature as a function of the latitude and longitude of a location. In economic applications we usually think of demand and supply functions as a relationship between prices and quantities of goods.

Definition of a function *Let A and B be sets. To each element $x \in A$ we associate some single element $y \in B$ and we write $y = f(x)$, $f : A \rightarrow B$, where f denotes* *the function. A is the domain of the function, B is its range, and f is a function mapping from A to B. Alternatively, we may say that f is a subset of $A \times B$ such that for each $x \in A$ there is one and only one $y \in B$ so that $(x, y) \in f$. This subset is also known as the* graph *of f.*

Note that for some $y \in B$ there may be no $x \in A$ such that $y = f(x)$. Conversely, if for every $y \in B$ there is $x \in A$ such that $y = f(x)$ then we say f maps A onto *B.*

The inverse of the function f is denoted f^{-1}; $f^{-1} : B \rightarrow A$. f^{-1} is defined as $f^{-1}(y) = \{x \mid x \in A, y = f(x)\}$. If $f^{-1}(y)$ has no more than one element for all $y \in B$ then we say that f is one-to-one.

2.4 $\mathbf{R}^N$: Real N-dimensional Euclidean space

Most of the sets, functions, and relations we will deal with are represented in real N-dimensional Euclidean space. The space is the N-fold Cartesian product of the real line, **R**, with itself, using the Euclidean metric (which is a measure of distance between points of the set). N is taken to be a (finite) positive integer. We typically take N as the number of commodities in the economy. We are familiar with $\mathbf{R}^2$ as the plane of the blackboard or the page and $\mathbf{R}^3$ as the conventional view of three-dimensional space. Visualizing $\mathbf{R}^N$ for large N may take rather more imagination but the mathematical principles of working in this space are the same as in $\mathbf{R}^2$ or $\mathbf{R}^3$.

Definition of R *Our understanding of $\mathbf{R}^N$ starts with our understanding of $\mathbf{R}$. **R** is the space of real numbers, positive and negative: the rationals, irrationals, and integers. It is the real line consisting of all finite (positive and negative) real numbers. Although $\pm\infty$ are not elements of **R**, there are elements of **R** that are arbitrarily large and positive and others arbitrarily small (negative). Addition, subtraction, multiplication, and division are useful operations on **R** and of course retain their familiar properties.*

We denote a **closed interval** in **R** as $[a, b] \equiv \{x \mid x \in R, a \leq x \leq b\}$. The reals, **R**, are said to be **complete**, that is, between any two distinct reals there is another real. This is formalized as the nested intervals property:

Consider a sequence of closed intervals in $\mathbf{R}$, $[x^\nu, y^\nu]$ with $x^\nu < y^\nu$ and $[x^{\nu+1}, y^{\nu+1}] \subseteq [x^\nu, y^\nu]$, $\nu = 1, 2, 3, \ldots$. Then there is $z \in \mathbf{R}$ so that z is an element of all of the intervals in the sequence of intervals, $z \in \cap_{\nu=1}^{\infty}[x^\nu, y^\nu]$. This is the nested intervals property, representing the completeness of **R**.

$\mathbf{R}^N$ is the N-fold Cartesian product of R. The typical element of $\mathbf{R}^N$, $x \in \mathbf{R}^N$, is an N-tuple of real numbers and will be denoted $x = (x_1, x_2, \ldots, x_N)$, where x_i is the ith coordinate of x. We can depict x as a point (or **vector**) in $\mathbf{R}^N$. In some applications, the notion of x as a vector emphasizes direction and magnitude.

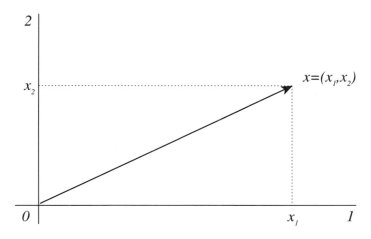

Fig. 2.1. A vector in $\mathbf{R}^2$.

We define the ith projection of x, or the projection of x on the ith axis, as x_i. Equivalently, the projection of x on the ith axis is the vector on the axis that results from dropping a perpendicular line to the axis from x. See Figure 2.1.

Algebra of elements of $\mathbf{R}^N$ We need to have well-defined, well-behaved, concepts of addition and subtraction in $\mathbf{R}^N$. We will define addition coordinatewise. Thus we define $x + y = (x_1 + y_1, x_2 + y_2, \ldots, x_N + y_N)$. We can depict the addition of x and y graphically as the parallel movement of the vector y to the end of the vector x, forming a parallelogram whose extreme point is $x + y$. See Figure 2.2.

The identity element under addition is the origin: the vector whose coordinates are all zero, traditionally denoted by the character 0.

We define vector subtraction by way of vector addition. Let $y \in \mathbf{R}^N$ and let $-y$ be the vector consisting of y with each of its coordinates multiplied by -1. Then we define $x - y \equiv x + (-y)$.

We will sometimes wish to multiply an element of $\mathbf{R}^N$, a vector, by an element of $\mathbf{R}$, a scalar. We define multiplication by a scalar in the obvious consistent fashion. Let

$$t \in \mathbf{R}, x \in \mathbf{R}^N, \quad \text{then } tx \equiv (tx_1, tx_2, \ldots, tx_N).$$

We define the dot product or scalar product of two elements of $\mathbf{R}^N$ as the sum of the products of the corresponding coordinates. Let $x, y \in \mathbf{R}^N$, then we define the dot product of x and y as $x \cdot y = \sum_{i=1}^{N} x_i y_i$. The economic application of the dot product is usually to evaluate an economic action at prevailing prices. Thus, if $p \in \mathbf{R}^N$ is a price vector and $y \in \mathbf{R}^N$ is an economic action, then $p \cdot y$ is the value of the action y at prices p.

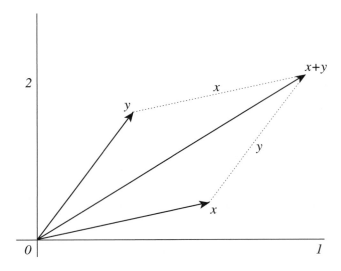

Fig. 2.2. Vector addition.

Norm in $\mathbf{R}^N$ It is very convenient to have a measure of distance and length in $\mathbf{R}^N$. Our concept of length comes from Euclidean geometry. It is measured by the root of the sum of the squared coordinates of a vector. We will define the length of a vector as the distance of the vector from the origin, 0. The distance between two vectors is the length of the difference (subtraction) between them. Let $x \in \mathbf{R}^N$. Then we say the length of x is

$$|x| \equiv \|x\| \equiv \sqrt{x \cdot x} \equiv \sqrt{\sum_{i=1}^{N} x_i^2}.$$

Let $x, y \in \mathbf{R}^N$. Then the distance between the two points x and y is $\|x - y\|$. That is, $|x - y| = \sqrt{\sum_i (x_i - y_i)^2}$. Note a few properties of this measure of distance that certainly represent a reasonable concept of distance: the distance between two points of $\mathbf{R}^N$ is always nonnegative; $\|x - y\| \geq 0$ all $x, y \in \mathbf{R}^N$; and the distance between two points of $\mathbf{R}^N$ is zero if and only if the points are identical (i.e., $|x - y| = 0$ if and only if $x = y$).

Now that we have a concept of distance, we have a corresponding concept of closeness. This leads to a most important concept in analysis: limiting behavior. We can characterize whether a sequence of points is getting close to another point (approaching a limit).

Limits of sequences We define a sequence in $\mathbf{R}$ as an ordered collection of real numbers. The elements of the sequence are numbered (indexed) by the positive integers, typically denoted by the index i or ν (the Greek n). We are interested only in infinite sequences, so i or ν take on the values 1, 2, 3, . . . and so on, indefinitely. The notion of their running on indefinitely will be denoted $\nu = 1, 2, 3, \ldots$. The limiting behavior of a sequence turns out to be a very powerful concept.

For example, consider the sequence x^ν, $\nu = 1, 2, 3, \ldots$, where x^ν is defined to have the value $1/\nu$. That is, the sequence x^ν runs 1, 1/2, 1/3, 1/4, 1/5, ... It is clear that the sequence x^ν is getting consistently closer to 0 as ν becomes larger. In the standard terminology, x^ν approaches 0 as a limit or, equivalently, $x^\nu \to 0$.

Formalizing this concept in **R**, let $x^i \in \mathbf{R}$, $i = 1, 2, \ldots$. We say that $x^i \to x^0$ if for any $\varepsilon > 0$ there is a positive integer $q(\varepsilon)$ (we use the functional notation to denote that $q(\varepsilon)$ necessarily depends on ε) so that for all $q' > q(\varepsilon)$, $|x^{q'} - x^0| < \varepsilon$. That is, we say that x^i approaches x^0 as a limit if we can always successfully perform the following exercise: Form a perimeter of radius ε about x^0, the proposed limiting value of the sequence x^i. Choose an index far enough out in the list of indices, i, and call it $q(\varepsilon)$. The choice of $q(\varepsilon)$ depends on ε. For smaller values of ε, we may need to go farther out in the sequence, so $q(\varepsilon)$ will be larger. For all index values i greater than $q(\varepsilon)$, check to see whether x^i is within ε of the proposed limit x^0. If so, then the sequence is said to approach x^0 as a limit. The idea is that for any radius $\varepsilon > 0$, no matter how small, if we go far enough out in the sequence, all of the elements of the sequence beyond that point will be within ε of the limit. If that is the case, then the sequence is said to approach the limit.

We have formalized the notion of a sequence of values approaching a limit in **R**. Now we do the same in $\mathbf{R}^N$. We define a sequence of points in $\mathbf{R}^N$ to converge to a limit in $\mathbf{R}^N$ if each of the coordinate sequences converges. This is a typical mathematical procedure reducing the analysis to a previously treated case. Let $x^i \in \mathbf{R}^N$, $i = 1, 2, \ldots$. We say that $x^i \to x^0$ if for each coordinate $n = 1, 2, \ldots, N$, $x_n^i \to x_n^0$.

Theorem 2.2, below, tells us that the identical definition and procedure for describing convergence of a sequence in **R** will work equally well in $\mathbf{R}^N$. That is, we can take a radius of size ε about the proposed limit point and see whether sufficiently far out in the sequence all points of the sequence are contained within a ball of radius ε centered at the proposed limit. If so, we have the limiting behavior that is sought.

Theorem 2.2 *Let $x^i \in \mathbf{R}^N$, $i = 1, 2, \ldots$. Then $x^i \to x^0$ if and only if for any ε there is $q(\varepsilon)$ such that for all $q' > q(\varepsilon)$, $\|x^{q'} - x^0\| < \varepsilon$.*

Proof Exercise 2.7.

Now that we have developed the notion of the limit of a sequence we can generalize it to the concept of a *cluster point* (or accumulation point). If we have a set or sequence

S in $\mathbf{R}^N$ so that there is an infinite sequence (or subsequence) in S approaching x° as a limit, then x° is a cluster or accumulation point of S. It is not quite correct to describe x° as a limit point (after all there may be many cluster points and S may not converge meaningfully to any one), but it can be approached as a limit by a sequence of points in S.

Open sets   We will now define open and closed subsets of $\mathbf{R}^N$. These concepts will prove to be extremely useful in describing our concepts of continuous functions and formalizing the idea of "closeness" of sets of points to each other. A set is said to be *open* if starting at any point of the set, the set contains all nearby points. More formally, centered at any point in the set, draw a ball of radius $\varepsilon > 0$. If the set is open, for positive ε sufficiently small, the ball will be contained entirely in the set. Formally,

Let $X \subset \mathbf{R}^N$; X is said to be open if for every $x \in X$ there is an $\varepsilon > 0$ so that $\|x - y\| < \varepsilon$ implies $y \in X$.

A typical example of an open set in $\mathbf{R}$ is an open interval, $(a, b) = \{x \mid x \in \mathbf{R}, a < x < b\}$. For any point in (a, b) there is a small positive radius so that all the values in $\mathbf{R}$ within that radius are included in (a, b).

Note: ϕ and $\mathbf{R}^N$ are open.

Closed sets   It is very useful to know when the limiting value of a sequence of points in a set is itself in the set. This issue arises naturally in economics since economic behavior is characterized by optimization – taking maximum or minimum values. It is important to know then whether the extremum is part of the opportunity set. For example, suppose we are trying to choose a point x in the closed interval $[a, b] = \{x \mid x \in \mathbf{R}, 0 \le a \le x \le b\}$ to maximize x^2. The choice would clearly be $x = b$. The maximum exists and is a member of the set $[a, b]$. Now consider the same problem where the opportunity set is the open interval $(a, b) = \{x \mid x \in \mathbf{R}, 0 \le a < x < b\}$. In this case there is no maximum in the opportunity set, since $b \notin (a, b)$. Maximizing behavior appears not to be well defined. The bottom line is that it is very convenient for us to have a characterization specifying when limits of points in a set will be included in the set. This is the concept of *closedness*.

We define a *closed* set in $\mathbf{R}^N$ as a set that includes the limit points of any sequence of points in the set. A set is closed if it contains all of its cluster points. Formally:

Let $X \subset \mathbf{R}^N$. X is said to be closed if for every sequence $x^i, i = 1, 2, 3, \ldots,$ satisfying

(i) $x^i \in X$ and
(ii) $x^i \to x^0$,

it follows that $x^0 \in X$.

Note: Closed and open are not antonyms among sets. Both ϕ and $\mathbf{R}^N$ are closed, as well as open.

We now define the *closure* of a set. Take any set X in $\mathbf{R}^N$. The closure of X is the smallest closed set containing X, that is, the set of X and all of its cluster points. Formally, let $X \subseteq \mathbf{R}^N$. Then we define the closure of X, denoted $\overline{X}$, as

$$\overline{X} = \{y \mid \text{there is } x^\nu \in X, \nu = 1, 2, 3, \ldots, \text{ so that } x^\nu \to y\}.$$

Theorem 2.3 *Let $X \subset \mathbf{R}^N$. X is closed if $\mathbf{R}^N \setminus X$ is open.*

Proof Exercise 2.10.

Theorem 2.4

(1) $X \subset \overline{X}$.
(2) $X = \overline{X}$ if and only if X is closed.

Proof Trivial.

Bounded sets Boundedness is another characteristic of subsets of $\mathbf{R}^N$ that proves useful in economic applications. As before, consider a simple optimization problem, finding the value of x in an opportunity set that maximizes x^2. We know from our examples above that it helps if the opportunity set is closed. Is that enough? No, we will need the opportunity set to be nonempty; there is no maximizer of x^2 in ϕ, the empty set. Is that all? Suppose the opportunity set is all of the reals, $\mathbf{R}$. Is there a choice of $x \in \mathbf{R}$ that achieves a maximum value of x^2 ? No. For any value of x chosen, there is a larger one elsewhere in $\mathbf{R}$ that gives a higher value of x^2. Once again the issue is the availability of a limiting value, which is where boundedness comes in. We will say that a subset of $\mathbf{R}^N$ is bounded if it can be contained inside a cube of finite size. Define the set

$$K(k) = \{x \mid x \in R^N, |x_i| \le k, i = 1, 2, \ldots, N\}$$

to be the cube of side $2k$ (centered at the origin).

Let $X \subset \mathbf{R}^N$. X is said to be bounded if there is $k \in \mathbf{R}$ so that $X \subset K(k)$.

Compact sets As the examples above suggested, when we look for well-defined maximizing behavior, it will be useful if our opportunity sets are both closed and bounded. That leads to the definition of compactness:

Let $X \subset \mathbf{R}^N$. X is said to be compact if X is closed and bounded.

Boundary, interior, etc. *Let $X \subset \mathbf{R}^N$. The interior of X is $\{y \mid y \in X$, there is $\varepsilon > 0$ so that $\|x - y\| < \varepsilon$ implies $x \in X\}$. The interior of X is the biggest open set contained in X.*

Boundary $X \equiv \overline{X} \setminus$ interior X. The boundary of X is its outer edge, its closure minus its interior.

Connectedness We say that S, $S \subseteq T \subseteq \mathbf{R}^N$, is "closed in T" if S includes all of its cluster points that are themselves in T. Thus, for example, every nonempty set S is closed in S. Similarly, the half open interval in $\mathbf{R}$, $(0, 1]$, which is trivially not a closed set in $\mathbf{R}$, is closed in the half open interval $(0,10]$. A set $S \subseteq \mathbf{R}^N$ is said to be connected if it cannot be expressed as the union of two disjoint nonempty subsets that are themselves closed in S. $\mathbf{R}^N$ is connected. Hence, the only two disjoint closed sets whose union is $\mathbf{R}^N$ are $\mathbf{R}^N$ and ϕ.

Set summation in $\mathbf{R}^N$ Let A and B be subsets of $\mathbf{R}^N$. That is, $A \subseteq \mathbf{R}^N$, $B \subseteq \mathbf{R}^N$. Then we define $A + B$ as

$$A + B \equiv \{x \mid x = a + b, a \in A, b \in B\}.$$

Thus, for example, if A is the line segment in $\mathbf{R}^2$ between $(0,0)$ and $(1,0)$ and B is the line segment between $(0,0)$ and $(0,1)$, then $A + B$ would be the square with corners $(0,0)$, $(1,0)$, $(0,1)$, and $(1,1)$.

The Bolzano-Weierstrass Theorem; completeness of $\mathbf{R}^N$ We stated without proof above that the reals, $\mathbf{R}$, are complete. That is, between any two distinct reals, there is another real number. We can now generalize this property to $\mathbf{R}^N$.

Theorem 2.5 (Nested Intervals Theorem) *By an interval in $\mathbf{R}^N$, we mean a set I of the form*

$$I = \{(x_1, x_2, \ldots, x_N) \mid a_1 \le x_1 \le b_1, a_2 \le x_2 \le b_2, \ldots,$$
$$a_N \le x_N \le b_N, a_i, b_i \in R\}.$$

Consider a sequence of nonempty closed intervals I_k such that

$$I_1 \supseteq I_2 \supseteq I_3 \supseteq \ldots \supseteq I_k \supseteq \ldots.$$

Then there is a point in $\mathbf{R}^N$ contained in all the intervals.

Proof The proof follows from the completeness of the reals, the nested intervals property on **R**.

Starting from the sequence x^ν we may select some infinite part of x^ν as a *subsequence*. Thus a subsequence might consist of every third element of x^ν or all of the odd-numbered elements of x^ν or the first, seventh, eighth, ..., and so forth elements of x^ν. The subsequence must itself be a sequence, that is, have an infinite number of elements, and the sequential order of the elements in the subsequence must be the same as in the original sequence, x^ν.

Corollary 2.1 (Bolzano-Weierstrass Theorem for sequences) *Let $x^i, i = 1, 2, 3, \ldots$ be a bounded sequence in $\mathbf{R}^N$. Then x^i contains a convergent subsequence.*

Proof (Exercise 2.12) There are two cases: either x^i assumes a finite number of values or x^i assumes an infinite number of values.

2.5 Continuous functions

The concept of continuity is essential to general equilibrium theory. We saw the tip-off to its importance in Section 1.4 where we applied the Brouwer Fixed-Point Theorem to prove the existence of equilibrium in the auctioneer's price-setting problem. It was essential there that we be able to describe the price adjustment procedure as continuous in prices. We used the property of the continuity of demand and supply functions to show that the price adjustment process was a continuous mapping from price space into itself. The idea of continuity of a function is that there should be no jumps in the values the function assumes as its argument [the x in $f(x)$] makes small changes. Small changes in the domain should correspond to small changes in the function value.

Definition of continuity *Let $f : A \to B$, $A \subset \mathbf{R}^m$, and $B \subset \mathbf{R}^p$. Let ε and $\delta(\varepsilon)$ be small positive real numbers; we use the functional notation $\delta(\varepsilon)$ to emphasize that the choice of δ depends on the value of ε. The function f is said to be continuous at $a \in A$ if*

*(i) for every $\varepsilon > 0$ there is $\delta(\varepsilon) > 0$ such that $|x - a| < \delta(\varepsilon) \Rightarrow |f(x) - f(a)| < \varepsilon$
or, equivalently,*
(ii) $x^\nu \in A, \nu = 1, 2, \ldots$ and $x^\nu \to a$ implies $f(x^\nu) \to f(a)$.

It will be an exercise below to prove that (i) and (ii) are equivalent.

The essence of continuity is that nearby points in the domain be mapped into nearby points in the range; there are no jumps. The definition in part (i) says that for every targeted small variation of function values by which we wish to limit values of the function, there is a corresponding small radius in the domain so that if the independent variable is restricted to remain within that radius, the variation in function values will remain within the desired limits. To see the power of this definition, think of a discontinuous function, for example,

$$g(x) = \begin{cases} -1 & \text{for } x < 0 \\ +1 & \text{for } x \geq 0. \end{cases}$$

The function g is discontinuous at 0. Set $\varepsilon = 1/2$. There is no $\delta > 0$ that when x is restricted to a radius of δ about 0 would keep $g(x)$ within a range of ε. Hence the function g is not continuous. This is the kind of behavior that the definition of continuity rules out. The equivalent definition, part (ii), describes continuity as the property of f that the image under f of a convergent sequence in the domain will be a convergent sequence of function values in the range.

Theorem 2.6 *Let* $f : A \rightarrow B$, *where* f *is continuous. Let* $S \subset B$, *with* S *closed. Then* $f^{-1}(S)$ *is closed.*

Proof Exercise 2.21.

Theorem 2.6 says that the inverse image of a closed set under a continuous mapping is closed.

Theorem 2.7 *Let* $f : A \rightarrow B$, *where* f *is continuous. Let* $S \subset A$, *with* S *compact. Then* $f(S)$ *is compact.*

Proof From part (ii) of the definition of continuity, closedness of S implies closedness of $f(S)$. From part (i) choose some positive ε. For each $x \in S$, there is a positive $\delta(x, \varepsilon)$ so that $|x - y| < \delta$ implies $|f(x) - f(y)| < \varepsilon$. For all x in S, consider the open ball centered at x with radius δ. This set of open balls covers S. It is a property of compactness (not proved here) that every open cover has a finite subcover, that is, that a finite subset of these open balls covers S. But then the maximum variation in $f(S)$ is ε times the number of open balls in the finite subcover – a finite number. This completes the proof.   QED

Theorem 2.7 says that the image of a compact set under a continuous mapping is compact.

The supremum of a set of real numbers (denoted sup) is the least upper bound of the set under $\geq$, when this bound exists. For a bounded set of reals, the sup will necessarily exist. It is equivalent to a maximum when the sup value is actually achieved in the set. The infimum of a set of real numbers (denoted inf) is the greatest lower bound of the set under $\geq$, when it exists. It is equivalent to a minimum when the inf value is actually achieved in the set.

Corollary 2.2 *Let* $f : A \rightarrow R$, *where* f *is continuous, and* $S \subset A$, *with* S *compact. Then there are* $\bar{x}, \underline{x} \in S$ *such that* $f(\bar{x}) = \sup\{f(x) \mid x \in S\}$ *and* $f(\underline{x}) = \inf\{f(x) \mid x \in S\}$.

This corollary is the most important single result for economic theory in the analysis of continuous functions. It gives us a very useful set of sufficient conditions to identify when a function has a well-defined extremum (maximum or minimum). The corollary says that two sufficient conditions allow us to say that a real-valued function f achieves its maximum and minimum on a set S. Those conditions are that f be continuous throughout S and that S be compact. As we develop the theory of the firm and the theory of the household in the rest of this volume, much of our effort will go into setting up the models so that we can characterize the opportunity sets of firms and households as compact and their maximands as continuous real-valued functions.

Homogeneous functions Let $f : \mathbf{R}^p \rightarrow \mathbf{R}^q$. The function f is said to be homogeneous of degree 0 if for every scalar (real number) $\lambda > 0$, we have $f(\lambda x) = f(x)$. f is said to be homogeneous of degree 1 if for every scalar $\lambda > 0$, we have $f(\lambda x) = \lambda f(x)$.

2.6 Convexity

Definition *A set of points* S *in* $\mathbf{R}^N$ *is said to be convex if the line segment between any two points of the set is completely included in the set, that is,* S *is* **convex** *if* $x, y \in S$ *implies* $\{z \mid z = \alpha x + (1 - \alpha)y, 0 \leq \alpha \leq 1\} \subseteq S$.
$\quad$ *S is said to be* **strictly convex** *if* $x, y \in S$, $x \neq y$, $0 < \alpha < 1$ *implies* $\alpha x + (1 - \alpha)y \in interior\ S$.

The notion of convexity is that a set is convex if it is connected, has no holes on the inside, and has no indentations on the boundary. Figure 2.3 displays convex and nonconvex sets. A set is strictly convex if it is convex and has a continuous strict curvature (no flat segments) on the boundary.

Properties of convex sets *Let* C_1 *and* C_2 *be convex subsets of* $\mathbf{R}^N$. *Then*

$C_1 \cap C_2$ *is convex*,
$C_1 + C_2$ *is convex*,
$\overline{C}_1$ *is convex*.

Proof See Exercise 2.14.

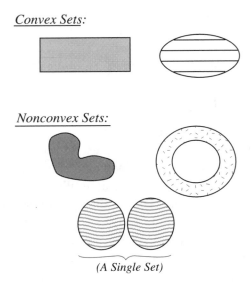

Fig. 2.3. Convex and nonconvex sets.

The concept of convexity of a set in $\mathbf{R}^N$ is essential in mathematical economic analysis. This reflects the importance of continuous point-valued optimizing behavior. To understand the importance of convexity, consider for a moment what will happen when it is absent. Suppose widgets are consumed only in discrete lots of 100, and suppose a typical widget eater at some prices to be indifferent between buying a lot of 100 and buying 0. He will definitely not buy a fractional lot. The insistence on discrete lots is a nonconvexity. At a low price, he will want to buy a lot of 100. As prices increase he will become indifferent a some price, say at p^*, between 0 and 100. At still higher prices, he will demand 0. The demand curve has a gap at p^*. Demand is set-valued (consisting of the two points 0 and 100) and appears discontinuous at p^*. With a gap that big in the demand curve, it is clear that there may be no intersection of supply and demand and hence no equilibrium. It is to prevent this family of difficulties that we will insist on convexity.

Strict convexity typically will assure uniqueness (point-valuedness) of maxima. Conversely, when opportunity sets or preferences are nonconvex (not convex), optimizing behavior of firms or households may jump between discrete noncontiguous points as prices vary.

2.7 Brouwer Fixed-Point Theorem

The Brouwer Fixed-Point Theorem is a profound and powerful result. It turns out to be essential in proving the existence of general equilibrium. We have already seen that it is convenient (in Section 1.4), but it can be shown to be indispensable (Chapter 11).

The Brouwer Fixed-Point Theorem says that a continuous function from a compact convex set into itself has a fixed point. There is at least one point that is left unchanged by the mapping. Note that the convexity is essential. For example, the fixed point property is not true (and the theorem is inapplicable) for a function mapping the circumference of a circle into itself.

In **R**, the Brouwer Fixed-Point Theorem takes a particularly simple form. Let f map the closed interval $[a, b]$ into itself. Then the theorem is equivalent to the assertion that every continuous curve $y = f(x)$ from one side of the square $[a, b] \times [a, b]$ to the opposite side must intersect the diagonal (the line $y = x$). See Figure 2.4.

Economic applications do not require that the economist know or understand the proof of the Brouwer Theorem. Because a combinatorial proof can be presented in elementary (though necessarily complex) form and because it is not generally included in introductory real analysis courses, it is presented below. Students who do not wish to follow the proof may skip, without loss of continuity, to the statement of the Brouwer Fixed-Point Theorem, below.

We will prove the Brouwer Fixed-Point Theorem on a simplex (the simplest of compact convex sets) in three steps:

(i) Prove Sperner's Lemma.

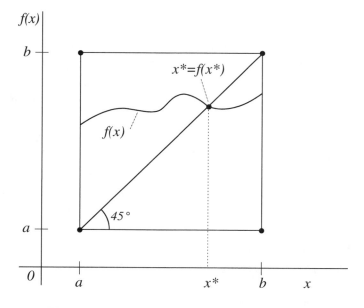

Fig. 2.4. The Brouwer Fixed-Point Theorem in **R**.

(ii) Use Sperner's Lemma to prove the Knaster-Kuratowski-Mazurkeiwicz (KKM) Theorem.

(iii) Use the KKM Theorem to prove the Brouwer Fixed-Point Theorem.[2]

Definition *Let* $x_1, x_2, \ldots, x_{N+1}$ *be* $N+1$ *points in* $\mathbf{R}^K$, $K \geq N$. *Any* N *of the points should be linearly independent[3]. Then the* N-*simplex defined by* $x_1, \ldots, x_{N+1}$ *is the set* S *of convex combinations of* $x_1, x_2, \ldots, x_{N+1}$:

$$S \equiv \left\{ x \mid x = \sum_{i=1}^{N+1} \lambda_i x_i, \lambda_i \geq 0, \sum_{i=1}^{N+1} \lambda_i = 1 \right\}.$$

For $x \in S$, λ_i *in the sum defining* x *is said to be the* ith **barycentric** *coordinate of* x. *The points* $x_1, x_2, x_3, \ldots, x_{N+1}$ *are the* **vertices** *of* S. *The subscript* i *is the* **index** *of the vertex* x_i. *For given* $x \in S$ *the set* $\{x_i \mid$ *the* ith *barycentric coordinate of* x, λ_i, *is positive*$\}$ *is said to be the* **carrier** *of* x. *We are already familiar with the case in which* S *is the unit simplex in* $\mathbf{R}^N$ *(from Section 1.4). In that case the* ith *barycentric coordinate of a point in the simplex is simply its* ith *coordinate, and its carrier is simply the set of vertices* i *so that the* ith *coordinate is positive. A* **face** *of the simplex is a simplex of lower dimension on the exterior of the simplex. More formally, a typical face,* F, *of the simplex* S *is defined as*

$$F \equiv \left\{ x \mid x = \sum_{i=1}^{N+1} \lambda_i x_i, \lambda_k \equiv 0 \text{ for one } k, \lambda_i \geq 0, \sum_{i=1}^{N+1} \lambda_i = 1 \right\}.$$

A **simplicial subdivision** *of* S *is a finite family of simplices* $\{S_j\}$ *so that (i) the elements of* $\{S_j\}$ *have disjoint interiors, (ii) if a vertex of* S_j *is an element of* S_k *then that point is also a vertex of* S_k, *and (iii)* $\cup S_k = S$. *Note that for any* $\varepsilon > 0$ *we can find a simplicial subdivision of* S *so that each subsimplex of the subdivision can be contained in a sphere of radius* ε. *That is, there exist subdivisions of arbitrarily fine mesh.*

Let $\{S_j\}$ *be a simplicial subdivision of* S. *We will label each vertex of each subsimplex with one of the numbers* $1, 2, \ldots, N+1$. *A labeling is said to be* **admissible** *if each vertex is labeled with the index of one of the elements of its carrier. Suppose we have an admissibly labeled simplicial subdivision of an* N-*simplex. Note that each face of the* N-*simplex is an* $(N-1)$-*simplex.*

Theorem 2.8 (Sperner's Lemma) *Let* $\{S_j\}$ *be a simplicial subdivision of the* N-*simplex* S. *Label* $\{S_j\}$ *by an admissible labeling. Then there is* $S^\circ \in \{S_j\}$ *so that*

---

[2] Useful references include Tompkins (1964) and Burger (1963).

[3] The points are linearly independent if none of them can be expressed as a linear combination of the others.

*S° carries a complete set of labels (i.e., there is a vertex of S° labeled 1, another
labeled 2, . . . , N + 1).*

Figure 2.5 depicts an admissibly labeled simplicial subdivision of a 2-simplex.
Where is (are) the subsimplex(ices) carrying the full set of labels?

The proof of Sperner's Lemma makes use of the *principle of mathematical induction*. This principle explains how to take an observation for a few positive integers
and generalize it to all integers, $n = 1, 2, 3, \ldots$. First show that the proposition is
true for $n = 1$. Then show that the property that the proposition is true for a value
n logically implies that the proposition is true for the value $n + 1$ as well. The
principle of mathematical induction says that once these properties are established,
then the proposition is true for all positive integers.

Proof of Sperner's Lemma It is convenient to prove the stronger result that the
number of subsimplices with a complete set of labels is an odd number. Since zero
is not odd, this result implies Sperner's Lemma. The proof proceeds by induction
on N, the dimension of the simplex. The 1-simplex is a line segment, and the
simplicial subdivision cuts it into nonoverlapping contiguous subsegments. The
labels are 1 and 2. We will use an elementary counting argument to show that
there is an odd number of subsimplices (subsegments) carrying a full set of labels

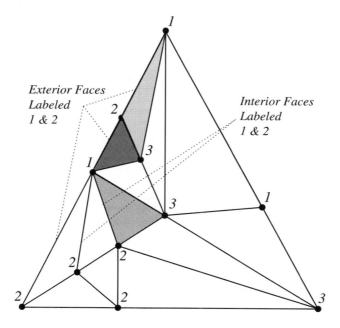

Fig. 2.5. An admissibly labeled simplicial subdivision of a simplex.

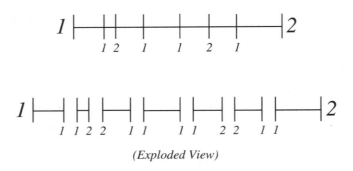

(Exploded View)

Fig. 2.6. Sperner's Lemma for $N = 1$.

(both labels 1 and 2). A typical admissibly labeled simplicial subdivision of the 1-simplex is shown in Figure 2.6.

Each vertex is labeled 1 or 2. One endpoint of the full segment is labeled 1 and the other labeled 2. Let there be a subsegments both of whose end points are labeled 1 and b subsegments whose end points are labeled 1 and 2. That is, there are b subsegments carrying a full set of labels. We need to prove that b is an odd number.

The way the proof proceeds is to enumerate the subsegments and endpoints. In particular, we will count up the endpoints labeled 1. We will perform the count in two ways: First we focus on the endpoints; then we focus on the subsegments. This will give us a count of the number of endpoints labeled 1 with the count performed in two distinct ways. We will show that since one count is necessarily odd, the other must be odd as well. This will imply that b is odd.

Count up the labels marked 1, once for each subsegment on which it appears. Each endpoint labeled 1 is counted once for each subsegment of which it is an element. Then the total number of 1s counted is $2a + b$. We think of a subsegment endpoint as being interior if it is not an endpoint of the original segment. Note that each interior endpoint labeled 1 of a subsegment is counted twice, once for each subsegment of which it is an element, and that each exterior endpoint labeled 1 is counted once (there is precisely one such endpoint). Now we will use an alternative counting procedure. Let c equal the number of interior endpoints labeled 1. Then the number of endpoints labeled 1 (again counting each endpoint once for each subsegment to which it is attached) is $1 + 2c$. Thus,

$$1 + 2c = 2a + b.$$

But $1 + 2c$ is certainly odd. Hence $2a + b$ is odd and therefore b is odd. This proves the lemma for the case for $N = 1$. Note that the 1-simplex in Figure 2.6 fulfills Sperner's Lemma. Examining the exploded view of the 1-simplex in the figure demonstrates how the counting argument takes place.

We now proceed by induction. Suppose for an $(N-1)$-simplex, any admissibly labeled simplicial subdivision of the $(N-1)$-simplex contains an odd number of subsimplices carrying a full set of labels. This is the inductive hypothesis. We must show that this property (that every admissibly labeled simplicial subdivision contains an odd number of subsimplices carrying a full set of labels) is then necessarily true as well of an N-simplex. Consider an admissibly labeled simplicial subdivision of an N-simplex. Note that each face of an N-simplex is an $(N-1)$-simplex, so an admissibly labeled subdivision of a face of the N-simplex will have an odd number of subsimplices carrying a full set of labels (of the face) by hypothesis. Figure 2.5 shows a 2-simplex (a triangle) with an admissibly labeled simplicial subdivision. Note that each face of the 2-simplex (side of the triangle) is a 1-simplex (a line segment) with an admissibly labeled simplicial subdivision resulting from the subdivision and labeling of the 2-simplex.

Let a be the number of elements (subsimplices) of the simplicial subdivision, $\{S_j\}$ of S, labeled with $1, \ldots, N$, but not labeled $N+1$. Then for each such element there are two faces of the subsimplex (each face is an $N-1$ simplex) whose vertices are labeled $1, \ldots, N$. Therefore, the number of such faces (faces of simplices of the subdivision, the simplices – and hence the faces – carrying the labels 1 to N) is $2a$. Let there be b subsimplices carrying all the labels, $1, \ldots, N+1$. These each have precisely one face with the labels $1, \ldots, N$. Thus the total number of faces of subsimplices with the labels $1, \ldots, N$ is $2a+b$. Some of these subsimplicial faces are interior to the main simplex, and some are on an exterior face of the main simplex. (See Figure 2.5 for an illustration on the 2-simplex.) Each of the subsimplicial interior faces are faces of precisely 2 adjacent subsimplices. As before, let $c =$ the number of interior faces carrying the labels $1, 2, 3, \ldots, N$. We now count the subsimplices of the simplicial subdivision with faces carrying the labels $1, \ldots, N$. Each interior face will be counted twice since it is the face of two adjacent subsimplices. An exterior face will be counted only once. In order to count the number of exterior faces of the subdivision with labels $1, 2, \ldots, N$, consider the face of the full simplex whose vertices are labeled $1, 2, \ldots, N$. Exterior faces of the simplicial subdivision that carry the labels $1, 2, \ldots, N$ lie on this face. By the inductive hypothesis, a simplicial subdivision of this face includes an odd number of subsimplices on the face defined by vertices $1, 2, \ldots, N$, which carry a full set of labels (relative to the face, i.e., $1, \ldots, N$). Denote this number d. By the inductive hypothesis, d is odd.

Recall that

$a =$ the number of subsimplices of the simplicial subdivision labeled with $1, \ldots, N$, but not labeled $N+1$;

$b =$ the number of subsimplices carrying all the labels $1, \ldots, N+1$;

c = the number of interior faces carrying the labels $1, 2, 3, \ldots, N$, but not $N + 1$;
d = number of subsimplices on the face defined by vertices $1, 2, \ldots, N$, carrying a full set of labels (relative to the face, i.e., $1, 2, \ldots, N$), which is an odd number by the inductive hypothesis.

We have

$$2a + b = 2c + d.$$

d is odd and so $2c + d$ is odd. Thus $2a + b$ is odd and hence b is odd.   QED

Theorem 2.9 (Knaster-Kuratowski-Mazurkewicz Theorem) *Let S be an N-simplex. Let the sets $C_1, C_2, \ldots, C_{N+1} \subset S$ be described as follows. Let C_j be closed and let vertex $j = x_j \in C_j$. For each $x \in S$, let $x \in C_i$ for some i such that x_i is one of x's carriers. Then*

$$\bigcap_{j=1}^{N+1} C_j \neq \phi.$$

Proof We can choose a sequence of simplicial subdivisions Λ^ν, indexed by ν, $\Lambda^\nu = \{S_k^\nu \mid k = 1, 2, \ldots.\}$, $\nu = 1, 2, 3, \ldots$. The index k is used to name each subsimplex within each subdivision Λ^ν. We construct the sequence Λ^ν, $\nu = 1, 2, 3, \ldots$, so that its mesh (the diameter of the subsimplices) becomes progressively finer and arbitrarily fine as ν increases. Label the vertices of each S_k^ν by j, where the vertex is an element of C_j for some j such that x_j is an element of the carrier of the vertex. This is an admissible labeling. Sperner's Lemma tells us that for each ν, there is some $S^\nu \in \Lambda^\nu$, so that S^ν has a complete set of labels. Let x_i^ν be the vertex of S^ν with label i. Then $x_i^\nu \in C_i$ for all ν. The sequence x_i^ν contains a convergent subsequence. Using the increasingly fine construction of the sequence Λ^ν and taking subsequences, the x_i^ν converge to the same x^0 for all i. But since C_i is closed, $x_i^\nu \to x^0$ means $x^0 \in C_i$ for all i and so $x^0 \in \cap_{i=1}^{N+1} C_i \neq \phi$.   QED

Theorem 2.10 (Brouwer Fixed-Point Theorem) *Let S be an N-simplex and let $f : S \to S$, where f is continuous. Then there is $x^* \in S$ so that $f(x^*) = x^*$.*

Proof Let $\lambda_j(x)$ be the jth barycentric coordinate of x. Define

$$C_j = \{x \mid \lambda_j(f(x)) \leq \lambda_j(x)\}.$$

Note that C_j fulfills the assumptions of the KKM Theorem inasmuch as

(i) C_j is closed by continuity of λ_j and f; and
(ii) vertex $j \in C_j$; and

(iii) if we let $x \in S$ and let $I(x)$ be the (set of) indices of the carrier of x, then there is $j \in I(x)$ so that $\lambda_j(x) \geq \lambda_j(f(x))$ since

$$\sum_{j \in I(x)} \lambda_j(x) = 1 \geq \sum_{j \in I(x)} \lambda_j(f(x)).$$

Then by the KKM Theorem there is $x^* \in S$ so that $x^* \in \cap_{j=1}^{N+1} C_j$. But then

$$\lambda_j(x^*) \geq \lambda_j(f(x^*)) \text{ for all } j$$

and $\sum \lambda_j(x^*) = \sum \lambda_j(f(x^*)) = 1$, so $\lambda_j(x^*) = \lambda_j(f(x^*))$ for all j, and hence $x^* = f(x^*)$. \hfill QED

Sperner's Lemma is ponderous in its geometric complexity, but the combinatorial proof of the Brouwer Fixed-Point Theorem is elementary and successful. There are simpler proofs, but they require more advanced mathematics. Note that the Brouwer Theorem, as a well-constructed mathematical statement, makes full use of its assumptions. Significantly weakening any of the assumptions invalidates the result. The fixed-point property (the quality that any continuous function from the set into itself has a fixed point) will fail for any set not topologically equivalent to the simplex (e.g., a domain with a hole in it), such as a circle or a torus or the union of two disjoint closed sets. The fixed-point property is false for a discontinuous function or for a domain that is not compact. The fixed-point property does generalize, however, from the simplex to any finite dimensional compact convex set, including any set that can be converted by a continuous transformation into such a set. As we will see below (Chapter 11), the Brouwer Fixed-Point Theorem is essential to proving the existence of general equilibrium.

2.8 Separation theorems

The Separating Hyperplane Theorem says that if we have two disjoint convex sets in $\mathbf{R}^N$ we can find a (hyper)plane between them so that one of the two sets is above the plane and the other below. The plane separates the convex sets. Because the plane is linear, it is defined by an equation that looks like a price system for N commodities. The Bounding Hyperplane Theorem leads to a similar interpretation. When the economy is described by the convex sets representing tastes (convex upper contour sets) or technology, we can use the separation theorems to characterize an efficient allocation as sustained by a price system. We'll see this in Chapters 12 and 14.

All of the sets and vectors we treat here will be in $\mathbf{R}^N$. Let $p \in \mathbf{R}^N$, $p \neq 0$. Then we define a hyperplane with normal p and constant k to be a set of the form $H \equiv \{x \mid x \in \mathbf{R}^N, p \cdot x = k\}$, where k is a real number. Note that for any two vectors, x and y, in H, $p \cdot (x - y) = 0$. H divides $\mathbf{R}^N$ into two subsets, the portion "above" H and the portion "below" as measured by the dot product of p with points of $\mathbf{R}^N$. The closed half space above H is defined as the set $\{x \mid x \in \mathbf{R}^N, p \cdot x \geq k\}$. The closed half space below H is defined as $\{x \mid x \in \mathbf{R}^N, p \cdot x \leq k\}$. H is said to be *bounding* for $S \subset \mathbf{R}^N$ if S is a subset of one of the two half spaces defined by H.

Lemma 2.1 *Let K be a nonempty closed convex subset of $\mathbf{R}^N$, and let $z \in \mathbf{R}^N$, $z \notin K$. Then there is $y \in K$ and $p \in \mathbf{R}^N$, $p \neq 0$, so that $p \cdot z < k = p \cdot y \leq p \cdot x$ for all $x \in K$.*

The lemma says that for a nonempty, closed, convex set K (not including the whole space) there is a hyperplane separating K from a point outside the set.

Proof of Lemma 2.1 Choose $y \in K$ as the closest point in K to z. That is, y minimizes $|x - z|$ for all $x \in K$ (continuity of the Euclidean norm and closedness of K ensure that a minimizer exists). Now we define $p = y - z$ and $k = p \cdot y$.

We must demonstrate that $p \cdot z < k$ and that $p \cdot x \geq k$ for all $x \in K$. The first of these follows directly: $p \cdot z = p \cdot z - p \cdot y + p \cdot y = -p \cdot p + p \cdot y < k$. Consider $x \in K$. We must show that $p \cdot x \geq k$. Since K is convex, we know that every point w on the line segment between x and y, $w = \alpha x + (1 - \alpha)y$, $1 \geq \alpha \geq 0$, is an element of K. We will show that the proposition $p \cdot x < k$ leads to a contradiction.
$$w = y + \alpha(x - y).$$
Consider
$$|z - y|^2 - |z - w|^2 = |z - y|^2 - |(z - y) - \alpha(x - y)|^2$$
$$= (z - y) \cdot (z - y) - [(z - y) \cdot (z - y) - 2\alpha(z - y) \cdot (x - y)$$
$$-\alpha^2(x - y) \cdot (x - y)]$$
$$= -2\alpha p \cdot (x - y) - \alpha^2(x - y) \cdot (x - y)$$
$$= -\alpha[2p \cdot (x - y) + \alpha(x - y) \cdot (x - y)].$$

Recall that $p \cdot y = k$. Suppose, contrary to hypothesis, that $p \cdot x < k$. Then $p \cdot (x - y) = p \cdot x - p \cdot y < 0$. Then for α sufficiently small, $|z - y|^2 - |z - w|^2 > 0$ and hence $|z - y| > |z - w|$. But this is a contradiction. The point y was chosen as the element of K closest to z. There can be no w in K closer to z than y.

The contradiction proves the lemma.   QED

Theorem 2.11 (Bounding Hyperplane Theorem (Minkowski)) *Let K be convex, $K \subset \mathbf{R}^N$. There is a hyperplane H through z and bounding for K if z is not interior to K.*

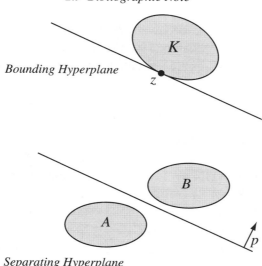

Fig. 2.7. Bounding and separating hyperplanes for convex sets.

Proof If $z \notin \overline{K}$, then the existence of H follows directly from the lemma. If $z \in$ boundary K, then consider a sequence $z^\nu \notin \overline{K}$, $z^\nu \to z$. Let p^ν be the corresponding sequence of normals to the supporting hyperplane, chosen to have length unity. The sequence is in a closed bounded set (the unit sphere). It thus has a convergent subsequence, whose limit is the required normal.   QED

Theorem 2.12 (Separating Hyperplane Theorem) *Let A, $B \subset \mathbf{R}^N$; let A and B be nonempty, convex, and disjoint, that is $A \cap B = \phi$. Then there is $p \in \mathbf{R}^N$, $p \neq 0$, so that $p \cdot x \geq p \cdot y$, for all $x \in A$, $y \in B$.*

Proof Consider $K = A - B$. K is convex. Since A and B are disjoint, $0 \notin K$. Then, by the lemma, there is p so that $p \cdot z \geq p \cdot 0 = 0$ for all $z \in K$. If we let $z = x - y$ then $p \cdot x \geq p \cdot y$.   QED

The hyperplane with normal p is said to separate A and B. Bounding and separating hyperplanes are presented in Figure 2.7.

2.9 Bibliographic Note

Chapter 1 of Debreu (1959), provides an excellent concise survey of the mathematical results presented here and in Chapter 16. Standard texts in real analysis include those by Bartle (1976), Bartle and Sherbert (1992), and Rudin (1976). Green and Heller (1981) provide a very thorough treatment of convexity. Separation theorems are well expounded in Hildenbrand and Kirman (1988). Useful references on the combinatorial proof of the Brouwer Fixed-Point Theorem include Tompkins (1964) and Burger (1963). Nikaido (1968) is also extremely helpful. Techniques for computation of fixed points are presented in Scarf and Hansen (1973).

Exercises

2.1   Prove that $A = B$ if and only if $A \subset B$ and $B \subset A$.

2.2   Recall **Theorem** 2.1 *Let A, B, and C be sets, then*

(a) $A \cap A = A$, $A \cup A = A$ (idempotency)

(b) $A \cap B = B \cap A$, $A \cup B = B \cup A$ (commutativity)

(c) $A \cap (B \cap C) = (A \cap B) \cap C$ (associativity)

    $A \cup (B \cup C) = (A \cup B) \cup C$

(d) $A \cap (B \cup C) = (A \cap B) \cup (A \cap C)$ (distributivity)

    $A \cup (B \cap C) = (A \cup B) \cap (A \cup C)$

Draw a diagram depicting Theorem 2.1.

2.3   Prove Theorem 2.1.

2.4   Let K be a set in $\mathbf{R}^N$. Recall that we denote the closure of K (K plus its cluster points, the smallest closed set including K) by $\overline{K}$. Suppose $\overline{K}$ is convex. Show that it does not follow that K is convex.

2.5   Give two examples of a reflexive relation and two examples of an irreflexive relation.

2.6   Give two examples of a transitive relation and two examples of an intransitive relation.

2.7   Prove Theorem 2.2. *Let $x^i \in \mathbf{R}^N$, $i = 1, 2, \ldots$. Then $x^i \to x^0$ if and only if for any $\varepsilon > 0$, there is $q(\varepsilon)$ such that for all $q' > q(\varepsilon)$, $\|x^{q'} - x^0\| < \varepsilon$.*

2.8   Give two examples of open sets in $\mathbf{R}$ and two examples of open sets in $\mathbf{R}^N$.

2.9   Give two examples of closed subsets of $\mathbf{R}$ and two examples of closed subsets of $\mathbf{R}^N$.

2.10   Prove Theorem 2.3. *Let $X \subset \mathbf{R}^N$. X is closed if $\mathbf{R}^N \setminus X$ is open.*

2.11   Find a nonempty set in $\mathbf{R}^N$ whose interior is empty. Find a nonempty set in $\mathbf{R}^N$ that is equal to its interior.

2.12   Prove the Bolzano-Weierstrass Theorem for sequences, the corollary to Theorem 2.5: *Let x^i be a bounded sequence in $\mathbf{R}^N$. Then x^i contains a convergent subsequence.*

2.13   Prove that forms (i) and (ii) of the definition of continuity of a function are equivalent.

2.14   Demonstrate the following properties of convex sets in $\mathbf{R}^N$. Let A and B be convex subsets of $\mathbf{R}^N$. Then $A \cap B$ is convex, $A + B$ is convex, and $\overline{A}$ is convex.

2.15   Show that the following sequences in $\mathbf{R}$ are convergent:

(i) $x^\nu = 3 + \left(-\frac{1}{10}\right)^\nu$, $\nu = 1, 2, 3, \ldots$

(ii) $x^\nu = \frac{2}{\nu} + 10^{-\nu}$, $\nu = 1, 2, 3, \ldots$.

2.16   Show that the following sequence in **R** is not convergent:

$$x^\nu = 3^\nu + (-1)^\nu 3^\nu, \quad \nu = 1, 2, 3, \ldots,$$

but find a convergent subsequence.

2.17   Consider a closed square (two-dimensional cube) in $\mathbf{R}^2$ with side $[0, 2]$:

$$C = [0, 2] \times [0, 2] = \{(x, y) | 0 \le x \le 2, 0 \le y \le 2\}.$$

Demonstrate that C is a convex set. That is, let (x^1, y^1) and $(x^2, y^2) \in C$. Let $0 \le \alpha \le 1$. Let $z = \alpha(x^1, y^1) + (1 - \alpha)(x^2, y^2)$. Show that $z \in C$.

2.18   The Brouwer Fixed-Point Theorem can be stated in the following way:

Let $S \subset \mathbf{R}^N$ be compact and convex. Let $f : S \to S$ be a continuous function. Then there is $x^* \in S$ so that $f(x^*) = x^*$.

Show how a fixed point would fail to exist when the assumptions of the Brouwer Fixed-Point theorem are not fulfilled, as specified in the following cases:

(i) Suppose S is not convex. Let $S = [1, 2] \cup [3, 4]$; $S \subset \mathbf{R}$. That is, S is the union of two disjoint closed intervals in **R**. Find continuous $f : S \to S$ so that there is no fixed point x^* fulfilling the theorem.

(ii) Suppose f is not continuous. Let $S = [1, 4]$; $S \subset \mathbf{R}$. Let

$$f(x) = \begin{cases} 4 - x & \text{for } x < 2, \\ x - 1 & \text{for } x \ge 2. \end{cases}$$

Show that although $f : S \to S$ there is no fixed point of f in S.

(iii) Suppose S is not compact. Let $S = \mathbf{R}$ and $f(x) = x + 1$. Note that $f : S \to S$ and f is continuous. Show that there is no fixed point of f in S.

2.19   Recall the Intermediate Value Theorem:

*Let $[a, b]$ be a closed interval in **R** and h a continuous real-valued function on $[a, b]$ so that $h(a) < h(b)$. Then for any real k so that $h(a) < k < h(b)$ there is $x \in [a, b]$ so that $h(x) = k$.*

Recall the Brouwer Fixed-Point Theorem:

Let $S \subset R^N$ be compact and convex. Let $f : S \to S$ be a continuous function. Then there is $x^* \in S$ so that $f(x^*) = x^*$.

Consider the special case $S = [0, 1]$, the unit interval in **R**, and let f be a continuous function from S into itself. Using the Intermediate Value

Theorem, prove the Brouwer Fixed-Point Theorem for this case. You may find the function $g(x) = x - f(x)$ useful.

2.20   Recall the Separating Hyperplane Theorem (Theorem 2.12):

Let A, $B \subset \mathbf{R}^N$, where A and B are nonempty convex sets, with disjoint interiors. Then there is $p \in \mathbf{R}^N$, $p \neq 0$, so that $p \cdot x \geq p \cdot y$ for all $x \in A$, $y \in B$.

(i) Show by (counter)example (a well-drawn figure is sufficient) that the convexity of both A and B are typically required to ensure this result. That is, show that if either of A or B is nonconvex then there may be no separating hyperplane.

(ii) Let A, $B \subset \mathbf{R}^2$. Let $A = \{(x, y) \mid x^2 + y^2 \leq 1\}$, the closed disk of radius one centered at the origin, and let $B = \{(x, y) \mid (x - 2)^2 + y^2 \leq 1\}$, the closed disk of radius one centered at (2,0). Show that A and B fulfill the conditions of the Separating Hyperplane Theorem and specify a separating hyperplane, including its normal.

2.21   Prove Theorem 2.6: Let $f : A \to B$, f continuous. Let $S \subset B$, S closed. Then $f^{-1}(S)$ is closed.

3

Prices and commodities

3.1 The market, commodities, and prices

We developed examples in Chapter 1 of general equilibrium economic systems characterized by N commodities. In Chapter 2 we developed the mathematics suitable for analyzing these economies using $\mathbf{R}^N$ as the commodity space. A typical point in $\mathbf{R}^N$, $x = (x_1, x_2, x_3, \ldots, x_N)$, represents a commodity bundle. That is, x is a shopping list, x_1 of good 1, x_2 of good 2, and so forth through x_N of good N. The coordinates x_i may be either positive or negative (subject to interpretation). What are these N commodities? That turns out to be rather a deeper question than it appears, so we postpone a full discussion until Chapter 15. Meanwhile, in order to fix ideas, we should give a bit of interpretation.

The market takes place at a single instant, prior to the rest of economic activity. We think of the market meeting, demands being expressed, equilibrium achieved, and allocations decided, all prior to actual consumption or production taking place. This may be unrealistic, but it serves to fix the economic environment.

We think of a commodity as a good or service completely specified by its characteristics. We assume there to be a finite positive integer number of commodities, N. In a model where there are several locations, the same good at different locations will be treated as different commodities. Otherwise identical goods at different locations may then trade at different prices, entering differently in preferences; converting one good to the other requires a production activity (transportation).

In a model over time, a commodity will be identified by its date in addition to other characteristics. This is sometimes referred to as "a full set of futures markets." The same good at different dates may be treated as different commodities. These commodities are regarded differently by consumers and it requires a production activity (storage) to convert them from one date to another. In a model with uncertainty, a commodity will be identified by the (uncertain) state of the world in which it is available. This is sometimes referred to as "a full set of contingent commodity markets."

The assumption of complete markets – that there is separate trade in all goods for all dates and all states – is very powerful and is far from fulfilled in actual economies. This will affect the applicability and interpretation of the results below, particularly with reference to the efficiency of equilibrium allocations. We will discuss this further in Chapter 15.

The price system consists of an N-tuple $p = (p_1, p_2, \ldots, p_N)$. $p_i \geq 0$ for all $i = 1, \ldots, N$. The value of a bundle $x \in \mathbf{R}^N$ at prices p is $p \cdot x$.

3.2 Bibliographic note

The treatment in this chapter parallels Chapter 2 of Debreu (1959). The notion of dated commodities is extremely powerful analytically; it is attributed to Hicks (1939).

Exercise

3.1   Review the "Commodities" section of the financial pages of the *Wall Street Journal* or other daily newspaper with extensive coverage. Note the availability of markets for the trade of goods for future delivery. How does the price vary with delivery date? Can you find price variation by location?

Part B

An economy with bounded production technology, supply and demand functions

In Chapters 4 – 7 we will develop a version of the complete Arrow-Debreu model of the economy. The theory of the firm and production sector is presented in Chapter 4 and that of households and demand in Chapter 5. We bring them together with the Walras' Law in Chapter 6 and existence of general equilibrium in Chapter 7.

As we noted in Chapter 2, the typical characterization of economic activity of firms and households is as a maximization subject to constraint. Recall the corollary to Theorem 2.7. In order for maximization to be well defined, sufficient conditions are that the maximand be a continuous function of its arguments and that the opportunity set be compact. That pretty well sets the agenda for characterizing firm and household behavior. We have to find continuous functions for them to maximize. We should find compact constraint sets for them to do it on. That will characterize firm supply and household demand behavior. Although these are not necessary conditions, they are the best generally sufficient conditions available.

Finding continuous functions for the firm and household to optimize does not pose a problem. For the firm, the obvious choice is profits. For the household the traditional maximand is utility, though we will go to some effort to derive the continuous utility function from the more primitive assumption of a preference ordering. The obvious constraint set for the firm is a representation of the firm's technically available possibilities – the possible input-output combinations based on available technology represented as a subset of $\mathbf{R}^N$. For the household, the obvious constraint set is a budget constraint. Are these constraint sets compact? If so we've satisfied the sufficient conditions for finding a well-defined maximum. Are the constraint sets closed and bounded?

Closedness is largely a technical concern and we don't really regard it as a problem. Boundedness is more difficult to establish. Is the firm's technology bounded? We will represent the firm's technology as a subset of $\mathbf{R}^N$. Any technically possible combination of inputs and outputs should be represented in the technology set. In a finite world with a finite economy, how could this set be unbounded? The answer is that in a finite world with a finite economy, realized outputs must be bounded in equilibrium. Firms and households should be led to these finite equilibrium outputs by prices. It should be a result in equilibrium, not an assumption at the outset of the study, that offered supplies by firms are finite. The firm should be in a position to consider what it would produce if it could afford to buy arbitrarily large amounts of inputs. Eventually, equilibrium prices should persuade the firm that arbitrarily large production plans would be unprofitable.

However, this leaves us with a difficult technical problem. How can we allow the firm to consider arbitrarily large (unbounded) production plans? If we allow the firm to try to optimize a profit function over an unbounded set (a noncompact set) we have no assurance that the firm's maximizing choice will be well defined. Without a well-defined maximum, we have no worthwhile theory of supply.

We face the same problem with the theory of the household. In equilibrium, the household will surely choose bounded consumption plans; after all, in a finite world bounded consumption is all that the economy will be able to produce so bounded demand will clear markets. That decision should however be the result of optimization led by prices, not the outcome of exogenous constraint. Conversely, at disequilibrium prices, the household may face an unbounded budget set (if some goods have zero prices at the price vector currently proposed by the Walrasian auctioneer). If the budget set is not compact, how can we describe the demand behavior of the household? There may be no well-defined utility maximum if the constraint set is not compact.

The solution to this nest of difficulties is a rather elaborate two-step procedure. At first we will consider an economy with bounded production technology. The firms will maximize profits over their bounded technology sets. Attainable outputs will necessarily be bounded as well. Households will face bounded choice sets that are carefully constructed to include the attainable consumptions as a proper subset. We will demonstrate the existence of a general equilibrium in this economy with bounded firm technology and bounded individual choice sets. That comprises the agenda for this Part B.

We will then extend the model to the case of unbounded firm technologies. The resource endowment of the economy is, however, finite. Under reasonable weak assumptions we can show that the attainable outputs of the economy are finite. We then show that we can artificially restrict the unbounded taste and technology sets of this economy to a bounded subset containing the attainable set as a proper subset. This essentially reduces the problem to the previous case of bounded technology. We will find an equilibrium in this artificially bounded economy. Then the rabbit comes out of the hat. We can show that the equilibrium of the artificially bounded economy is also an equilibrium of the original unbounded economy. That's the plan for Part C.

4

Production with bounded firm technology

4.1 Firms and production technology

We will represent production as organized in firms. A firm is characterized by its name, by the production technology to which it has access, and by who owns it, the shareholders. We postpone discussion of the ownership and distribution of profits to Chapter 6. The population of firms is the finite set F, indexed $j = 1, \ldots, \#F$. The typical firm is $j \in F$. Firm j's most distinctive characteristic is its production technology, represented by the set $\mathcal{Y}^j \subset \mathbf{R}^N$.

The set $\mathcal{Y}^j$ represents the technical possibilities of firm j. A typical element y of the technology set, $y \in \mathcal{Y}^j$, is a vector representing a technically possible combination of inputs and outputs. Negative coordinates of y are inputs; positive coordinates are outputs. For example, say $y \in \mathcal{Y}^j$, $y = (-2, -3, 0, 0, 1)$; this $y \in \mathcal{Y}^j$ means that an input of two units of good 1 and three units of good 2 will allow firm j to produce one unit of good 5. Each element y of $\mathcal{Y}^j$ is like a recipe in a cookbook or one of many blueprint plans for production, which can be implemented as a matter of choice by the firm. There is no guarantee that the economy can provide the inputs $y \in \mathcal{Y}^j$ specifies, either from endowment or from the output of other firms. Rather, $y \in \mathcal{Y}^j$ represents the technical output possibilities of production by firm j if the specified inputs are provided. A typical $\mathcal{Y}^j$ is illustrated in Figure 4.1. A point y in $\mathcal{Y}^j$ represents the answer to a hypothetical question: If the inputs specified in y were available what outputs could firm j produce? The answer includes the outputs (positive coordinates) specified in y.

We are used to seeing a firm's production technology depicted as a production function. How does a production function relate to a technology set $\mathcal{Y}^j$? The answer is that the production function embodies a concept of efficiency; the production function is the equation of the upper boundary of $\mathcal{Y}^j$. In Figure 4.1, the curve depicting the implied production function is the line 0A. Suppose, for example, the production function $w = f^j(x)$ represents the production technology of firm j, where x represents a (scalar) input to production and w represents a scalar output.

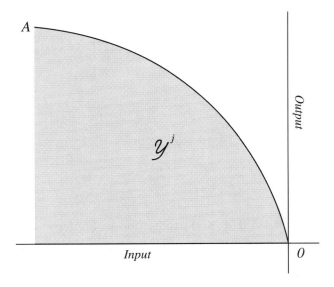

Fig. 4.1. $\mathcal{Y}^j$: Technology set of firm j.

We could also represent j's production technology by the set $\mathcal{Y}^j$. The relation between $f^j(\cdot)$ and $\mathcal{Y}^j$ is

$$f^j(x) \equiv \max\{w \mid (-x, w) \in \mathcal{Y}^j\}.$$

4.2 The form of production technology

We now formalize the analytic properties of $\mathcal{Y}^j$ as a subset of $\mathbf{R}^N$. We will use these assumptions to develop the theory of production and firm supply.[1]

(P.I) $\mathcal{Y}^j$ *is convex for each* j.
(P.II) $0 \in \mathcal{Y}^j$.
(P.III) $\mathcal{Y}^j$ *is closed.*

P.I is the convexity assumption. It corresponds to the idea of increasing marginal costs and diminishing marginal product. It says (when combined with P.II) that if a particular production plan is possible, then it is also possible at half the original scale. Hence P.I is an assumption that there are no scale economies and no indivisibilities.

P.II is the assumption that it is always possible to run a firm at a nil output level with nil inputs as well. That means that the worst the owners of the firm can do

---

[1] We will designate assumptions on the structure of production by "P." and those on the structure of consumption by "C." followed by a roman numeral. The numbering of the assumptions will differ from their order of appearance (resulting in consecutive low-numbered assumptions in the most general model, Chapter 17).

in terms of profits is zero. The firm is never required to operate at a loss. As a mathematical formality, this convention allows us to treat the formation of "new" firms in a quite general fashion as a special case of the ordinary analysis of firm production choices. At some prices the firm will find it unprofitable to produce; it will set output at zero and have zero profits. Prices may then change, making it attractive to produce at a positive output level instead of zero. This looks very much like the founding of a new firm, based on the renewed profitability of its line of work. In the formal statement of the model, the "new" firm has always been there, operating at a nil level.

P.III is essentially technical, helping to assure us of a well-defined profit-maximizing production plan for the firm and of the continuity of output decisions with prices.

We will introduce P.IV and P.V later. Here we will skip to P.VI:

(P.VI) $\mathcal{Y}^j$ is a bounded set for each $j \in F$.

P.VI is a very convenient assumption; it is also very restrictive. The convenience comes from our notions of how to describe firm behavior – profit maximization. P.III says that $\mathcal{Y}^j$ is closed and now P.VI says that it is bounded. Hence, under P.III and P.VI, $\mathcal{Y}^j$ is a compact set. Maximizing profits over this domain should result in a well-defined answer (Corollary 2.2).

4.3 Strictly convex production technology

We wish to describe firm supply behavior as profit maximization subject to technology constraint. In order to discuss the simplest possible case of firm supply behavior we introduce:

(P.V) For each $j \in F$, $\mathcal{Y}^j$ is strictly convex.

The assumption of *strict* convexity assures us of a unique (point-valued) profit-maximizing choice of production plan. Supply will be a function rather than set-valued (Theorem 4.1 below). This is very convenient and significantly simplifies the exposition and mathematics used. Note that P.V implies P.I; thus it is redundant to assume both. We can generalize to the case of weak convexity and set-valued supply behavior at some increase in technical detail. This exercise is performed in Part G (Chapters 16 and 17). Figure 4.2 illustrates three possible forms of $\mathcal{Y}^j$: strictly convex[2] (consistent with P.I and P.V), weakly convex (consistent with P.I but not P.V), and nonconvex (inconsistent with both).

---

[2] Since profit-maximizing choices will typically occur at the origin or above the horizontal axis, the figure illustrates the technology sets only in this region. In Figure 4.2a, please use your imagination to fill in the set below the axis to maintain strict convexity.

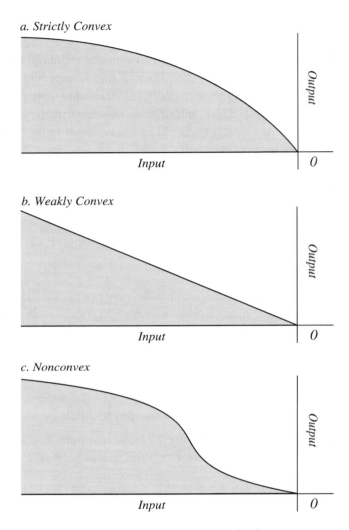

Fig. 4.2. Convex and nonconvex technology sets.

We are now ready to develop a supply function for firm j. We start with a space of possible price vectors. We will describe prices by a vector $p \in \mathbf{R}^N_+$, $p = (p_1, p_2, \ldots, p_N)$, $p \neq 0$, where 0 denotes the zero vector in $\mathbf{R}^N$. $\mathbf{R}^N_+$ denotes the nonnegative orthant (quadrant) of $\mathbf{R}^N$. Thus the price vector is taken to have no negative coordinates and some strictly positive coordinates. Taking price vector $p \in \mathbf{R}^N_+$ as given,[3] each firm j "chooses" $y^j \in \mathcal{Y}^j$ such that $p \cdot y^j$ maximizes $p \cdot y$, the profits of the firm at production plan y, subject to inclusion in $\mathcal{Y}^j$. We define

---

[3] Nonnegativity of prices reflects monotone preferences (desirability of goods), a concept to be introduced in the next chapter.

the supply function[4] of firm j as

$$\tilde{S}^j(p) = \{y^{*j} \mid y^{*j} \in \mathcal{Y}^j, \; p \cdot y^{*j} \geq p \cdot y \text{ for all } y \in \mathcal{Y}^j\}.$$

Then we have :

Theorem 4.1 *Assume P.II, P.III, P.V, and P.VI. Let $p \in \mathbf{R}_+^N$, $p \neq 0$. Then $\tilde{S}^j(p)$ is a well-defined, nonempty, continuous point-valued function.*

Proof Well defined: $\tilde{S}^j(p)$ consists of the maximizer of a continuous function on a compact, strictly convex set. The function is well defined since a continuous real-valued function achieves its maximum on a compact set (by Corollary 2.2).

Point-valued: We will demonstrate that the strict convexity of $\mathcal{Y}^j$ (P.V) implies that $\tilde{S}^j(p)$ is point-valued. We wish to show that there is a unique $y^0 \in \mathcal{Y}^j$ that maximizes $p \cdot y$ in $\mathcal{Y}^j$. Suppose such is not the case. Then there are $y^1, y^2 \in \mathcal{Y}^j$, $y^1 \neq y^2$, so that $p \cdot y^1 = \max_{y \in \mathcal{Y}^j} p \cdot y = p \cdot y^2$. Now consider the profitability of a convex combination of y^1 and y^2 : $p \cdot (\alpha y^1 + (1-\alpha)y^2) = p \cdot y^1 = p \cdot y^2$. But, by strict convexity of $\mathcal{Y}^j$ (P.V) for $0 < \alpha < 1$, $\alpha y^1 + (1-\alpha)y^2 \in$ interior $\mathcal{Y}^j$. This would mean that in a neighborhood of $\alpha y^1 + (1-\alpha)y^2$ there is $y^3 \in \mathcal{Y}^j$ so that $p \cdot y^3 > p \cdot y^1 = p \cdot y^2$, which is a contradiction. Hence, we conclude that $\tilde{S}^j(p)$ is point-valued and we can now validly represent $\tilde{S}^j(p)$ as a function.

Continuity: We now wish to demonstrate continuity of $\tilde{S}^j(p)$. Let $p^\nu \in \mathbf{R}_+^N$, $\nu = 1, 2, \ldots$, $p^\nu \neq 0$, $p^\nu \rightarrow p^0 \neq 0$. We must show that $\tilde{S}^j(p^\nu) \rightarrow \tilde{S}^j(p^0)$. Because $\tilde{S}^j(p^\nu)$ is a sequence in the compact set $\mathcal{Y}^j$, it contains a convergent subsequence. We claim that the sequence itself converges, that is, the cluster point of the convergent subsequence(s) is unique. To demonstrate uniqueness we will use a proof by contradiction. Suppose there are two distinct cluster points, y^* and y^{**}, where $y^* \neq y^{**}$. Then $p^\nu \cdot \tilde{S}^j(p^\nu) \rightarrow p^0 \cdot y^* = p^0 \cdot y^{**}$. However, the strict convexity of $\mathcal{Y}^j$ would then imply that there is $y^{***} \in \mathcal{Y}^j$ such that $p^0 \cdot y^{***} > p^0 \cdot y^{**} = p^0 \cdot y^*$. But this is a contradiction, since for ν large $p^\nu \cdot y^{***} > p^\nu \cdot y^*$ and hence $p^\nu \cdot y^{***} > p^\nu \cdot \tilde{S}^j(p^\nu)$, which contradicts the definition of $\tilde{S}^j(p^\nu)$. The contradiction proves that there is only one limit point, $y^* = y^{**} = y^{***}$.

We have now that $\tilde{S}^j(p^\nu)$ converges. We must show that it converges to $\tilde{S}^j(p^0)$. Suppose it does not. Then $p^0 \cdot \tilde{S}^j(p^0) > p^0 \cdot y^*$. But the dot product is a continuous function of its arguments, so for ν large, this implies that $p^\nu \cdot \tilde{S}^j(p^0) > p^\nu \cdot \tilde{S}^j(p^\nu)$, which is a contradiction. Hence $\tilde{S}^j(p^\nu) \rightarrow \tilde{S}^j(p^0)$.

This completes the proof.   QED

---

[4] The superscript tilde (˜) notation emphasizes that the supply function is defined over the *bounded* domain $\mathcal{Y}^j$.

Lemma 4.1 (homogeneity of degree 0) *Assume P.II, P.III, P.V, and P.VI. Let* $\lambda > 0$, $p \in \mathbf{R}_+^N$. *Then* $\tilde{S}^j(\lambda p) = \tilde{S}^j(p)$.

4.4 Attainable production plans

We now wish to move from the behavior of the individual firm to production plans of the whole productive sector. Recall

Definition *A sum of sets* $\mathcal{Y}^j$ *in* $\mathbf{R}^N$ *is defined as*

$$\mathcal{Y} = \sum_j \mathcal{Y}^j \quad \text{is the set } \left\{ y \mid y = \sum_j y^j \text{ for some } y^j \in \mathcal{Y}^j \right\}.$$

We will now define the economy's *aggregate technology* set as $\mathcal{Y} \equiv \sum_{j \in F} \mathcal{Y}^j$. This definition says that production decisions of the individual firms can be combined additively, that is, that they are independent of one another. We are interested in the array of outputs that can be achieved by the economy. There are initial inputs to production $r \in \mathbf{R}_+^N$; they are supplied to the production sector, characterized by the firms in F and their technology sets $\mathcal{Y}^j$, and summarized by $\mathcal{Y}$. Let $r \in \mathbf{R}_+^N$ be the vector of total initial resources or endowments ($\mathbf{R}_+^N$ denotes the nonnegative orthant – quadrant – of $\mathbf{R}^N$).

Definition *Let* $y \in \mathcal{Y}$. *Then* y *is said to be* ***attainable*** *if* $y + r \geq 0$.

That is, a production plan is attainable if the economy's initial resources are sufficient to provide its net input requirements. Note that attainability is defined for $\mathcal{Y}$, the aggregate technology, not for $\mathcal{Y}^j$, the individual firm technologies.

Restating the definition, $y \in \mathcal{Y}$ is attainable if $x = y + r$, where $x \in [\mathcal{Y} + \{r\}] \cap \mathbf{R}_+^N$. This definition takes the aggregate production technology set $\mathcal{Y}$, translates it by the endowment vector r, and then takes the intersection with the nonnegative orthant of $\mathbf{R}^N$, $\mathbf{R}_+^N$. The intersection is the set of x attainable as outputs or aggregate consumptions (attainable production plans plus endowment). This intersection corresponds to the 90° wedge-shaped attainable set bounded by the coordinate axes and the production frontier in the Robinson Crusoe model, the set (designating it by points on its boundary) 0ABCDMSHGFE in Figures 1.1 and 1.2.

Since the attainable production vectors are those that can be produced with the available resources (and hence do not create unsatisfiable excess demands in factor markets), it is among these that an equilibrium vector is to be found (if it exists). Since $\mathcal{Y}^j$ is bounded by P.VI, $\mathcal{Y}$ (as the finite sum of $\mathcal{Y}^j$) is bounded and therefore trivially, so is the attainable subset of $\mathcal{Y}$.

4.5 Bibliographic note

The presentation of production technology in this chapter parallels that of Arrow (1962) and Arrow and Debreu (1954). It is simplified here – the full Arrow-Debreu treatment appears in Chapters 8 and 17.

Exercises

4.1 Consider the model of the firm and production presented in Chapter 4. Theorem 4.1 (or parts of it) is false if we omit P.VI, boundedness of $\mathcal{Y}^j$.

(i) Explain mathematically how and why Theorem 4.1 fails.

(ii) Demonstrate by example that Theorem 4.1 fails. Explain the example.

4.2 Consider the following production function representing the technology of one firm. Production of y involves a set-up cost, $S > 0$, which is the initial amount of input required before any positive production can take place. We have

$$y = \begin{cases} 0 & \text{if } L \leq S \\ a(L - S) & \text{if } L > S, \end{cases}$$

where L is the amount of labor used as an input to y, and a is a positive constant. This production function (like any production function) is the upper boundary of a technology set.

Show that this production function or its technology set violates the (weak) convexity assumption (P. I). Discuss.

4.3 In the Robinson Crusoe model of Chapter 1, we implicitly used the assumption of convex technology, describing the production possibility set as convex. Consider a Robinson Crusoe economy with a nonconvex production possibility set.

(i) Diagram the possibility that there is a competitive equilibrium (despite the nonconvexity).

(ii) Is the equilibrium established in (i) Pareto efficient? Explain.

(iii) Diagram the possibility that there is no competitive equilibrium (due to the nonconvexity). Explain.

(iv) In the nonconvex Robinson Crusoe economy, can a Pareto efficient allocation generally be sustained as a competitive equilibrium? Diagram and explain.

5

Households

5.1 The structure of household consumption sets and preferences

A household is thought of as an individual or a family with a single well-defined preference quasi-ordering, interacting with the rest of the economy through the market. The household sells its endowment, but it does not sell any commodity it produces. Production for sale takes place in firms. We maintain the convention introduced in Chapter 1 that the household sells all of its endowment. Any part of the endowment desired for personal use (in particular as leisure) is then repurchased from the market. Production for sale takes place in firms. Households are elements of the finite set H numbered $1, 2, \ldots, \#H$. A household $i \in H$ will be characterized by its possible consumption set $X^i \subseteq \mathbf{R}^N_+$, its preferences $\succsim_i$, and its endowment $r^i \in \mathbf{R}^N_+$.

5.1.1 Consumption sets

A typical element of X^i represents the consumption plans of the household (not net trade) and is hence necessarily nonnegative. We introduce the following assumptions on the possible consumption sets.

(C.I) X^i is closed and nonempty.

(C.II) $X^i \subseteq \mathbf{R}^N_+$. X^i is bounded below and unbounded above. That is, $x \in X^i$ and $y \geq x$ (the inequality holds coordinatewise) implies $y \in X^i$.

(C.III) X^i is convex.

It is usually simplest to take X^i to be the nonnegative orthant (quadrant) of $\mathbf{R}^N$, denoted $\mathbf{R}^N_+$. We will take the possible aggregate consumption set to be $X = \sum_{i \in H} X^i$.

5.1.2 Preferences

Each household $i \in H$ has a preference quasi-ordering on X^i, denoted $\succsim_i$. For typical $x, y \in X^i$, "$x \succsim_i y$" is read "x is preferred or indifferent to y (according to i)." We introduce the following terminology:

If $x \succsim_i y$ and $y \succsim_i x$ then $x \sim_i y$ ("x is indifferent to y"),
If $x \succsim_i y$ but not $y \succsim_i x$ then $x \succ_i y$ ("x is strictly preferred to y").

We will assume $\succsim_i$ to be *complete* on X^i, that is, any two elements of X^i are comparable under $\succsim_i$. For all $x, y \in X^i$, $x \succsim_i y$, or $y \succsim_i x$ (or both). Since we take $\succsim_i$ to be a quasi-ordering, $\succsim_i$ is assumed to be transitive and reflexive.

The conventional alternative to describing the quasi-ordering $\succsim_i$ is to assume the presence of a utility function $u^i(x)$ so that $x \succsim_i y$ if and only if $u^i(x) \geq u^i(y)$. We will show below that the utility function can be derived from the quasi-ordering. Readers who prefer the utility function formulation may use it at will. Just read $u^i(x) \geq u^i(y)$ wherever you see $x \succsim_i y$.

The assumption that household preferences can be characterized by a transitive, reflexive, complete relation, $\succsim_i$, is very strong. It says that the household knows what it wants and (transitivity) that its preferences are well defined and consistent (they do not cycle but rather represent a true ordering).

The traditional alternative to specifying the preference ordering $\succsim_i$ is to assume household preferences to be characterized by a utility function $u^i(\cdot)$. There is nothing wrong with this approach; indeed we will adopt it in part below. It communicates an unfortunate message, however, that there is a numerical index of which individuals are aware that characterizes their level of satisfaction with consumption plans. Typically, this is a fable that only economists can believe. It is unfortunately subject to the misinterpretation that u^i represents intensity of preference (cardinality) and that because it exists, the values of u^i are comparable among households (comparability). None of these properties is actually required for a theory of utility or choice. Further, the utility function is not a needed primitive element of the theory of household choice. It is possible to fully develop the theory of choice using preferences $\succsim_i$ as the primitive notion. A corresponding utility function u^i will be introduced in Section 5.2 merely as a convenient representation of $\succsim_i$, adding no informational content to the notion of preferences embodied in $\succsim_i$.

5.1.3 Weak monotonicity

We will assume that there is always at least one good that household i wants more of, and there are no noxious goods, that is,

(C.IV) (Weak Monotonicity) Let x, $y \in X^i$, with $x \gg y$, (that is, $x_i > y_i$, $i = 1, \ldots, N$). Then $x \succ_i y$.

The assumption of weak monotonicity says that adding more of everything to the household consumption makes the household better off (i.e., moves it to a strictly preferred consumption). There are a few economic implications of this assumption. First, some good or goods are really desirable. This formalizes the notion of scarcity. No matter where you are in your consumption space, you always want more of something. The assumption also sneaks in an idea about excess goods: Not all of the goods may be desirable, but none is noxious. This can be interpreted as a notion of free disposability. Even if you don't want some of the goods, having an excess does not reduce household satisfaction. The assumption is "weak" in the sense that it does not require that all goods be desirable – an assumption that would characterize strong monotonicity.

5.1.4 Continuity

We now introduce the principal technical assumption on preferences, the assumption of continuity.

(C.V) (Continuity) For every $x^0 \in X^i$, the sets $A^i(x^0) = \{x \mid x \in X^i, x \succsim_i x^0\}$ and $G^i(x^0) = \{x \mid x \in X^i, x^0 \succsim_i x\}$ are closed.

Although C.V is more technical than economic, it proves to be extremely useful. The structure of the upper and lower contour sets of $\succsim_i$ assumed in C.V is precisely the behavior we'd expect if $\succsim_i$ were defined by a continuous utility function. In fact, we will show that we can derive a *continuous* utility function representing $\succsim_i$ while assuming C.V. This leads to a considerable simplification of the theory of household choice. It also allows us to derive demand behavior as a continuous function of prices. Continuity of demand is, of course, very helpful in proving the existence of equilibrium.

The economic content of C.V is the following description of the structure of preferences: Begin with a typical point x in X^i, consider a line segment in X^i starting at one end with elements superior to x according to $\succsim_i$ and progressing eventually to points inferior to x. Then the line segment must include points indifferent to x as well. As we pass from superior to inferior according to $\succsim_i$, we must touch on indifference. This would seem trivially obvious except that there are otherwise well-behaved preference quasi-orderings that violate C.V and can generate discontinuities in demand. The classic example is the lexicographic ordering.

Example 5.1 (Lexicographic preferences) The lexicographic (dictionary-like) ordering on $\mathbf{R}^N$ (let's denote it $\succsim_L$) is described in the following way. Let

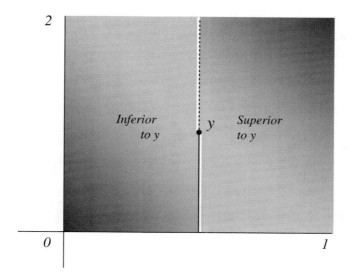

Fig. 5.1. Lexicographic preferences.

$x = (x_1, x_2, \ldots, x_N)$ and $y = (y_1, y_2, \ldots, y_N)$.

$\quad x \succ_L y \quad$ if $x_1 > y_1$, or

$\qquad\qquad$ if $x_1 = y_1$ and $x_2 > y_2$, or

$\qquad\qquad$ if $x_1 = y_1$, $x_2 = y_2$, and $x_3 > y_3$, and so forth $\ldots$.

$\quad x \sim_L y \quad$ if $x = y$.

$\succsim_L$ fulfills weak monotonicity, trivially fulfills strict convexity (C.VII, introduced below), but does not fulfill continuity (C.V). This is easiest to see graphically (see Figure 5.1). Consider $\succsim_L$ on $\mathbf{R}_+^2$. For any x in $\mathbf{R}_+^2$, the points superior to x are those above and to the right of x, those inferior are those below and to the left. The only point indifferent to x is x itself. Consequently, while traveling along a line segment, it is perfectly possible to go from better than x to worse than x without passing through indifference. It is left as an exercise (5.1) to show that preferences like these can generate discontinuous demand behavior.

5.1.5 Convexity of preferences

We introduce now the notions of weak and strict convexity of preferences. These assumptions correspond to the idea of diminishing marginal rate of substitution (in which the indifference curves have the usual convex to the origin shape). Weak convexity (C.VI) includes the possibility of flat segments on the indifference curves, admitting perfect substitutability between goods. This opens the possibility of set-valued, rather than point-valued, demands, a technically tricky issue we post-pone to Chapters 16 and 17. For the present chapter, we concentrate on the strictly convex case (C.VII), where demands are necessarily point-valued.

(C.VI) $x \succsim_i y$ implies $((1 - \alpha)x + \alpha y) \succsim_i y$, for $0 \le \alpha \le 1$.

An immediate consequence of C.VI is that $A^i(x^0)$ is convex for every $x^0 \in X^i$.

Proof Exercise 5.6.

5.1.6 Strict convexity of preferences

We now seek to characterize preferences that will result in a point-valued demand function. Consider

(C.VII) (Strict Convexity of Preferences): Let $x \succsim_i y$, (note that this includes $x \sim_i y$), $x \ne y$, and let $0 < \alpha < 1$. Then

$$\alpha x + (1 - \alpha)y \succ_i y.$$

Equivalently, if preferences are characterized by a utility function $u^i(\cdot)$, then we can state C.VII as

$$u^i(x) \ge u^i(y), \ x \ne y, \quad \text{implies} \quad u^i[\alpha x + (1 - \alpha)y] > u^i(y).$$

Assumption C.VII says that the indifference curves are strictly curved. There are no flat segments in them. This corresponds economically to the idea that there are no perfect substitutes.

5.2 Representation of $\succsim_i$: Construction of a continuous utility function

Starting from the household preference ordering $\succsim_h$, we can now very conveniently represent the household preferences by a continuous real-valued function $u^h(\cdot)$. The reason we want a utility function is to use it to help construct the household demand function. We would like to be able to characterize household demand behavior as utility maximization subject to a budget constraint. The alternative, already available to us, is to characterize demand as going as high as possible in the preference quasi-ordering subject to budget constraint. Because the utility function we will develop is actually just a representation of the preference ordering, this is really the same idea. However, the mathematics of maximizing a continuous function subject to constraint is very well developed. In particular, we can apply Corollary 2.2. We can save considerable effort by showing that preferences can be well represented by a continuous utility function.

Classical economists sometimes attributed very strong significance to the numerical values taken by a utility function, suggesting that these represented the intensity of preference experienced – either by an individual at different consumptions (a property known as cardinality of the utility function) or between individuals (comparability). For our purposes, neither of these conditions is useful. On a principle of parsimony (using the weakest – and hence most general – possible assumptions to achieve desired analytic ends) we will demonstrate a weaker property, ordinality (representing an ordering). The utility function can represent the idea of preference without necessarily displaying interpersonal comparability or intensity. The essential point is to allow preferences on consumption plans to be represented by a numerical function so that higher values correspond to more preferred consumption plans.

Let $u^h: X^h \to \mathbf{R}$. Then u^h is a utility function.

Definition *We will say that the utility function $u^h(\cdot)$ **represents** the preference ordering $\succsim_h$ if for all x, $y \in X^h$, $u^h(x) \geq u^h(y)$ if and only if $x \succsim_h y$. This implies that $u^h(x) > u^h(y)$ if and only if $x \succ_h y$.*

We are interested in showing that under reasonable assumptions on $\succsim_h$, $u^h()$ exists and is a continuous function of its arguments. It is possible to prove this result using C.I, C.II, C.III, and C.V only, without using any assumption on scarcity or desirability of commodities (Debreu (1959), Section 4.6). There is a much simpler proof available, however, if we also assume weak monotonicity (C.IV); this is the approach we take below.

Theorem 5.1 (Existence of a continuous real-valued utility function) *Let X^h and $\succsim_h$ fulfill all of C.I – C.V. Then there is $u^h(\cdot)$, a real-valued continuous function, $u^h : X^h \to \mathbf{R}$, so that u^h represents $\succsim_h$.*

Proof Let $x^\nu \in X^h$, $\nu = 1, 2, 3, \dots, x^\nu \to x^0$. First we need to define a suitable utility function $u^h(\cdot)$. We must then show that $u^h(x^\nu) \to u^h(x^0)$.

Our first job is to find $u^h(\cdot)$. The strategy is to use weak monotonicity to simplify the problem. In particular, we will argue that movement upward along the 45° line is always in the direction of increasing preference. Furthermore, for each point $x \in X^h$, there exists a unique point on the 45° line precisely indifferent to x. We will then define $u^h(x)$ as the length of the vector (point) on the 45° line indifferent to x. We will then at last show that $u^h(\cdot)$ is continuous. This construction is illustrated in Figure 5.2.

First we must formally define $u^h(x)$ and show that it is well defined. Define the 45° line as $L = \{y \mid y \in \mathbf{R}^N, y = t(1, 1, 1, \dots, 1), t \geq 0\}$. We now define $u^h(x)$

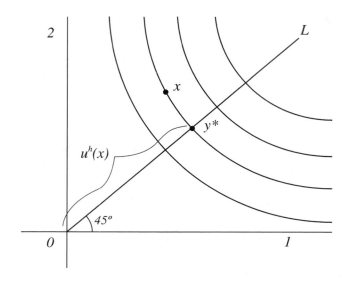

Fig. 5.2. Constructing the utility function.

in the following way. Let $x \in X^h$. Recall the upper and lower contour preference sets $A^h(x)$ and $G^h(x)$. Let y^* be the point at the intersection,

$$\{y^*\} = L \cap A^h(x) \cap G^h(x).$$

We know this intersection is nonempty since X^h is closed and connected (by C.III, convexity) and because $A^h(x)$ and $G^h(x)$ are closed and nonempty and their union equals X^h (by completeness of $\succsim_h$). That is, by connectedness of X^h, $A^h(x)$ and $G^h(x)$ cannot be disjoint (even along L). By weak monotonicity of $\succsim_h$, there is only a single point in this intersection. For each $x \in X^h$, let

$$u^h(x) \equiv |y^*|,$$

where y^* is defined as above. That is, we define $u^h(x)$ to be the Euclidean length of the element of the 45° line indifferent to x. Then $u^h(x)$ is well defined.

We now must demonstrate that $u^h(\cdot)$ is a continuous function. Let $x^\nu \in X^h$, $\nu = 1, 2, 3, \ldots$. Let $x^\nu \to x^\circ$. We must then show that $u^h(x^\nu) \to u^h(x^\circ)$.

First we note that there is a corresponding sequence $y^\nu \in L$, $y^\nu \sim x^\nu$. Let $y^\circ \in L$, $y^\circ \sim x^\circ$. It is sufficient to show that $y^\nu \to y^\circ$. The sequence y^ν is bounded (since the sequence x^ν is bounded so that all but a finite number of elements are in a neighborhood of x° and $y^\nu \sim x^\nu$). To show that $y^\nu \to y^\circ$, note that the sequence contains one or more convergent subsequences. It is sufficient to show that all of the convergent subsequences converge to y°. Suppose, on the contrary, there is a subsequence $y'^\nu \to y'^\circ \neq y^\circ$. Without loss of generality, suppose

$|y'^\circ| > |y^\circ|$. Then there is a corresponding subsequence of x^ν, $x'^\nu \sim y'^\nu$. But then for ν sufficiently large,

$$x'^\nu \succsim_h (y'^\circ + y^\circ)/2 \succ_h y^\circ \sim_h x^\circ.$$

This observation uses both the continuity and the monotonicity of preferences. That is, x'^ν is bounded away from x°. Hence x'^ν cannot converge to x°, which is a contradiction. The contradiction implies that, on the contrary, no such alternative limit point y'°, exists and $y^\nu \to y^\circ$, as was to be shown.   QED

The function $u^i(\cdot)$ in Theorem 5.1, i's *utility* function, is merely a representation of i's preference ordering $\succsim_i$; $u^i(\cdot)$ contains no additional information. In particular, it does not represent strength or intensity of preference. Utility functions like $u^i(\cdot)$ that represent an ordering $\succsim_i$, without embodying additional information or assumptions, are called *ordinal* (i.e., representing an *ordering*). In this sense, any monotone (order-preserving) transformation of $u^i(\cdot)$, $v^i(\cdot)$, is equally appropriate as a representation of $\succsim_i$.

5.3 Choice and boundedness of budget sets, $\tilde{B}^i(p)$

We think of the household choosing a consumption plan in its budget set to maximize its utility subject to budget constraint. This maximization exercise generates two values: a maximum utility (a real number) and a consumption choice (a nonnegative N-dimensional vector) that maximizes the utility subject to constraint. Remember that when we try to maximize a continuous real-valued function over a compact set, we are assured of the existence in the compact set of a point that is a well-defined maximizer of the continuous function in that set. We will suppose that the household's budget set, $\tilde{B}^i(p)$, is a closed bounded set, but not too bounded.[1] We need it to be bounded so that the opportunity set will be compact and hence so that there will be a well-defined optimum behavior for the household. We need it to be large enough (preferably containing all of the attainable consumptions in the economy consistent with budget constraint) so that there will be scope for scarcity – so that demand may exceed attainable production.

Definition x *is an **attainable** aggregate consumption if $y + r \geq x \geq 0$, where $y \in \mathcal{Y}$ and $r \in \mathbf{R}_+^N$ is the economy's initial resource endowment, so that y is an attainable production plan. Note that the set of attainable consumptions is bounded under P.II, P.III, P.V, and P.VI.*

---

[1] As before, the superscript tilde notation ($\sim$), emphasizes that the budget set is defined as a bounded set. This is a restriction that we will wish to relax below (in Chapter 11 and rather obliquely in Lemma 7.1) inasmuch as at zero prices the budget set can quite reasonably be unbounded.

We are interested in describing the demand behavior of the household subject to budget constraint in a well-defined fashion. We know from the Corollary 2.2 that compactness of the opportunity set is a sufficient condition so that a continuous maximand will have a well-defined maximum on the set. The opportunity set here is a budget set. When some prices are nil, the opportunity set may be unbounded (and hence not compact). Using the production model of Chapter 4, however, we know that attainable consumption plans are bounded. In equilibrium, boundedness of opportunities is information to be conveyed to consumers through prices, but in searching for equilibrium we will let it be embodied as well in a bound on their opportunity sets.

Choose $c \in \mathbf{R}_+$ so that $|x| < c$ (a strict inequality) for all attainable consumptions x. Choose c sufficiently large that $X^i \cap \{x \mid x \in \mathbf{R}^N, c > |x|\} \neq \phi$; c is then a very suitable bound on individual consumptions in the household opportunity sets. It is small enough (i.e., finite) so that the opportunity sets will be bounded. It is large enough so that consumption plans constrained by this bound can be well defined and can reflect scarcity.

We assign to household i, a budget at prices p of $\tilde{M}^i(p)$. This is the value (in units of account) that the household can spend on purchases. The budget itself will be defined more fully in Chapter 6. We now characterize a bounded budget set $\tilde{B}^i(p)$. Let

$$\tilde{B}^i(p) = \{x \mid x \in \mathbf{R}^N, p \cdot x \leq \tilde{M}^i(p)\} \cap \{x \mid |x| \leq c\}.$$

This is the budget set of household i. Consumption plans in this budget set must fulfill a budget constraint and have a maximum length of c (all attainable consumption plans will lie within this length). To represent household consumption choice, we ask the household to optimize consumption with regard to its preferences – equivalently, to maximize utility – subject to budget and the possible consumption set.[2] Define

$$\tilde{D}^i(p) \equiv \{x \mid x \in \tilde{B}^i(p) \cap X^i, x \succsim_i y \quad \text{for all } y \in \tilde{B}^i(p) \cap X^i\}$$

$$\equiv \{x \mid x \in \tilde{B}^i(p) \cap X^i, x \text{ maximizes } u^i(y) \quad \text{for all } y \in \tilde{B}^i(p) \cap X^i\}.$$

---

[2] We ignore the issue of occupational choice in this treatment. It is possible to use a convention on income and consumption to treat the issue of occupational choice as part of the household demand decision. We could say that the household is endowed with several different kinds of labor, each attributed to a possible occupation the household can pursue. The household will sell all of its labor endowment, contributing to household income. We can then require that the household repurchase all but (at most) 24 hours per day worth of the labor it has sold. The household – which could be a professor of classics or an investment banker, but lacks the time to pursue both as full-time occupations – sells both forms of labor and then repurchases the labor of the occupation that it does not wish to pursue, leaving the household a net seller of labor of the occupation it actually follows. For a more technical expression of this treatment see Arrow and Hahn (1971).

To characterize market demand let

$$\tilde{D}(p) = \sum_{i \in H} \tilde{D}^i(p).$$

Lemma 5.1 $\tilde{B}^i(p)$ *is a closed set.*

We will restrict attention to models where $\tilde{M}^i(p)$ is homogeneous of degree one, that is, where $\tilde{M}^i(\lambda p) = \lambda \tilde{M}^i(p)$. It is immediate then that $\tilde{B}^i(p)$ is homogeneous of degree zero.

Lemma 5.2 *Let* $\tilde{M}^i(p)$ *be homogeneous of degree 1. Then* $\tilde{B}^i(p)$ *and* $\tilde{D}^i(p)$ *are homogeneous of degree* 0.

Monotonicity of preferences (C.IV) assures us that prices in equilibrium will be non-negative. Homogeneity of degree zero of both $\tilde{D}^i(p)$ and $\tilde{S}^j(p)$ (from Lemma 4.1) allows us to simplify significantly the space of prices. We do not need to use the full nonnegative orthant of $\mathbf{R}^N$. Instead, we can restrict prices to the unit simplex in $\mathbf{R}^N$. Economically speaking, this restriction represents that homogeneity of degree zero in p implies that only *relative* prices (price ratios) matter in forming supply and demand in this economy. The numerical values in which prices are quoted (dollars, yen, guineas, ...) are irrelevant. We will confine attention to price vectors on the set P, the unit simplex in $\mathbf{R}^N$,

$$P \equiv \left\{ p \mid p \in \mathbf{R}^N, \ p_i \geq 0, \ i = 1, 2, 3, \ldots, N, \ \sum_{i=1}^{N} p_i = 1 \right\}.$$

5.3.1 Positivity of income

To avoid possibly empty budget sets $\tilde{B}^i(p)$ and discontinuities in demand behavior at the boundary of X^i we will assume

(C.VIII) $\tilde{M}^i(p) \gg \min_{x \in X^i \cap \{y \mid y \in \mathbf{R}^N, c \geq |y|\}} p \cdot x \geq 0$ *for all* $p \in P$.

C.VIII can be fulfilled in a variety of ways: i's endowment r^i could be strictly interior to X^i or i's share of firm profits could ensure positive income everywhere. Assumption C.VIII allows us to avoid discontinuities that may occur when the budget set coincides with the boundary of X^i (the Arrow corner). The term "corner" here refers to the terminology that an economic solution on the boundary of a constraint set, typically against a nonnegativity constraint, is said to be a corner solution. Alternatively, a weaker sufficient condition than C.VIII could be used, guaranteeing sufficiently high income on a subset of P where equilibria might

arise, but this requires more structure than we wish to develop. The next example
illustrates the difficulty we have assumed away.

Example 5.2 (The Arrow Corner) Consider household i in a 2-commodity economy with sale of endowment as i's only source of income (i has no share in firm
profits). Let the household consumption set X^i be the nonnegative quadrant, with
i endowed with one unit of good 1 and none of good 2. Consider consumption
behavior in the neighborhood of a zero price of good 1. We have

$$X^i = \mathbf{R}^2_+,$$

$$r^i = (1, 0),$$

$$\tilde{M}^i(p) = p \cdot r^i.$$

Let $p^0 = (0, 1)$. Then

$$\tilde{B}^i(p^0) \cap X^i = \{(x, y) \mid c \geq x \geq 0, y = 0\},$$

the truncated nonnegative x axis. Consider the sequence $p^\nu = (1/\nu, 1 - 1/\nu)$.
$p^\nu \to p^0$. We have

$$\tilde{B}^i(p^\nu) \cap X^i = \left\{(x, y) \mid p^\nu \cdot (x, y) \leq \frac{1}{\nu}, (x, y) \geq 0, c \geq |(x, y)| \geq 0\right\},$$

$(c, 0) \in \tilde{B}^i(p^0)$, but there is no sequence $(x^\nu, y^\nu) \in \tilde{B}^i(p^\nu)$ so that
$(x^\nu, y^\nu) \to (c, 0)$. On the contrary, for any sequence $(x^\nu, y^\nu) \in \tilde{B}^i(p^\nu)$ so that
$(x^\nu, y^\nu) = \tilde{D}^i(p^\nu)$, (x^ν, y^ν) will converge to some $(x^*, 0)$, where $0 \leq x^* \leq 1$.
For suitably chosen $\succsim_i$, we may have $(c, 0) = \tilde{D}^i(p^0)$. Hence $\tilde{D}^i(p)$ need not be
continuous at p^0. This completes the example.

Example 5.2 demonstrates that when the budget constraint coincides with the
boundary of the consumption set, discontinuities in the budget set (a large change
in the consumption choices available in response to a small change in prices) and
corresponding discontinuity in demand behavior may result. Hence, to ensure
continuity of demand (C.VIII), positivity of income (sufficient income to stay off
the boundary of the consumption set) may be required.

5.4 Demand behavior under strict convexity

We have now developed enough structure to characterize demand behavior for the
household as a continuous (point-valued) function of prices. As noted in Chapter 1
this is an essential step in developing sufficient conditions for existence of a well-
defined general equilibrium. In order for demand to be point valued, strict convexity
of preferences (C.VII) is essential. With only weak convexity (C.VI), the possibility

of perfect substitutes in consumption would allow there to be a linear segment of equally satisfactory, equally affordable consumption plans so that demand would be set valued rather than point valued. This case is treated in Chapters 16 and 17.

Theorem 5.2 *Assume C.I – C.V, C.VII, and C.VIII. Let $\tilde{M}^i(p)$ be a continuous function for all $p \in P$. Then $\tilde{D}^i(p)$ is a well-defined, point-valued, continuous function for all $p \in P$.*

Proof $\tilde{B}^i(p) \cap X^i$ is the intersection of the closed set $\{x \mid p \cdot x \le \tilde{M}^i(p)\}$ with the compact set $\{x \mid |x| \le c\}$ and the closed set X^i. Hence it is compact. It is nonempty by C.VIII. Because $\tilde{D}^i(p)$ is characterized by the maximization of a continuous function, $u^i(\cdot)$, on this compact nonempty set, there is a well-defined maximum value, $u^0 = u^i(x^0)$, where x^0 is the utility-optimizing value of x in $\tilde{B}^i(p) \cap X^i$. We must show that x^0 is unique for each $p \in P$ and that x^0 is a continuous function of p.

We will now demonstrate that *uniqueness* follows from strict convexity of preferences (C.VII). Suppose there are $x', x'' \in \tilde{B}^i(p) \cap X^i$, $x' \ne x''$, $x^0 \sim_i x' \sim_i x''$. We must show that this leads to a contradiction. But now consider a convex combination of x' and x''. Choose $0 < \alpha < 1$. The point $\alpha x' + (1 - \alpha)x'' \in \tilde{B}^i(p) \cap X^i$ by convexity of X^i and $\tilde{B}^i(p)$. But C.VII, strict convexity of preferences, implies that $\alpha x' + (1 - \alpha)x'' \succ_i x' \sim_i x^0 \sim_i x''$. This is a contradiction, since x^0, x', and x'' are all elements of $\tilde{D}^i(p)$. Hence x^0 is the unique element of $\tilde{D}^i(p)$. We can now, without loss of generality, refer to $\tilde{D}^i(p)$ as a (point-valued) function.

Note that under C.VIII, $\tilde{M}^i(p) > 0$ for all $p \in P$.

To demonstrate continuity, let $p^\nu \in P$, $\nu = 1, 2, 3, \ldots$, $p^\nu \to p^0$. We must show that $\tilde{D}^i(p^\nu) \to \tilde{D}^i(p^0)$. $\tilde{D}^i(p^\nu)$ is a sequence in a compact set. Without loss of generality take a convergent subsequence, $\tilde{D}^i(p^\nu) \to x^0$. We must show that $x^0 = \tilde{D}^i(p^0)$. We will use a proof by contradiction.

Define

$$\hat{x} = \underset{x \in X^i \cap \{y \mid y \in \mathbf{R}^N, c \ge |y|\}}{\arg\min} p^0 \cdot x.$$

The expression "$\hat{x} = \arg\min_{x \in X^i \cap \{y \mid y \in \mathbf{R}^N, c \ge |y|\}} p^0 \cdot x$" defines $\hat{x}$ as the minimizer of $p^0 \cdot x$ in the domain $X^i \cap \{y \mid y \in \mathbf{R}^N, c \ge |y|\}$. $\hat{x}$ is well defined (though it may not be unique) since it represents a minimum of a continuous function taken over a compact domain.

Note that under C.IV and C.VIII, $p^0 \cdot \tilde{D}^i(p^0) > p^0 \cdot \hat{x}$.

Let

$$\alpha^\nu = \min\left[1, \frac{\tilde{M}^i(p^\nu) - p^\nu \cdot \hat{x}}{p^\nu \cdot (\tilde{D}^i(p^0) - \hat{x})}\right].$$

For ν large, the denominator is positive, α^ν is well defined (this is where C.VIII enters the proof), and $0 \le \alpha^\nu \le 1$. Let $w^\nu = (1 - \alpha^\nu)\hat{x} + \alpha^\nu \tilde{D}^i(p^0)$. Note that $\tilde{M}^i(p)$ is continuous in p. Then $w^\nu \to \tilde{D}^i(p^0)$ and $w^\nu \in \tilde{B}^i(p^\nu) \cap X^i$. Suppose, contrary to the theorem, $x^0 \ne \tilde{D}^i(p^0)$. Then $u^i(x^0) < u^i(\tilde{D}^i(p^0))$, so that for ν large, $u^i(w^\nu) > u^i(\tilde{D}^i(p^\nu))$. But this is a contradiction, since $\tilde{D}^i(p^\nu)$ maximizes $u^i(\cdot)$ in $\tilde{B}^i(p^\nu) \cap X^i$. The contradiction proves the result. This completes the demonstration of continuity.   QED

Theorem 5.2 gives a family of sufficient conditions for demand behavior of the household to be very well behaved. It will be a continuous (point-valued) function of prices if preferences are continuous and convex and if income is a continuous and sufficiently positive function of prices.

What will household spending patterns look like? What is the value of household expenditures, $p \cdot \tilde{D}^i(p)$? There are two significant constraints on $p \cdot \tilde{D}^i(p)$, budget and length: $p \cdot \tilde{D}^i(p) \le \tilde{M}^i(p)$ and $|\tilde{D}^i(p)| \le c$. In addition, of course, $\tilde{D}^i(p)$ must optimize consumption choice with regard to preferences $\succsim_i$ or equivalently with regard to the utility function $u^i(\cdot)$. We have enough structure on preferences and the budget set to actually say a fair amount about the character of spending and where $\tilde{D}^i(p)$ is located. This is embodied in

Lemma 5.3 *Assume C.I – C.V, C.VII, and C.VIII. Then $p \cdot \tilde{D}^i(p) \le \tilde{M}^i(p)$. Further, if $p \cdot \tilde{D}^i(p) < \tilde{M}^i(p)$ then $|\tilde{D}^i(p)| = c$.*

Proof $\tilde{D}^i(p) \in \tilde{B}^i(p)$ by definition. However, that ensures $p \cdot \tilde{D}^i(p) \le \tilde{M}^i(p)$ and hence the weak inequality surely holds. Suppose, however, $p \cdot \tilde{D}^i(p) < \tilde{M}^i(p)$ and $|\tilde{D}^i(p)| < c$. We wish to show that this leads to a contradiction. Recall C.IV (Weak Monotonicity) and C.VII (Strict Convexity). By C.IV there is $w^* \in X^i$ so that $w^* \succ_i \tilde{D}^i(p)$. Clearly, $w^* \notin \tilde{B}^i(p)$ so one (or both) of two conditions holds: (a) $p \cdot w^* > \tilde{M}^i(p)$, (b) $|w^*| > c$.

Set $w' = \alpha w^* + (1 - \alpha)\tilde{D}^i(p)$. There is an $\alpha(1 > \alpha > 0)$ sufficiently small so that $p \cdot w' \le \tilde{M}^i(p)$ and $|w'| \le c$. Thus $w' \in \tilde{B}^i(p)$. Now $w' \succ_i \tilde{D}^i(p)$ by C.VII, which is a contradiction since $\tilde{D}^i(p)$ is supposed to be the preference optimizer in $\tilde{B}^i(p)$. The contradiction shows that we cannot have both $p \cdot \tilde{D}^i(p) < \tilde{M}^i(p)$ and $|\tilde{D}^i(p)| < c$. Hence, if the first inequality holds, we must have $|\tilde{D}^i(p)| = c$. QED

5.5 Bibliographic note

The treatment of the household, preferences, and demand here parallels the presentations of Arrow (1962), Arrow and Debreu (1954), and Debreu (1959). The construction of the utility function as the length of a ray from the origin to the indifference curve is presented in Arrow and Hahn (1971) (with a technical over-sight – a weaker monotonicity assumption – corrected in the treatment here). Debreu (1959) provides a more general derivation of the utility function that does not depend on monotonicity but at the cost of greater complexity in exposition (using the connectedness of $\mathbf{R}^N$ and the density of the rationals in the reals).

Exercises

5.1   The lexicographic (dictionary-like) ordering on $\mathbf{R}_+^N$ (let's denote it $\succsim_L$) is described in the following way. Let $x = (x_1, x_2, \ldots, x_N)$, $y = (y_1, y_2, \cdots, y_N)$.

$$x \succ_L y \quad \text{if } x_1 > y_1, \text{ or}$$
$$\text{if } x_1 = y_1 \text{ and } x_2 > y_2, \text{ or}$$
$$\text{if } x_1 = y_1, x_2 = y_2, \text{ and } x_3 > y_3, \text{ and so forth} \ldots .$$
$$x \sim_L y \quad \text{if } x = y.$$

$\succsim_L$ fulfills weak monotonicity, trivially fulfills strict convexity (trivially since the only point indifferent to x is x), and does not fulfill continuity. Consider a two-commodity ($N = 2$) economy. Consider a household (we'll omit a subscript for its name to save notation) with a lexicographic preference ordering. Let the possible consumption set X be the nonnegative quadrant. We give the household endowment, $r = (1, 1)$, 1 unit of each good. Note that with this endowment, household income will always be positive, so C.VIII is fulfilled. Let the constant c as before indicate a large real number used to bound the length of a prospective consumption vector. The household bounded budget set is then described as

$$\tilde{B}(p) = \{x \mid x \in \mathbf{R}_+^N, \ p \cdot x \le p \cdot (1, 1)\} \cap \{x \mid |x| \le c\}$$

and demand behavior is described as

$$\tilde{D}(p) \equiv \{x \mid x \in \tilde{B}(p) \cap X, x \succsim_L y \text{ for all } y \in \tilde{B}(p) \cap X\}.$$

Consider the price sequence in the unit simplex

$$p^v = (1 - (1/v), 1/v), \quad v = 1, 2, \ldots .$$

As v becomes large, p^v converges to $(1, 0)$; that is, as v increases, x_1 (the lexicographically preferred good) becomes consistently more expensive and x_2 (the lexicographically less preferred good) becomes consistently less expensive.

Describe the demand behavior at p^v and in the limit at $(1, 0)$. Show that demand is discontinuous at $(1, 0)$.

5.2   Recall our definition of how a utility function represents a preference or-
        dering:

> **Definition** *We will say that the utility function $u^h(\cdot)$* **represents** *the prefer-*
> *ence ordering $\succsim_h$ if for all $x, y \in X^h$, $u^h(x) \geq u^h(y)$ if and only if $x \succsim_h y$.*
> *This implies that $u^h(x) > u^h(y)$ if and only if $x \succ_h y$.*

We noted that this concept of a utility function is *ordinal* in the sense
that it represents an ordering on the commodity bundles without additional
information regarding the intensity of preference.

The function $u^i(\cdot)$ in theorem 5.1, i's *utility* function, is merely a representation of i's preference ordering $\succsim_i$. $u^i(\cdot)$ contains no additional information.
In particular, it does not represent strength or intensity of preference. A utility function, like $u^i(\cdot)$, that represents an ordering $\succsim_i$, without embodying
additional information or assumptions, is called *ordinal* (i.e., representing
an *ordering*).

Let $a, b \in \mathbf{R}_+$ be positive real numbers. Define $v^i(x) = a + b \cdot u^i(x)$.

Show that if $u^i(\cdot)$ represents the preference ordering $\succsim_i$ then so does $v^i(\cdot)$.
This is known as invariance under a monotone transformation.

5.3   We wish to demonstrate the importance of the adequacy of income assump-
        tion (C.VIII) in avoiding a discontinuity of demand behavior (the Arrow
        Corner). Let household i's possible consumption set X^i be the nonnegative
        quadrant in $\mathbf{R}^2$ translated by (1,1). That is,

$$X^i = \{(x, y) \mid x \geq 1, y \geq 1\}.$$

Note that X^i fulfills C.I – C.III. Let household i have no share of any firm.
Let i have endowment $r^i = (2, 1)$.

(i) Show that this situation violates C.VIII (consider $p = (0, 1)$).

Let i's preferences be represented by the utility function $u^i(x_1, x_2) = x_1 + x_2$ (this utility function violates strict convexity but fulfills weakly convex
preferences; no confusion should result). Define i's demand behavior as

$$\tilde{D}^i(p) \equiv \{x \mid x \in \tilde{B}^i(p) \cap X^i, u^i(x) \geq u^i(y) \text{ for all } y \in \tilde{B}^i(p) \cap X^i\},$$

where

$$\tilde{B}^i(p) = \{x \mid x \in \mathbf{R}^N, p \cdot x \leq p \cdot r^i\} \cap \{x \mid |x| \leq c\}.$$

(ii) Consider the price sequence in the unit simplex, $p^v = [(1/v, 1-(1/v)]$,
$v = 1, 2, \ldots$. As v becomes large, p^v converges to (0,1). Describe the
demand behavior (i.e., describe $\tilde{D}^i(p)$ at p^v and in the limit at (0,1)).
Show that demand is discontinuous at (0,1).

5.4 Consider Theorem 5.1. Arrow and Hahn try to prove it by the same approach used in this chapter using a weaker version of monotonicity,
(*C.IV′*) (*Very Weak Monotonicity*) *Let* x, $y \in X^i$, *with* $x \gg y$. *Then* $x \succsim_i y$.
Their proof is fallacious. Show that under C.IV′ there may be thick bands of indifference along the 45° line. We define

$$u^i(x) = \min_{y \in L, y \sim_i x} |y|.$$

Show that the construction of $u^i(x)$ can then lead to discontinuities in $u^i(x)$.

5.5 Recall that in defining household demand behavior we used the truncated budget set

$$\tilde{B}^i(p) = \{x \mid x \in \mathbf{R}^N, p \cdot x \leq \tilde{M}^i(p)\} \cap \{x \mid |x| \leq c\}.$$

We defined demand behavior as

$$\tilde{D}^i(p) \equiv \{x \mid x \in \tilde{B}^i(p) \cap X^i, x \succsim_i y \text{ for all } y \in \tilde{B}^i(p) \cap X^i\}.$$

We then established in Theorem 5.2 that, under a variety of additional assumptions, $\tilde{D}^i(p)$ is well defined (nonempty).
Show that this result depends on the truncation of $\tilde{B}^i(p)$. That is, define

$$B^i(p) = \{x \mid x \in \mathbf{R}^N, p \cdot x \leq \tilde{M}^i(p)\}$$

and

$$D^i(p) \equiv \{x \mid x \in B^i(p) \cap X^i, x \succsim_i y \text{ for all } y \in B^i(p) \cap X^i\}.$$

Show that for some prices (in particular with $p_k = 0$ for some goods k) and preferences, $D^i(p)$ may not be well defined under the same circumstances where $\tilde{D}^i(p)$ will be well defined.

5.6 Show under Assumption C.VI that $A^i(x^0)$ is convex for every $x^0 \in X^i$.

6

A market economy

6.1 Firms, profits, and household income

It is now time to bring the firms of Chapter 5 and the households of Chapter 6 together to form a private ownership economy. The link between firms and households will be in household income. The firms are owned by the households. Thus, firm profits are transmitted to households as part of income. This essential step ensures fulfillment of the Walras' Law and hence provides for the existence of general equilibrium.

The economy is characterized by the agents in it: households (the set H) and firms (the set F). For each firm j, there is a list of households that are shareholders in j. We let $\alpha^{ij} \in \mathbf{R}_+$ represent i's share of firm j. We assume $\sum_{i \in H} \alpha^{ij} = 1$ for each $j \in F$ and $\alpha^{ij} \geq 0$ for all $i \in H$, $j \in F$. That is, we assume that every firm is 100% owned by some one or several shareholders and that there is no negative ownership of firms (no short sales). A household $i \in H$ is characterized by its endowment of goods $r^i \in \mathbf{R}_+^N$, by its endowed shares $\alpha^{ij} \in \mathbf{R}_+$ of firms $j \in F$, and by $\succsim_i$. The initial resource endowment of the economy, designated r in Chapters 4 and 5 is now identified as

$$r \equiv \sum_{i \in H} r^i.$$

A firm $j \in F$ is characterized by its possible production set $\mathcal{Y}^j$. Firm j's profit function is $\tilde{\pi}^j(p) = \max_{y \in \mathcal{Y}^j} p \cdot y = p \cdot \tilde{S}^j(p)$.

Theorem 6.1 *Assume P.II, P.III, and P.VI. $\tilde{\pi}^j(p)$ is a well-defined continuous function of p for all $p \in \mathbf{R}_+^N$, $p \neq 0$.*

Proof Exercise 6.2.

Household i's income is now defined as $\tilde{M}^i(p) = p \cdot r^i + \sum_{j \in F} \alpha^{ij} \tilde{\pi}^j(p)$. Note that this expression is homogeneous of degree one in p. Specifying $\tilde{M}^i(p)$ in this form means that household i has income from two sources: sale of endowment and a share of profits of firms in which it is a shareholder. Assuming P.I–P.VI, $\tilde{M}^i(p)$ is continuous, real valued, nonnegative, and well defined for all $p \in \mathbf{R}^N_+$, $p \neq 0$. Recalling Lemma 5.2 and using this definition of $\tilde{M}^i(p)$, we have that $\tilde{B}^i(p)$ and $\tilde{D}^i(p)$ are homogeneous of degree 0 in p. We can then, without loss of generality, restrict the price space to the unit simplex in $\mathbf{R}^N$, denoted P,

$$
P = \left\{ p \mid p \in \mathbf{R}^N, \, p_k \geq 0, k = 1 \ldots, N, \sum_{k=1}^{N} p_k = 1 \right\}.
$$

6.2 Excess demand and Walras' Law

We can now define the excess demand function of the economy. It consists of the demand function defined in Chapter 6 minus the supply function defined in Chapter 5 minus the endowment of initial resources. General equilibrium will consist in prices that make this function the zero vector (or in the case of free goods, a nonpositive vector).

Definition *The excess demand function at prices $p \in P$ is*

$$
\tilde{Z}(p) = \tilde{D}(p) - \tilde{S}(p) - r = \sum_{i \in H} \tilde{D}^i(p) - \sum_{j \in F} \tilde{S}^j(p) - \sum_{i \in H} r^i.
$$

Recall that by definition $\tilde{D}^i(p)$ and $\tilde{S}^j(p)$ are bounded. Then their finite sums are bounded as well. Theorems 5.1 and 6.2 established sufficient conditions for $\tilde{D}^i(p)$ and $\tilde{S}^j(p)$ to be continuous functions of their arguments. These sufficient conditions carry over to $\tilde{Z}(p)$ as well.

Lemma 6.1 *Assume C.I–C.V, C.VII, C.VIII, P.I–P.III, P.V, and P.VI. The range of $\tilde{Z}(p)$ is bounded. $\tilde{Z}(p)$ is continuous and well defined for all $p \in P$.*

Proof Apply Theorems 5.1 and 6.2. The finite sum of bounded sets is bounded. The finite sum of continuous functions is continuous.

We saw in Chapter 1 that the Walras' Law is helpful in proving the existence of general equilibrium. Unfortunately, the classic Walras' Law is not strictly true in this model. This reflects the boundedness restriction on household demand developed in Chapter 6. The classic Walras' Law applies only when the budget constraint is the binding constraint on household expenditure. In the model of Chapter 6, the length restriction, c, may instead be the binding constraint. This leads us to

Theorem 6.2 (Weak Walras' Law) *Assume C.I–C.V, C.VII, C.VIII, P.I–P.III, P.V,
and P.VI. For all $p \in P$, $p \cdot \tilde{Z}(p) \leq 0$. For p such that $p \cdot \tilde{Z}(p) < 0$, there is
$k = 1, 2, \ldots, N$ so that $\tilde{Z}_k(p) > 0$.*

Proof Recall two properties of the market economy. For each household i, we have
the budget constraint on demand, $p \cdot \tilde{D}^i(p) \leq \tilde{M}^i(p) = p \cdot r^i + \sum_{j \in F} \alpha^{ij} \tilde{\pi}^j(p)$.
For each firm j, we have that it is fully owned by households i, $\sum_{i \in H} \alpha^{ij} = 1$ for
each $j \in F$.

The proof starts with a string of identities:

$$p \cdot \tilde{Z}(p) = p \cdot \left[\sum_{i \in H} \tilde{D}^i(p) - \sum_{j \in F} \tilde{S}^j(p) - \sum_{i \in H} r^i \right]$$

$$= p \cdot \sum_{i \in H} \tilde{D}^i(p) - p \cdot \sum_{j \in F} \tilde{S}^j(p) - p \cdot \sum_{i \in H} r^i$$

$$= \sum_{i \in H} p \cdot \tilde{D}^i(p) - \sum_{j \in F} p \cdot \tilde{S}^j(p) - \sum_{i \in H} p \cdot r^i$$

$$= \sum_{i \in H} p \cdot \tilde{D}^i(p) - \sum_{j \in F} \tilde{\pi}^j(p) - \sum_{i \in H} p \cdot r^i$$

$$= \sum_{i \in H} p \cdot \tilde{D}^i(p) - \sum_{j \in F} \left[\sum_{i \in H} \alpha^{ij} \tilde{\pi}^j(p) \right] - \sum_{i \in H} p \cdot r^i$$

$$= \sum_{i \in H} p \cdot \tilde{D}^i(p) - \sum_{i \in H} \left[\sum_{j \in F} \alpha^{ij} \tilde{\pi}^j(p) \right] - \sum_{i \in H} p \cdot r^i$$

$$= \sum_{i \in H} p \cdot \tilde{D}^i(p) - \sum_{i \in H} \tilde{M}^i(p) \leq 0.$$

The last inequality holds by the budget constraint, $p \cdot \tilde{D}^i(p) \leq \tilde{M}^i(p)$, that applies
to each household i. This proves the weak inequality as required.

We now must demonstrate the positivity of some coordinate of $\tilde{Z}(p)$ when the
strict inequality holds. Let $p \cdot \tilde{Z}(p) < 0$. Then
$p \cdot \sum_{i \in H} \tilde{D}^i(p) < p \cdot r + p \cdot \sum_{j \in F} \tilde{S}^j(p) = \sum_{i \in H} \tilde{M}^i(p)$, so for some $i \in H$,
$p \cdot \tilde{D}^i(p) < \tilde{M}^i(p)$. Now we apply Lemma 5.3. By weak monotonicity (C. IV),
$p \cdot \tilde{D}^i(p) = \tilde{M}^i(p)$ or $|\tilde{D}^i(p)| = c$. Hence we must have $|\tilde{D}^i(p)| = c$. Recall that
c is chosen so that $|x| < c$ (a strict inequality) for all attainable x. But then $\tilde{D}^i(p)$
is not attainable. For *no* $y \in Y$ do we have $\tilde{D}^i(p) \leq y + r$. Therefore, $\tilde{Z}_k(p) > 0$,
for some $k = 1, 2, \ldots, N$.   QED

The Weak Walras' Law performs the following exercise. For any price vector
p, we evaluate the excess demand function $\tilde{Z}(p)$. That is, we take the dot product

$p \cdot \tilde{Z}(p)$. The Weak Walras' Law tells us that this product will have one of two characteristics. Either the value of excess demand, evaluated at prevailing prices, is nil or the value is negative and there is positive excess demand for one or several of the N goods. The Weak Walras' Law applies to the excess demand function $\tilde{Z}(p)$ of the economy constrained to keep individual household demand inside a sphere of radius c. This restriction ensures that the excess demand function is well defined for all $p \in P$. Theorem 6.2 differs from the more conventional Walras' Law (Theorem 10.2). Theorem 10.2 is defined on a market excess demand function $Z(p)$ with no requirement that household demands stay inside a sphere of radius c; absent that restriction, $Z(p)$ may not be well defined. Theorem 6.2 above and Theorem 10.2 below will coincide where the restriction to the ball of radius c is not a binding constraint, since in that case $p \cdot \tilde{Z}(p) \le 0$ holds as an equality.

6.3 Bibliographic note

Explicit development of the behavior of the artificially bounded economy, in particular the Weak Walras' Law, is distinctive with the treatment in this volume. The approach of developing the equilibrium of an unbounded economy as a consequence of the equilibrium of the bounded economy is pursued successfully in Arrow and Debreu (1954) and expounded in Arrow (1962).

Exercises

6.1   An economy is generally said to be "competitive" if no agent in the economy has a significant effect in determining equilibrium prices. They cannot be price-setters. Is it an assumption or a conclusion in Chapters 4 through 6 that agents are competitive in this sense? If it is an assumption, where is it made? If a conclusion, where does it appear and what hypotheses is it based on?

6.2   Prove Theorem 6.1: Assume P.II, P.III, P.VI. $\tilde{\pi}^j(p)$ is a well-defined continuous function of p for all $p \in \mathbf{R}_+^N$, $p \ne 0$.

7

General equilibrium of the market economy with an excess demand function

7.1 Existence of equilibrium

In this chapter we will consider the existence of general equilibrium of an economy where demands $\tilde{D}^i(\cdot)$ and supplies $\tilde{S}^j(\cdot)$ come from bounded opportunity sets, $\tilde{B}^i(p)$ and $\mathcal{Y}^j$, and are point valued. From Chapters 4 and 5 we know that a sufficient condition for point-valuedness is strict convexity of tastes and technologies, P.V and C.VII. As noted in Chapter 6, homogeneity of degree zero of $\tilde{D}^i(\cdot)$ and $\tilde{S}^j(\cdot)$ in p means that we may, without loss of generality, restrict the price space to be the unit simplex in

$$P = \left\{ p \mid p \in \mathbf{R}^N, p_k \geq 0, k = 1 \ldots, N, \sum_{k=1}^{N} p_k = 1 \right\}.$$

From Chapter 6, the market excess demand function is defined

$$\tilde{Z}(p) = \sum_{i \in H} \tilde{D}^i(p) - \sum_{j \in F} \tilde{S}^j(p) - r.$$

We are now in a position to define the general equilibrium of the market economy.

Definition $p^0 \in P$ is said to be an equilibrium price vector if $\tilde{Z}(p^0) \leq 0$ *(the inequality holds coordinatewise) with $p_k^0 = 0$ for k such that $\tilde{Z}_k(p^0) < 0$.*

That is, an equilibrium is characterized by market clearing for all goods except perhaps free goods that may be in excess supply in equilibrium. To find sufficient conditions and to prove the existence of a general equilibrium, we have to focus on the excess demand function, $\tilde{Z}(p)$, $\tilde{Z} : P \to \mathbf{R}^N$. We have the following observations on $\tilde{Z}(p)$:

Weak Walras' Law (Theorem 6.2): For all $p \in P$, $p \cdot \tilde{Z}(p) \leq 0$. For p such that $p \cdot \tilde{Z}(p) < 0$, there is $k = 1, 2, \ldots, N$ so that $\tilde{Z}_k(p) > 0$, under assumptions C.I–C.V, C.VII, and C.VIII, P.I–P.III, P.V, and P.VI.

Continuity: $\tilde{Z}(p)$ is a continuous function, assuming P.II, P.III, P.V, P.VI, C.I–C.V, and C.VII, C.VIII (Theorems 4.1, 5.2, and 6.1).

Our approach to proving the existence of general equilibrium follows the plan used in Chapter 1. We establish sufficient conditions so that excess demand is a continuous function of prices and fulfills the Weak Walras's Law (Theorem 6.2). The rest of the proof involves the mathematics of an economic story. Suppose the Walrasian auctioneer starts out with an arbitrary possible price vector (chosen at random, *crié au hasard*, in Walras's phrase) and then adjusts prices in response to the excess demand function $\tilde{Z}(p)$. He raises the price of goods, k, in excess demand, $\tilde{Z}_k(p) > 0$, and reduces the price of goods, k, in excess supply, $\tilde{Z}_k(p) < 0$. He performs this price adjustment as a continuous function of excess demands and supplies while staying on the price simplex. Then the price adjustment function $T(p)$ is a continuous mapping from the price simplex into itself. From the Brouwer Fixed-Point Theorem (Theorem 2.10), there is a fixed point p^0 of the price adjustment function, so that $T(p^0) = p^0$. Using the Weak Walras' Law we can then show that p^0 is not merely a fixed point of the price adjustment function, but it is a general equilibrium as well.

Theorem 7.1[1] *Assume P.II, P.III, P.V, P.VI, C.I–C.V, C.VII, and C.VIII. There is $p^* \in P$ so that p^* is an equilibrium.*

Proof We formulate a price adjustment function, $T : P \to P$. Define $T(p)$ in the following fashion for each coordinate $k = 1, 2, 3, \ldots, N$:

$$T_k(p) \equiv \frac{p_k + \max[0, \tilde{Z}_k(p)]}{1 + \sum_{n=1}^{N} \max[0, \tilde{Z}_n(p)]} = \frac{p_k + \max[0, \tilde{Z}_k(p)]}{\sum_{n=1}^{N} \{p_n + \max[0, \tilde{Z}_n(p)]\}}.$$

The price adjustment function T raises the relative price of goods in excess demand and reduces that of goods in excess supply while keeping the price vector on the simplex. The denominator is trivially positive.

By Lemma 6.1, $\tilde{Z}(p)$ is a continuous function. Then $T(p)$ is a continuous function from the simplex into itself since continuity is preserved under the operations of max, addition, and division by a positive-valued continuous function. An illustration of the notion of a continuous function from P into P is presented in Figure 7.1. By the Brouwer Fixed-Point Theorem there is $p^* \in P$ so that $T(p^*) = p^*$. But

[1] I acknowledge and thank John Roemer and Li Li for help in formulating the proof.

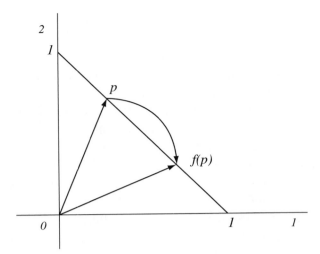

Fig. 7.1. Mapping from P into P.

then for all $k = 1, \ldots, N$,

$$p_k^* = \frac{p_k^* + \max[0, \tilde{Z}_k(p^*)]}{1 + \displaystyle\sum_{n=1}^{N} \max[0, \tilde{Z}_n(p^*)]}.$$

Thus, either $p_k^* = 0$ or

$$p_k^* = \frac{p_k^* + \max[0, \tilde{Z}_k(p^*)]}{1 + \displaystyle\sum_{n=1}^{N} \max[0, \tilde{Z}_n(p^*)]} > 0.$$

CASE 1 $p_k^* = 0 = \max[0, \tilde{Z}_k(p^*)]$. Hence $\tilde{Z}_k(p^*) \leq 0$.

CASE 2

$$p_k^* = \frac{p_k^* + \max[0, \tilde{Z}_k(p^*)]}{1 + \displaystyle\sum_{n=1}^{N} \max[0, \tilde{Z}_n(p^*)]} > 0.$$

To avoid repeated tedious notation, let

$$0 < \alpha = \frac{1}{1 + \displaystyle\sum_{n=1}^{N} \max[0, \tilde{Z}_n(p^*)]} \leq 1.$$

This case now resolves into two subcases:

CASE 2A $\alpha = 1$ implies $\tilde{Z}_k(p^*) \leq 0$, for all k.

CASE 2B $\alpha < 1$.

We have

$$p_k^* = \alpha p_k^* + \alpha \max[0, \tilde{Z}_k(p^*)]$$

or

$$(1 - \alpha) p_k^* = \alpha \max[0, \tilde{Z}_k(p^*)].$$

Multiplying through by $\tilde{Z}_k(p^*)$, we get

$$(1 - \alpha) p_k^* \tilde{Z}_k(p^*) = \alpha (\max[0, \tilde{Z}_k(p^*)]) \tilde{Z}_k(p^*).$$

We can restate the Weak Walras' Law as

$$0 \geq p^* \cdot \tilde{Z}(p^*) = \sum_{k \in \text{Case 1}} p_k^* \tilde{Z}_k(p^*) + \sum_{k \in \text{Case 2}} p_k^* \tilde{Z}_k(p^*)$$

$$= 0 + \sum_{k \in \text{Case 2}} p_k^* \tilde{Z}_k(p^*)$$

$$= \sum_{k \in \text{Case 2}} p_k^* \tilde{Z}_k(p^*).$$

Simplifying, multiplying through by $(1 - \alpha)$, and substituting we get

$$0 \geq (1 - \alpha) \sum_{k \in \text{Case 2}} p_k^* \tilde{Z}_k(p^*) = \alpha \sum_{k \in \text{Case 2}} (\max[0, \tilde{Z}_k(p^*)]) \tilde{Z}_k(p^*).$$

But this means that $\tilde{Z}_k(p^*) \leq 0$, for all k in Case 2. However, then, there is no k, either in Case 1 or 2, so that $\tilde{Z}_k(p^*) > 0$. From the Weak Walras' Law it follows that $p^* \cdot \tilde{Z}(p^*) = 0$. Hence for k so that $\tilde{Z}_k(p^*) < 0$, it follows that $p_k^* = 0$. This completes the proof. QED

It is useful to remark on the character of the equilibrium in Theorem 7.1. We formalize this as

Lemma 7.1 *Assume P.II, P.III, P.V, P.VI, C.I–C.V, CVII, and C.VIII. Let p^* be an equilibrium. Then $|\tilde{D}^i(p^*)| < c$, where c is the bound on the Euclidean length of demand, $\tilde{D}^i(p)$. Further, in equilibrium, Walras' Law holds as an equality: $p^* \cdot \tilde{Z}(p^*) = 0$.*

Proof Since $\tilde{Z}(p^*) \leq 0$ (coordinatewise), we know that $\sum_{i \in H} \tilde{D}^i(p^*) \leq \sum_{j \in F} \tilde{S}^j(p^*) + \sum_{i \in H} r^i$, coordinatewise. However, that implies that the aggregate consumption $\sum_{i \in H} \tilde{D}^i(p^*)$ is attainable, so for each household i, $|\tilde{D}^i(p^*)| < c$, where c is the bound on demand, $\tilde{D}^i(p)$.

We have for all p, $p \cdot \tilde{Z}(p) \le 0$. In equilibrium, at p^*, we have $\tilde{Z}(p^*) \le 0$ with $p_k^* = 0$ for k so that $\tilde{Z}_k(p^*) < 0$. Therefore $p^* \cdot \tilde{Z}(p^*) = 0$.   QED

We have now demonstrated the existence of equilibrium in the strictly convex bounded economy. Note how boundedness has entered the argument above. The technology sets of the firms, $\mathcal{Y}^j$, were assumed to be bounded. It follows that the technology set for the economy as a whole, $\mathcal{Y}$, is also bounded. In defining the opportunity sets of the households $\tilde{B}^i(p)$ we constrained the household to choose a consumption plan in a bounded set (the closed ball of radius c) that contained the attainable points as a proper subset.

In the next several chapters, Part C, we will weaken the assumptions of boundedness used here. We consider there firms that recognize that their technology includes the possibility that with unbounded inputs they could produce unbounded outputs – prices will then nevertheless guide them to bounded inputs and outputs. We would like to weaken the boundedness restriction on household choice. Households should feel free to choose arbitrarily large consumption plans. In equilibrium, prices will lead the households to bounded plans, but it should be prices, not definitions, that do so. Indeed, according to Lemma 7.1, prices have already done that job in the equilibrium developed above. The typical household equilibrium consumption plan does not face a binding constraint on the Euclidean length of the consumption vector in equilibrium. That is, $|\tilde{D}^i(p^*)| < c$. We take advantage of this observation in Part C. We will demonstrate that putting that much faith in the price system is indeed confidence well placed.

7.2 Bibliographic note

The major mathematical insight of modern general equilibrium theory is the importance of the fixed-point theorem in proving the existence of equilibrium. It appears first in Arrow and Debreu (1954) and McKenzie (1954). The mapping used here appears in Varian (1992).

Exercises

7.1   Consider a two-commodity economy with an excess demand function $\tilde{Z}(p)$. $p \in P = \{p \mid p \in \mathbf{R}^2, p \ge 0, p_1 + p_2 = 1\}$. Let $\tilde{Z}(p)$ be continuous, bounded, and fulfill Walras' Law as an equality ($p \cdot \tilde{Z}(p) = 0$), and assume $\tilde{Z}_1(0, 1) > 0$, $\tilde{Z}_2(1, 0) > 0$. Without using the Brouwer Fixed-

Point Theorem, show that the economy has an equilibrium. (Note: You may find the Intermediate Value Theorem useful.)

We use the following model (paralleling the model of Chapters 4–7) in Exercises 7.2 and 7.3. There is thought to be a finite set of firms denoted F. Each firm j is characterized by a production technology set $Y^j \subset \mathbf{R}^N$. There is a finite set of households H. Each household i is characterized by an endowment vector $r^i \in \mathbf{R}^N_+$, ownership share of firm j, α^{ij}, and preferences depicted equivalently by the quasi-order $\succsim_i$ or by a utility function $u^i(\cdot)$, defined on a possible consumption set $X^i \subseteq \mathbf{R}^N$. In a private ownership economy, i's income is characterized as $M^i(p) = p \cdot r^i + \sum_{j \in F} \alpha^{ij} p \cdot y^{0j}$, where y^{0j} is firm j's profit-maximizing production plan. We will generally assume (except as noted in the questions) the standard conditions:

for households: income sufficient to keep consumption interior to the possible consumption set, weak monotonicity, continuity, and strict convexity of preferences;

for firms: continuity (closedness) and strict convexity of technology.

We use the following definition.

Definition $\{p^0, x^{0i}, y^{0j}\}$, $p^0 \in \mathbf{R}^N_+$, $i \in H$, $j \in F$, $x^{0i} \in \mathbf{R}^N$, $y^{0j} \in \mathbf{R}^N$ *is said to be a competitive equilibrium if*

(i) $y^{0j} \in Y^j$ and $p^0 \cdot y^{0j} \ge p^0 \cdot y$ for all $y \in Y^j$, for all $j \in F$,

(ii) $x^{0i} \in X^i$, $p^0 \cdot x^{0i} \le M^i(p^0)$ and $x^{0i} \succsim_i x$ for all $x \in X^i$ with $p^0 \cdot x \le M^i(p^0)$ for all $i \in H$, and

(iii) $0 \ge \sum_{i \in H} x^{0i} - \sum_{j \in F} y^{0i} - \sum_{i \in H} r^i$ with $p^0_k = 0$ for coordinates k so that the strict inequality holds.

7.2 Consider the general competitive equilibrium of a production economy with redistributive taxation of income from endowment. Half of each household's income from endowment (based on actual endowment, not net sales) is taxed away. The proceeds of the tax are then distributed equally to all households. We thus have

$$M^i(p) = p \cdot (.5r^i) + \sum_{j \in F} \alpha^{ij} p \cdot y^j + T,$$

where T is the transfer of tax revenues to the household,

$$T = (1/\#H) \sum_{h \in H} p \cdot (.5r^h).$$

Does there exist a competitive equilibrium in the economy with redistributive income taxation? Explain.

7.3   Consider the general competitive equilibrium of a production economy with excise taxation. In addition to the prices of goods $p \in \mathbf{R}^N_+$, there is a vector of excise taxes $\tau \in \mathbf{R}^N_+$. Proceeds of the tax are then distributed to households as a lump sum. Household income then is

$$M^i(p) = p \cdot r^i + \sum_{j \in F} \alpha^{ij} p \cdot y^j + T,$$

where T is the transfer of tax revenues to the household. The household budget constraint is

$$(p + \tau) \cdot x^i \leq M^i(p).$$

The transfer to the typical household, T, is then characterized as

$$T = (1/\#H) \sum_{h \in H} \tau \cdot x^h.$$

Does there exist a competitive equilibrium in the economy with excise taxation? Explain.

7.4   In an economy with an excess demand function $Z(\cdot)$, $Z : P \to \mathbf{R}^N$, we usually define an equilibrium price vector as $p \in P$ so that $Z(p) \leq 0$ (where 0 is the zero vector, and the weak inequality holds coordinatewise), with $p_k = 0$ for any good k so that $Z_k(p) < 0$.

Some authors use an alternate definition:

p^* so that $Z(p^*) \leq 0$. That is, p^* is a Walrasian equilibrium if there is no good for which there is a positive excess demand.

The alternate definition imposes no requirement that $p_k^* = 0$ for k so that $Z_k(p^*) < 0$.

 (i) Show that under this definition of equilibrium there may be excess supplies at positive prices in equilibrium.
 (ii) What is the behavior of the market price adjustment process (Walrasian auctioneer) with excess supplies implied by this concept of equilibrium?
(iii) Discuss. Is this a desirable concept of equilibrium?

7.5   The usual U-shaped cost curve model of undergraduate economics includes a small nonconvexity (diminishing marginal cost at low output levels). This is a violation of our usual convexity assumptions on production (P.I or P.V). Consider the general equilibrium of an economy displaying U-shaped cost curves. It is possible that a general equilibrium exists despite the small violation of convexity. After all, P.I and P.V are sufficient, not necessary, conditions. Draw a diagram or give an example (partial equilibrium is acceptable). Explain. Nevertheless, it is also possible that an equilibrium fail to exist in this setting. Draw a diagram or give an example. Explain.

7.6　In Chapter 7 we used the mapping $T : P \to P$ as a price adjustment function whose fixed points are competitive equilibria. Consider instead using the mapping $Q : P \to P$, where the ith coordinate mapping of Q is

$$Q_i(p) = \frac{\max[0,\, p_i + p_i \tilde{Z}_i(p)]}{\displaystyle\sum_{j=1}^{N} \max[0,\, p_j + p_j \tilde{Z}_j(p)]}.$$

Assume that Walras' Law holds as an equality, that is, that $p \cdot \tilde{Z}(p) = 0$.
(i) Show that every competitive equilibrium price vector p^0 is a fixed point of Q.
(ii) Show that every vertex of the price simplex P is also a fixed point of Q.
(iii) Under suitably chosen sufficient conditions on the economy, $Q(\cdot)$ can be shown to have a fixed point, $p^* = Q(p^*)$. Does this prove that the economy – under those sufficient conditions – has a competitive equilibrium?

7.7　*Consider the following definition:* $\{p^0, x^{0i}, y^{0j}\}$, $p^0 \in \mathbf{R}_+^N$, $i \in H$, $j \in F$, *is said to be a competitive equilibrium if*
　(i) $y^{0j} \in Y^j$ *and* $p^0 \cdot y^{0j} \geq p^0 \cdot y$ *for all* $y \in Y^j$, *for all* $j \in F$,
　(ii) $x^{0i} \in X^i$, $p^0 \cdot x^{0i} \leq M^i(p^0) = p^0 \cdot r^i + \sum_{j \in F} \alpha^{ij} p^0 \cdot y^{0j}$ *and* $x^{0i} \succsim_i x$ *for all* $x \in X^i$ *with* $p^0 \cdot x \leq M^i(p^0)$ *for all* $i \in H$, *and*
　(iii) $0 \geq \sum_{i \in H} x^{0i} - \sum_{j \in F} y^{0i} - \sum_{i \in H} r^i$ *with* $p_k^0 = 0$ *for coordinates* k *so that the strict inequality holds.*

(a) The concept of competitive equilibrium is supposed to reflect *decentralization* of economic behavior. Explain how this definition embodies the concept of decentralization.
(b) The concept of competitive equilibrium is supposed to reflect market clearing. Explain how this definition includes market clearing.

7.8　The style of analysis we have been using is known as "axiomatic," involving precisely stated assumptions, detailed modeling, and logically derived conclusions. What are the strengths and weaknesses of this approach?

7.9　A two-person, two-commodity, pure exchange (no production) economy is known as an Edgeworth box (discussed more fully in Section 1.3 – you should not need to consult this material). Use the model of Chapters 4 to 7 to demonstrate the existence of equilibrium in an Edgeworth box. Present the following argument:

(1) Set $\mathcal{Y}^j \equiv \{0\}$ for all $j \in F$, where 0 is the zero vector in $\mathbf{R}^N$. Explain why this represents the case of a pure exchange economy. Explain why the usual assumptions on production are fulfilled by this choice of $\mathcal{Y}^j$.

(2) Define an equilibrium in this setting.

(3) Show that Theorem 7.1 applies and ensures the existence of equilibrium. State any additional assumptions you need.

Part C

An economy with unbounded production technology, supply and demand functions

Our plan in Chapters 8 to 11 is to weaken the boundedness restrictions built into the model of Chapters 4 to 7. We will allow firm technology sets to be unbounded and allow households to choose from budget sets limited only by income and not by direct limits on the size of consumption plans. In equilibrium, prices will guide firms and households to well-defined (bounded) equilibrium allocations.

Remember the principal characterization of firm and household behavior: maximization of a criterion function (profit or utility) subject to a constraint (technology or budget). This results in a well-defined outcome, a supply or demand function, if the criterion is a continuous function of its arguments and the constraint set is compact and hence bounded (Corollary 2.2). In Chapters 4 to 7 we achieved boundedness of the constraint sets by assumption P.VI and definition (the restriction $|x| \leq c$ in the definition of $\tilde{B}^i(p)$ prevents budget sets from being unbounded when some prices are zero). This is inadequate. Unbounded production technology sets make sense and our theory should be able to deal with them; if a firm could acquire arbitrarily large inputs it would find it technically possible to produce arbitrarily large outputs. Scarcity – the limits of available inputs – should be communicated by prices, not by the modeler's assumptions. Price incentives should lead firms to choose finite inputs and outputs as an optimizing choice. On the household side, it should be prices, not an arbitrary constraint, that alert households that they cannot afford unbounded consumption.

In Chapters 8 to 11 we will repeat the exercise of characterizing household demand and firm supply behavior and market equilibrium, this time without the boundedness constraints. We will do this in a slightly tricky two-part argument. We first characterize an economy with unbounded firm and household opportunity sets. Unfortunately, since constraint sets are unbounded, demand and supply may not be well defined. We will show that (under reasonable conditions, P.IV, to be developed below) attainable outputs of the economy are nevertheless bounded. We will then reintroduce the bound c that we developed above, representing a loose upper bound on the Euclidean length of attainable outputs and consumptions. We will artificially bound technology and budget sets using this bound. Thus the model is reduced to the previous case (a common mathematician's trick) of Chapters 4 to 7. Just as we found an equilibrium in Theorem 7.1, we can find it again in this artificially bounded model. We are not really interested in the artificially bounded model; it represents merely a reflection of the true model of Chapters 8 to 11. But recall Lemma 7.1. The bound c is not binding in equilibrium! Hence, we will show that the equilibrium of the artificially bounded economy is also an equilibrium of the full unbounded economy of Chapters 8 to 11. Thus, the existence of general equilibrium in the unbounded economy will be demonstrated as a generalization of the bounded existence of equilibrium result (Theorem 7.1).

The relationship between the model economy and its more tractable artificially bounded counterpart is summarized in Table C.1.

Table C.1. *Model economy vs. artificially bound economy.*

	Model economy	Artificially bounded economy
Strict upper bound on length of attainable output	c	
j's production technology	Y^j	$\tilde{Y}^j = Y^j \cap \{x \mid \lvert x \rvert \leq c\}$
j's supply function	$S^j(p)$, may not exist	$\tilde{S}^j(p)$, always exists
i's income function	$M^i(p)$, may not exist	$\tilde{M}^i(p)$, always exists
i's demand function	$D^i(p)$, may not exist	$\tilde{D}^i(p)$, always exists
Excess demand function	$Z(p)$, may not exist	$\tilde{Z}(p)$, always exists

We use the model of Chapters 4–7 to establish the existence of equilibrium prices p^* for the artificially bounded economy, $\tilde{Z}(p^*) \leq 0$. We then show that at prices p^*, the supply and demand functions of the model economy and the artificially bounded economy coincide so that the equilibrium of the artificially bounded economy is also an equilibrium of the model economy. That is, $\tilde{S}^j(p^*) = S^j(p^*)$, $\tilde{D}^i(p^*) = D^i(p^*)$, and $\tilde{Z}(p^*) = Z(p^*) \leq 0$ with $p_k^* = 0$ for k so that $Z_k(p^*) < 0$. This is the plan we will follow in Chapters 8–11.

8

Theory of production: The unbounded technology case

8.1 Unbounded production technology

We will introduce here a model of firms and production decisions that is formally identical to the model introduced in Chapter 4, except that we omit the assumption of boundedness of production technology (P.VI). Remember why we need boundedness. Sufficient conditions for well-defined optimizing behavior include a compact (hence bounded) opportunity set. We will introduce a weaker assumption (P.IV) below and show that the set of attainable allocations is still bounded.

Our modeling plan is to reduce the study of general equilibrium in the economy with unbounded technology sets to the case of bounded technologies of Chapters 4–7. We will define an artificially restricted firm sector consisting of the unbounded production technologies restricted to a bounded subset that includes their attainable portions as a proper subset. Of course, actual equilibria and successful production plans have to be located in this attainable region, but the inducement of firms to choose to operate there should not be from exogenous constraint; it should be the result of incentives provided by the price system. We will show this to be the case in the equilibrium of the artificially restricted firm sector using Lemma 7.1. In equilibrium, artificial bounds on production will not be a binding constraint.

We now (re)state a generalized form of the model of the production sector introduced in Chapter 4. Production is organized in firms; these are represented by technology sets Y^j rather than the bounded technology sets $\mathcal{Y}^j$ of Chapter 4. The population of firms is the finite set F, indexed $j = 1, \ldots, \#F$. $Y^j \subseteq R^N$. The set Y^j represents the technical possibilities of firm j. $y \in Y^j$ is a possible combination of inputs and outputs. Negative coordinates of y are inputs; positive coordinates are outputs. For example, if $y \in Y^j$, $y = (-2, -3, 0, 0, 1)$, then an input of two units of good 1 and three units of good 2 will allow firm j to produce one unit of good 5. Y^j is like a list of recipes or a collection of blueprint plans for production, to be implemented as a matter of choice by the firm. There is no guarantee that the economy can provide the inputs $y \in Y^j$ specifies, either from endowment or from the output of other firms. Rather, $y \in Y^j$ represents the technical output possibilities of production by firm j if the specified inputs are provided. With this slightly new notation we reintroduce the mathematical structure first presented in Chapter 4.

We restate for the technologies Y^j the assumptions P.I–P.III on production technologies introduced in Chapter 4 for the technology sets $\mathcal{Y}^j$:

(P.I) Y^j is convex for each j.
(P.II) $0 \in Y^j$.
(P.III) Y^j is closed.

The *aggregate technology* set is $Y = \sum_{j \in F} Y^j$.

8.2 Boundedness of the attainable set

Assumptions P.I, P.II, and P.III refer to the possible production plans of individual firms. We now introduce P.IV, an assumption on the set of possible production plans for the economy as a whole. P.IV is designed to give us weak sufficient conditions (not including boundedness of individual firm technologies) that will ensure that the set of outputs attainable from the economy and from individual firms is bounded. This will be true even though the technology sets of the firms and the economy may be unbounded. With finite endowments and convex technologies, of course, we expect that plans attainable for the economy will be bounded (we will demonstrate this below). Nevertheless, this is information that we expect to be communicated to the firms and households through the price system, not by an exogenously assumed restriction on firm technology. The firm technology is a blueprint for what the firm could produce with inputs hypothetically provided. It is perfectly reasonable then for the technology to specify that *if* infinite inputs were provided, *then* infinite outputs would be possible. With finite resource endowments, of course, we do not ordinarily expect that an unbounded plan can be an equilibrium outcome. Weak and economically meaningful technical assumptions under which a bounded attainable set is assured are formalized as: P.IV(a) is the "no free lunch" postulate – there are no outputs without inputs. P.IV(b) is the irreversibility postulate – there exists no way to transform an output back to the original quantities of all inputs.

(P.IV) (a) if $y \in Y$ and $y \neq 0$, then $y_k < 0$ for some k.
      (b) if $y \in Y$ and $y \neq 0$, then $-y \notin Y$.

P.IV enunciates two quite reasonable sounding notions regarding production. P.IV(a) says we cannot expect outputs without inputs. There's no free lunch. This is a fundamental notion of scarcity appearing throughout economics. P.IV(b) says that production is irreversible. You can't unscramble an egg. You cannot take labor and capital to produce an output and then take the output and transform it back into labor and capital. Let $r \in \mathbf{R}_{+}^{N}$ be the vector of total initial resources or endowments. Finiteness of r and P.IV imply that there can never be an infinite production. We will demonstrate this below in Theorems 8.1 and 8.2.

Definition *Let $y \in Y$. Then y is said to be attainable if $y + r \geq 0$.*

We will show that the set of attainable vectors y is bounded under P.I–P.IV. In particular, this demonstration will not use P.VI; boundedness of the individual firm production technologies is not required for boundedness of the attainable set. Because the attainable production vectors are those that can be produced with the available resources (and hence do not create unsatisfiable excess demands in factor markets), it is among these that an equilibrium production plan is to be found (if it exists). However, individual firms should have no need to decide whether a planned production is attainable. All of the information needed by firms regarding the availability of needed inputs to production should be embodied in prevailing prices.

In an attainable production plan $y \in Y$, $y = y^1 + y^2 + \ldots + y^{\#F}$, any particular individual firm vector y^j might not satisfy $y^j + r \geq 0$. Thus

Definition *We say that y^j is **attainable in Y^j** if there exists a $y^k \in Y^k$ for each of the firms $k \in F$, $k \neq j$, such that $y^j + \sum_{k \in F,\ k \neq j} y^k$ is attainable.*

We wish to show, in Theorem 8.1 below, that this definition and P.I–P.IV imply boundedness for the set of plans y^j attainable in Y^j. Here is the strategy of proof. The argument is by contradiction. We use the convexity of Y and each Y^j to concentrate on a subset of Y^j (for suitably chosen j) contained in a sphere of radius 1. How could there be an attainable plan in Y^j that is unbounded? We will show that this could occur only in two possible ways: Either firm j could be producing outputs without inputs (contradicting P.IV(a)) or firm j's unbounded production plan could be partly reversed by the plans of the other firms, so that the net effect is a bounded attainable sum even though there is an unbounded attainable sequence in Y^j. We map back into a bounded set and take a limit – using both convexity and closedness of Y^j. Then, in the limit, it follows that other firms' production plans precisely reverse those of firm j. But this contradicts the assumption of irreversibility, P.IV(b). The contradiction completes the proof.

Theorem 8.1 *Under P.I, P.II, P.III, and P.IV, for each $j \in F$, the set of vectors attainable in Y^j is bounded.*

Proof We will use a proof by contradiction. Suppose contrary to the theorem that the set of vectors attainable in Y^j is not bounded for some $j \in F$. Then, for each

$j \in F$, there exists a sequence $\{y^{\nu j}\} \subset Y^j$, $\nu = 1, 2, 3, \ldots$, such that:

(1) $|y^{\nu j'}| \to +\infty$, for some $j' \in F$,
(2) $y^{\nu j} \in Y^j$, for all $j \in F$, and
(3) $y^{\nu} = \sum_{j \in F} y^{\nu j}$ is attainable; that is, $y^{\nu} + r \geq 0$.

We show that this contradicts P.IV. Recall P.II, $0 \in Y^j$, for all j. Let $\mu^{\nu} = \max_{j \in F} |y^{\nu j}|$. For ν large, $\mu^{\nu} \geq 1$. By (1) we have $\mu^{\nu} \to +\infty$. Consider the sequence $\tilde{y}^{\nu j} \equiv \frac{1}{\mu^{\nu}} y^{\nu j} = \frac{1}{\mu^{\nu}} y^{\nu j} + (1 - \frac{1}{\mu^{\nu}})0$. By P.I, $\tilde{y}^{\nu j} \in Y^j$. Let $\tilde{y}^{\nu} = \frac{1}{\mu^{\nu}} y^{\nu} = \sum_{j \in F} \tilde{y}^{\nu j}$. By (3) and P.I we have

(4) $\tilde{y}^{\nu} + \frac{1}{\mu^{\nu}} r \geq 0$.

The sequences $\tilde{y}^{\nu j}$ and $\tilde{y}^{\nu}$ are bounded ($\tilde{y}^{\nu}$ as the finite sum of vectors of length less than or equal to 1). Without loss of generality, take corresponding convergent subsequences so that $\tilde{y}^{\nu} \to \tilde{y}^0$ and $\tilde{y}^{\nu j} \to \tilde{y}^{0j}$ for each j, and $\sum_j \tilde{y}^{\nu j} \to \sum_j \tilde{y}^{0j} = \tilde{y}^0$. Of course, $\frac{1}{\mu^{\nu}} r \to 0$. Taking the limit of (4), we have

$$\tilde{y}^0 + 0 = \sum_{j \in F} \tilde{y}^{0j} + 0 \geq 0.$$

By P.III, $\tilde{y}^{0j} \in Y^j$, so $\sum_{j \in F} \tilde{y}^{0j} = \tilde{y}^0 \in Y$. But, by P.IV(a), we have that $\sum_{j \in F} \tilde{y}^{0j} = 0$. Choose a distinct $j' \in F$ so that $\tilde{y}^{0j} \neq 0$. We know such a j' exists since for all ν there is $j' \in F$ so that $|\tilde{y}^{0j'}| = 1$. This gives us

$$\tilde{y}^{0j'} + \sum_{j \in F, j \neq j'} \tilde{y}^{0j} = 0.$$

But then

$$\tilde{y}^{0j'} = - \sum_{j \in F, j \neq j'} \tilde{y}^{0j} \neq 0,$$

However, $\tilde{y}^{0j'} \in Y$ and $\sum_{j \in F, j \neq j'} \tilde{y}^{0j} \in Y$. This family of results violates P.IV(b). The contradiction proves the theorem. QED

We have shown that under P.I–P.IV, the set of production plans attainable in Y^j is bounded. We can now conclude that the attainable subset of Y is compact (closed and bounded).

Theorem 8.2 *Under P.I–P.IV, the set of attainable vectors in Y is compact, that is, closed and bounded.*

Proof We will demonstrate the result in two steps.

Boundedness: $y \in Y$ attainable implies $y = \sum_{j \in F} y^j$ where $y^j \in Y^j$ is attainable in Y^j. However, by Theorem 8.1, the set of such y^j is bounded for each j. Attainable y then is the sum of a finite number ($\#F$) of vectors, y^j, each taken from a bounded subset of Y^j, so the set of attainable y in Y is also bounded.

Closedness: Consider the sequence $y^\nu \in Y$, y^ν attainable, $\nu = 1, 2, 3, \ldots$. We have $y^\nu + r \geq 0$. Suppose $y^\nu \to y^0$. We wish to show that $y^0 \in Y$ and that y^0 is attainable. We write the sequence as $y^\nu = y^{\nu 1} + y^{\nu 2} + \ldots + y^{\nu j} + \ldots + y^{\nu \# F}$, where $y^{\nu j} \in Y^j$, $y^{\nu j}$ attainable in Y^j for all $j \in F$. Since the attainable points in Y^j constitute a bounded set (by Theorem 8.1), without loss of generality, we can find corresponding convergent subsequences $y^\nu, y^{\nu 1}, y^{\nu 2}, \ldots, y^{\nu j}$ so that for all $j \in F$ we have $y^{\nu j} \to y^{0j} \in Y^j$, by P.III. We have then $y^0 = y^{01} + y^{02} + \ldots + y^{0j} + \ldots + y^{0 \# F}$ and $y^0 + r \geq 0$. Hence, $y^0 \in Y$ and y^0 is attainable. QED

8.3 An artificially bounded supply function

We wish to describe firm supply behavior as profit maximization subject to technology constraint. Since Y^j may not be bounded, maximizing behavior may not be well defined. However, we have shown above that attainable production plans do lie in a bounded set. Hence we can describe well-defined profit-maximizing behavior subject to technology and boundedness constraints. Eventually, we will wish to eliminate the boundedness constraint – not because we are interested in firms producing at unattainable levels but rather because the resource constraints that define attainability should be communicated to firms in prevailing prices rather than in an additional constraint on firm behavior.

Assume P.I, P.II, P.III, and P.IV. Choose a positive real number c, sufficiently large so that for all $j \in F$, $|y^j| < c$ (a strict inequality) for all y^j attainable in Y^j. Let $\tilde{Y}^j = Y^j \cap \{y | |y| \leq c\}$. Note the weak inequality in the definition of $\tilde{Y}^j$. Restricting attention to $\tilde{Y}^j$ in describing firm j's production plans allows us to remain in a bounded set so that profit maximization will be well defined. Note that $\tilde{Y}^j$ is closed, bounded (hence compact), and convex. A typical artificially bounded technology set, $\tilde{Y}^j$, is depicted in Figure 8.1. Note that under P.I.–P.IV, using $\tilde{Y}^j$ as $\mathcal{Y}^j$, $\tilde{Y}^j$ fulfills P.I–P.III, and P.VI of Chapter 4. That is, we have reduced the study of supply in $\tilde{Y}^j$ to the formally identical case of supply in $\mathcal{Y}^j$ studied in Chapter 4.

The strategy of proof for demonstrating the existence of equilibrium in the economy characterized by the production technologies Y^j is then:

(1) demonstrate that the artificially restricted economy defined by the production technologies $\tilde{Y}^j$ fulfills the assumptions of the model of Part B;
(2) use Theorem 7.1 to establish the existence of equilibrium, with price vector p^*, in the artificially restricted economy; and then

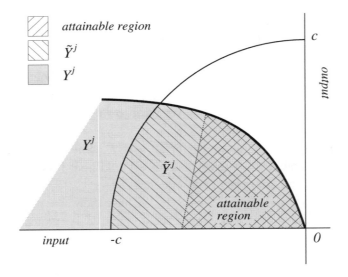

Fig. 8.1. Bounding firm j's production technology.

(3) show that the artificial restrictions are not binding constraints in the equilibrium developed in (2), as noted in Lemma 7.1, so that p^* is also an equilibrium price vector of the unrestricted economy.

This amounts to reducing the study of the economy whose production technology is characterized by Y^j to the previously treated case characterized by $\mathcal{Y}^j$.

In order to discuss the simplest possible case of firm supply behavior we continue to use

(P.V) For each $j \in F$, Y^j is strictly convex.

Note that P.V is identical to P.V of Chapter 4. Under P.V, $\tilde{Y}^j$ is strictly convex. Hence, again setting $\tilde{Y}^j = \mathcal{Y}^j$, $\tilde{Y}^j$ fulfills P.V of Chapter 4.

Taking price vector $p \in \mathbf{R}_+^N$ as given, each firm j "chooses" $y^j \in Y^j$ such that $p \cdot y^j$ maximizes $p \cdot y$. We will consider two cases: a restricted supply function where the supply behavior of firm j is required to be contained in $\tilde{Y}^j$, the artificially bounded subset of Y^j, and an unrestricted supply function where the supply behavior is not so restricted. Any attainable planned supply will be in both Y^j and $\tilde{Y}^j$, but very large (unattainable) planned supply will be in Y^j only. There are many points of Y^j and some of $\tilde{Y}^j$ that are not attainable. When the firm's intended supply is unattainable, it cannot, of course, be fulfilled and cannot represent an equilibrium. It is the role of the price system to lead the firm toward attainable plans and to value unattainable production plans as unprofitable. We use the restricted supply function because it is very convenient: it is always well defined even if the planned production is unattainable. It is an essential step to show that the restriction of the supply function is only a technical convenience and has no constraining effect on the economic analysis or on the set of equilibria. The restricted supply function is denoted $\tilde{S}^j(p) \in \tilde{Y}^j$, and the unrestricted supply function is $S^j(p) \in Y^j$. They are defined as follows.

Define the restricted supply function of firm j as

$$\tilde{S}^j(p) = \{y^{*j} \mid y^{*j} \in \tilde{Y}^j, \, p \cdot y^{*j} \geq p \cdot y^j \text{ for all } y^j \in \tilde{Y}^j\}.$$

Define the (unrestricted) supply function of firm j as

$$S^j(p) = \{y^{*j} \mid y^{*j} \in Y^j, \, p \cdot y^{*j} \geq p \cdot y \text{ for all } y \in Y^j\}.$$

Note that $\tilde{S}^j(p)$ here is identical to the same function defined in Chapter 4 when we identify $\mathcal{Y}^j$ with $\tilde{Y}^j$. Then we have:

Theorem 8.3 *Assume P.II, P.III, P.IV, and P.V. Let $p \in \mathbf{R}_+^N$, $p \neq 0$. Then*

(a) $\tilde{S}^j(p)$ is a well-defined (nonempty) continuous (point-valued) function, and
(b) if $\tilde{S}^j(p)$ is attainable in Y^j, then $\tilde{S}^j(p) = S^j(p)$.

Proof There are two ways to prove part (a). We can either prove it directly or note that it has already been proved in a different context. In fact part (a) is simply Theorem 4.1 inasmuch as under assumptions P.II–P.V, $\tilde{Y}^j$ fulfills all of the properties in Theorem 4.1 required of $\mathcal{Y}^j$. Nevertheless, we include a direct proof of part (a) for completeness.

Part (a):
Well defined: $\tilde{S}^j(p)$ consists of the maximizer of a continuous function on a compact strictly convex set. The function is well defined since a continuous real-valued function achieves its maximum on a compact set.

Point valued: We will demonstrate that the strict convexity of $\tilde{Y}^j$ implies that $\tilde{S}^j(p)$ is point valued. We wish to show that there is a unique $y^0 \in \tilde{Y}^j$ that maximizes $p \cdot y$ in $\tilde{Y}^j$. If we suppose that such is not the case then there are $y^1, y^2 \in \tilde{Y}^j$, $y^1 \neq y^2$ so that $p \cdot y^1 = p \cdot y^2 = \max_{y \in \tilde{Y}^j} p \cdot y$. But by strict convexity of $\tilde{Y}^j$ (P.V) for $0 < \alpha < 1$, $\alpha y^1 + (1 - \alpha)y^2 \in \text{interior } \tilde{Y}^j$. We have $p \cdot (\alpha y^1 + (1-\alpha)y^2) = p \cdot y^1 = p \cdot y^2$. However, in a neighborhood of $\alpha y^1 + (1-\alpha)y^2$ there is $y^3 \in \tilde{Y}^j$ with $p \cdot y^3 > p \cdot y^1 = p \cdot y^2$. This is a contradiction. Hence we conclude that $\tilde{S}^j(p)$ is point valued.

Continuity: We now wish to demonstrate continuity of $\tilde{S}^j(p)$. Let $p^\nu \in \mathbf{R}_+^N$, $\nu = 1, 2, \ldots$, $p^\nu \neq 0$, $p^\nu \to p^0 \neq 0$. We must show that $\tilde{S}^j(p^\nu) \to \tilde{S}^j(p^0)$. Suppose this is not-true. Since $\tilde{Y}^j$ is compact, if we take a subsequence, there is $y^0 \in \tilde{Y}^j$ so that $\tilde{S}^j(p^\nu) \to y^0 \neq \tilde{S}^j(p^0)$. $p^\nu \cdot \tilde{S}^j(p^\nu) \geq p^\nu \cdot \tilde{S}^j(p^0)$, by the definition of $\tilde{S}^j(p)$. But the dot product is a continuous function. $p^\nu \cdot \tilde{S}^j(p^\nu) \to p^0 \cdot y^0$. So $p^0 \cdot y^0 \geq p^0 \cdot \tilde{S}^j(p^0)$, which is a contradiction. Hence there is no such y^0, and $\tilde{S}^j(p)$ is continuous. This completes the proof of part (a).

For part (b):
  Suppose $\tilde{S}^j(p)$ is attainable in Y^j, but $\tilde{S}^j(p) \neq S^j(p)$. Then there is $\bar{y}^j \in Y^j$ so that $p \cdot \bar{y}^j > p \cdot \tilde{S}^j(p)$. Then

$$p \cdot [\alpha \bar{y}^j + (1 - \alpha)\tilde{S}^j(p)] > p \cdot \tilde{S}^j(p) \quad \text{for any } \alpha, 0 < \alpha \leq 1.$$

  Now $\tilde{S}^j(p)$ being attainable implies $|\tilde{S}^j(p)| < c$, so we can choose some $\alpha > 0$ that is sufficiently small so that $|\alpha \bar{y}^j + (1 - \alpha)\tilde{S}^j(p)| \leq c$. But then $\alpha \bar{y}^j + (1 - \alpha)\tilde{S}^j(p) \in \tilde{Y}^j$; thus $\tilde{S}^j(p)$ is not a profit maximizer in $\tilde{Y}^j$, a contradiction that proves the theorem.   QED

The intuition behind part (b) of Theorem 8.3 is that when $\tilde{S}^j(p)$ is attainable, the constraint that $|\tilde{S}^j(p)| \leq c$ is not binding. Removing the constraint leaves firm j's profit-maximizing plan at price vector p unchanged, but the optimizing choice is precisely $S^j(p)$, so the two functions coincide.

Lemma 8.1 (homogeneity of degree 0) *Assume P.II–P.V. Let $\lambda > 0, p \in \mathbf{R}_+^N$. Then $S^j(\lambda p) = S^j(p)$ and $\tilde{S}^j(\lambda p) = \tilde{S}^j(p)$.*

In this chapter we have developed two closely related notions of the supply function of firm j, $S^j(p)$ and $\tilde{S}^j(p)$. The first, $S^j(p)$, represents the supply behavior of firm j based on j's technology set Y^j. The second, $\tilde{S}^j(p)$, is based on a bounded subset of Y^j, $\tilde{Y}^j$. By design, $\tilde{S}^j(p)$ fulfills all of the properties of the function of the same name in Chapter 4. Since these are useful properties, being well defined and continuous, we're delighted to have them. What makes $\tilde{S}^j(p)$ useful is the relationship between the two. For those values of p so that $\tilde{S}^j(P)$ is attainable in Y^j, $S^j(p) = \tilde{S}^j(p)$. That is the result proved in Theorem 8.3(b). We will use this relationship in Chapter 11 to establish the existence of an equilibrium in the economy characterized by the production technology Y^j.

8.4 Bibliographic note

The use of the artificially bounded economy and the argument that the twin assumptions of irreversibility and no free lunch imply boundedness appear in Arrow and Debreu (1954). The treatment here in part follows that of Arrow (1962).

Exercises

8.1   Consider production without P.IV(b), but fulfilling P.I–P.III and P.IV(a). Formulate an example of Y^1 and Y^2 in $\mathbf{R}^2$ so that the set of points attainable in Y^1 is not bounded.

8.2   The convexity assumption is essential in proving Theorems 8.1 and 8.2. Formulate an example fulfilling P.II, P.III, and P.IV but not P.I where the theorems are false, that is, where the set of attainable points in Y^j and Y are unbounded.

9

Households: The unbounded technology case

9.1 Households

Most of the theory of the household developed in Chapter 5 remains unchanged with consideration of an unbounded production technology. However, we will want to consider an unbounded budget set, $B^i(p)$, in place of the bounded budget set, $\tilde{B}^i(p)$, introduced in Chapter 5. Our strategy of proof and investigation will be to reduce the study of the unbounded case to the previously completed bounded case, showing that they coincide in equilibrium.

Theorem 8.2 reassures us of boundedness of the attainable set assuming P.IV. The constant c, restated and used in Chapter 8, representing a (strict) upper bound on the size of any attainable allocation, is just as defined in Chapter 4 and used in Chapter 5. Consequently, the theory of production introduced in Chapter 8 leaves the household model of Chapter 5 unchanged. The functions $\tilde{B}^i(p)$ and $\tilde{D}^i(p)$ remain formally as developed in Chapter 5 and the fundamental theory of the household introduced in Chapter 5 remains unchanged.

9.2 Choice in an unbounded budget set

It is at this point that our treatment of household consumption choice behavior begins to differ from that of Chapter 5. Instead of taking the household budget set to be bounded in part by a sphere of radius c, designed to strictly contain all of the attainable set (recall the definition of $\tilde{B}^i(p)$ above), we will take the budget set to be determined by household income $M^i(p)$ only, as $B^i(p)$. It will nevertheless be convenient to consider the bounded budget set, $\tilde{B}^i(p)$, because demand behavior in this compact set will be well defined even when $B^i(p)$ is unbounded and demand behavior may be undefined. It is then essential for us to show that optimizing demand behavior in $\tilde{B}^i(p)$ is the same as in $B^i(p)$ when demand is in the attainable set.

We will denote the household budget or income as a real number, $M^i(p) \geq 0$.

Then the household budget constraint set is

$$B^i(p) \equiv \{x \mid x \in \mathbf{R}^N, p \cdot x \leq M^i(p)\}.$$

Lemma 9.1 $B^i(p)$ *is a closed convex set.*

We characterize the demand behavior of household i as optimizing household satisfaction from consumption based on preferences $\succsim_i$ (or, equivalently, optimizing utility u^i) subject to budget constraint and the possible consumption set X^i. Although in equilibrium, the household will choose an attainable consumption, we do not wish to impose attainability as a constraint on individual consumption choice. Attainability should be a result, not an assumption, in equilibrium. It is the job of the price system to lead consumers away from unattainable consumption plans by informing them that the plans are prohibitively expensive. Let the household demand function, $D^i : \mathbf{R}^N_+ \to \mathbf{R}^N_+$, be defined in the following way:

$$D^i(p) \equiv \{y \mid y \in B^i(p) \cap X^i, y \succsim_i x \text{ for all } x \in B^i(p) \cap X^i\}$$

$$\equiv \{y \mid y \in B^i(p) \cap X^i, u^i(y) \geq u^i(x) \text{ for all } x \in B^i(p) \cap X^i\}.$$

We will restrict attention to models where $M^i(p)$ is homogeneous of degree one, that is, where $M^i(\lambda p) = \lambda M^i(p)$. It is immediate then that $B^i(p)$ is homogeneous of degree zero.

Lemma 9.2 *Let* $B^i(p)$ *be homogeneous of degree* 0. *Then* $D^i(p)$ *is homogeneous of degree* 0 *also.*

Recall that homogeneity of degree zero of both $D^i(p)$ and $S^j(p)$ (from Lemma 8.1) allows us significantly to simplify the space of prices. We will confine attention to price vectors on the set P, the unit simplex in $\mathbf{R}^N$,

$$P \equiv \left\{ p \mid p \in \mathbf{R}^N, p_i \geq 0, i = 1, 2, 3, \ldots, N, \sum_{i=1}^{N} p_i = 1 \right\}.$$

Even with a well-defined budget set, we still have a problem in defining demand behavior for typical $h \in H$. For some $p \in P$, household i's opportunity set $(B^i(p) \cap X^i)$ may not be compact. Unbounded $B^i(p) \cap X^i$ will arise typically when some goods' prices are zero so that the budget constraint is consistent with unbounded consumption of some goods. In an economy with a bounded attainable set, such consumptions could never be equilibria, but during the process of price adjustment the Walrasian auctioneer should be free to search through the nil prices and households should be free to demand the unbounded consumption plans. It should be a conclusion – not an assumption – that such points are not equilibria, and this information should be communicated to agents in the economy through prices, not by assumption. As an intermediate step in characterizing household consumption behavior, we use the same technical device that we used on the production side in a similar setting. We create an artificially bounded budget set containing as a proper subset all of the economy's attainable points consistent with budget constraint. The strategy of proof will then be:

- to characterize demand behavior in the artificially bounded economy,
- to show that it coincides with demand of the unbounded economy throughout the attainable set,
- to find an equilibrium for the artificially bounded economy and show that the equilibrium is attainable, and finally
- to show that it is also an equilibrium for the unbounded economy.

We wish now to characterize a bounded subset of $B^i(p)$ containing the consumption plans that are both within the budget $\tilde{M}^i(p) > 0$ (where $\tilde{M}^i(p)$ equals $M^i(p)$ when the latter derives from attainable firm production plans) and that are also attainable. We have not yet fully described this budget.

Definition $x \in X$ is an **attainable** consumption if $y + r \geq x \geq 0$, where $y \in Y$ and r is the economy's initial resource endowment, so that y is an attainable production plan.

Note that Theorem 8.2 says that the set of attainable consumptions is bounded under P.I–P.IV.

Choose c so that $|x| < c$ (a strict inequality) for all attainable consumptions x. Let

$$\tilde{B}^i(p) = \{x \mid x \in \mathbf{R}^N, p \cdot x \leq \tilde{M}_i(p)\} \cap \{x \mid |x| \leq c\}.$$

Note that $\tilde{B}^i(p)$ is defined just as in Chapter 5. We now define

$$\tilde{D}^i(p) \equiv \{x \mid x \in \tilde{B}^i(p) \cap X^i, x \succsim_i y \text{ for all } y \in \tilde{B}^i(p) \cap X^i\}$$

$$\equiv \{x \mid x \in \tilde{B}^i(p) \cap X^i, x \text{ maximizes } u^i(y) \text{ for all } y \in \tilde{B}^i(p) \cap X^i\}.$$

Note that $\tilde{D}^i(p)$ is also as defined in Chapter 5. Sets $\tilde{B}^i(\cdot)$ and $\tilde{D}^i(\cdot)$ are homogeneous of degree 0 as are $B^i(\cdot)$ and $D^i(\cdot)$. Let $D(p) = \sum_{i \in H} D^i(p)$ and, as before, $\tilde{D}(p) = \sum_{i \in H} \tilde{D}^i(p)$.

9.3 Demand behavior under strict convexity

We will now more fully characterize demand. Theorem 9.1 below says that $\tilde{D}^i(p)$, the artificially restricted demand behavior, is continuous and well defined everywhere on the price space P. This is merely the repetition of the corresponding result from Chapter 5. In addition, $\tilde{D}^i(p)$ and $D^i(p)$ coincide throughout the relevant range where equilibria may be found.

Theorem 9.1 *Assume C.I–C.V, C.VII, and C.VIII. Let $\tilde{M}^i(p)$ be a continuous function for all $p \in P$. Then*

(a) $\tilde{D}^i(p)$ is a well-defined (point-valued) continuous function for all $p \in P$. Furthermore,
(b) if $\tilde{D}^i(p)$ is attainable and if $\tilde{M}^i(p) = M^i(p)$ then $\tilde{D}^i(p) = D^i(p)$.

Proof Part (a) was already proved in the proof of Theorem 5.2. We repeat the proof here merely for completeness.

$\tilde{B}^i(p) \cap X^i$ is the intersection of a closed set, $\{x \mid p \cdot x \leq \tilde{M}^i(p)\}$, a compact set (the closed ball of radius c), and the closed set X^i. Hence it is compact. It is nonempty by C.VIII. Because $\tilde{D}^i(p)$ is characterized by the maximization of a continuous function, $u^i(\cdot)$, on this compact nonempty set, there is a well-defined maximum. There is a well-defined maximum value, $u^0 = u^i(x^0)$, where x^0 is the optimizing value of x in $\tilde{B}^i(p) \cap X^i$. We must show that x^0 is unique for each $p \in P$ and a continuous function of p.

We will now demonstrate that *uniqueness* follows from strict convexity of preferences (C.VII). Suppose there are $x', x'' \in \tilde{B}^i(p) \cap X^i$, $x' \neq x''$, $x^0 \sim x' \sim x''$. We must show that this leads to a contradiction. But now consider a convex combination of x' and x''. Choose $0 < \alpha < 1$. The point $\alpha x' + (1 - \alpha)x'' \in \tilde{B}^i(p) \cap X^i$ by convexity of X^i and $\tilde{B}^i(p)$. But C.VII, strict convexity of preferences, implies that $\alpha x' + (1 - \alpha)x'' \succ_i x' \sim_i x^0 \sim_i x''$. This is a contradiction, since x^0, x', and x'' are all elements of $\tilde{D}^i(p)$. Hence x^0 is the unique element of $\tilde{D}^i(p)$. We can now, without loss of generality, refer to $\tilde{D}^i(p)$ as a (point-valued) function.

To demonstrate continuity, let $p^\nu \in P$, $\nu = 1, 2, 3, \ldots$, $p^\nu \to p^0$. We must show that $\tilde{D}^i(p^\nu) \to \tilde{D}^i(p^0)$. $\tilde{D}^i(p^\nu)$ is a sequence in a compact set. Without loss of generality take a convergent subsequence, $\tilde{D}^i(p^\nu) \to x^0$. We must show that $x^0 = \tilde{D}^i(p^0)$. We will use a proof by contradiction.

Define

$$\hat{x} = \operatorname*{arg\,min}_{x \in X^i \cap \{y \mid y \in \mathbf{R}^N, c \geq |y|\}} p^0 \cdot x.$$

The expression "$\hat{x} = \arg\min_{x \in X^i \cap \{y \mid y \in R^N, c \geq |y|\}} p^0 \cdot x$" defines $\hat{x}$ as the minimizer of $p^0 \cdot x$ in the domain $X^i \cap \{y \mid y \in R^N, c \geq |y|\}$. $\hat{x}$ is well defined (though it may not be unique) since it represents a minimum of a continuous function taken over a compact domain.

Note that under C.IV and C.VIII, $p^0 \cdot \tilde{D}^i(p^0) > p^0 \cdot \hat{x}$.

Let

$$\alpha^\nu = \min\left[1, \frac{\tilde{M}^i(p^\nu) - p^\nu \cdot \hat{x}}{p^\nu \cdot (\tilde{D}^i(p^0) - \hat{x})}\right].$$

For ν large, the denominator is positive, α^ν is well defined (this is where C.VIII enters the proof), and $0 \leq \alpha^\nu \leq 1$. Let $w^\nu = (1 - \alpha^\nu)\hat{x} + \alpha^\nu \tilde{D}^i(p^0)$. Note that $\tilde{M}^i(p)$ is continuous in p. Then $w^\nu \to \tilde{D}^i(p^0)$ and $w^\nu \in \tilde{B}^i(p^\nu) \cap X^i$. Suppose, contrary to the theorem, $x^0 \neq \tilde{D}^i(p^0)$. Then $u^i(x^0) < u^i(\tilde{D}^i(p^0))$, so that for ν large, $u^i(w^\nu) > u^i(\tilde{D}^i(p^\nu))$. But this is a contradiction, since $\tilde{D}^i(p^\nu)$ maximizes $u^i(\cdot)$ in $\tilde{B}^i(p^\nu) \cap X^i$. The contradiction proves the result. This completes the demonstration of continuity and of part (a).

Part (b) has not previously been proved. We now wish to demonstrate the equivalence of $D^i(p)$ and $\tilde{D}^i(p)$ when $M^i(p) = \tilde{M}^i(p)$ and $\tilde{D}^i(p)$ is attainable. In this case the sets $B^i(p)$ and $\tilde{B}^i(p)$ differ only by the constraint $|x| \leq c$. The informal argument here is to note that all the attainable points are strictly contained in this ball. That is, for all attainable points, the constraint $|x| \leq c$ is not binding. Therefore, if the constraint is not binding for $\tilde{D}^i(p)$, the optimum is left unchanged by it's relaxation in $B^i(p)$. Formally, suppose $D^i(p)$ and $\tilde{D}^i(p)$ do not coincide. Then $D^i(p) \neq \tilde{D}^i(p)$. Since $\tilde{D}^i(p)$ is attainable, $|\tilde{D}^i(p)| < c$. Since $B^i(p)$ contains $\tilde{B}^i(p)$ we must have $D^i(p) \succ_i \tilde{D}^i(p)$. Then, using the convexity of the budget sets and of preferences, for any $0 < \alpha < 1$, $\alpha D^i(p) + (1-\alpha)\tilde{D}^i(p) \succ_i \tilde{D}^i(p)$. However, since $M^i(p) = \tilde{M}^i(p)$, for α sufficiently small, we have $\alpha D^i(p) + (1-\alpha)\tilde{D}^i(p) \in \tilde{B}^i(p)$.

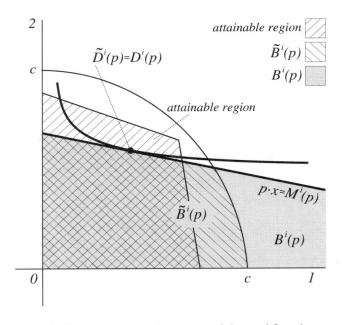

Fig. 9.1. Household i's budget sets and demand functions.

(This is illustrated in Figure 9.1.) But then contrary to hypothesis, $\tilde{D}^i(p)$ is not the optimizer of $\succsim_i$ in $\tilde{B}^i(p)$. The contradiction shows that the hypothesis is false, and $D^i(p) = \tilde{D}^i(p)$.   QED

Theorem 9.1 here establishes the link between two closely related demand functions for each household $i \in H$, $D^i(p)$ and $\tilde{D}^i(p)$. $D^i(p)$ is i's demand function; unfortunately, it may not be well defined if the corresponding budget is ill defined or if the budget set is unbounded. Thus we use $\tilde{D}^i(p)$, i's artificially restricted demand function, which would be i's demand function when i's optimization is restricted to a bounded set containing the attainable points as a proper subset. $\tilde{D}^i(p)$ is always well defined. Moreover, when $\tilde{D}^i(p)$ is attainable and $\tilde{M}^i(p) = M^i(p)$ is well defined, then $\tilde{D}^i(p) = D^i(p)$. Theorem 9.1(b) shows that the two functions coincide for prices leading to household choice in the bounded subset including the attainable set. That is, they coincide at all prices $p \in P$ where an equilibrium can occur.

9.4 Bibliographic note

The treatment here – emphasizing choice in a bounded domain and then extending it to an unbounded domain – parallels that in Arrow and Debreu (1954) and Arrow (1962).

Exercise

9.1   Formulate an example demonstrating the importance of considering $\tilde{D}^i(p)$ in $\tilde{B}^i(p)$ rather than $D^i(p)$ in $B^i(p)$. Consider $p' = (0, 1)$. Let $M^i(p') = \tilde{M}^i(p') = 10$, $X^i = \mathbf{R}_+^2$. Let $u(x_1, x_2) = x_1 + x_2 + (x_1 \cdot x_2)^{1/2}$. Show that $D^i(p)$ is undefined. Show that $\tilde{D}^i(p)$ is well defined.

10

A market economy: The unbounded technology case

10.1 Firms and households

We now bring the elements of Chapters 8 and 9 together to describe the market economy and to develop the Walras' Law. As before, the economy is characterized by the agents in it: households (the set H) and firms (the set F). A household $i \in H$ is characterized by its endowment of goods $r^i \in \mathbf{R}_+^N$, by its endowed share α^{ij} of firms $j \in F$, and by $\succsim_i$. We assume $\sum_{i \in H} \alpha^{ij} = 1$ for each $j \in F$ and $\alpha^{ij} \geq 0$ for all $i \in H$, $j \in F$. Each firm is 100% owned by one or more shareholders, and there is no negative ownership (no short sales). The initial resource endowment of the economy, designated $r \in \mathbf{R}_+^N$ is $r \equiv \sum_{i \in H} r^i$.

10.2 Profits

A firm $j \in F$ is characterized by its possible production technology set Y^j. Firm j's profit function is $\pi^j(p) = \max_{y \in Y^j} p \cdot y = p \cdot S^j(p)$. Considering that we need to discuss artificially restricted firm technology sets $\tilde{Y}^j$, it is convenient to have a concept of the profit function for the firm so restricted,

$$\tilde{\pi}^j(p) = \max_{y \in \tilde{Y}^j} p \cdot y = p \cdot \tilde{S}^j(p).$$

Note that the definition of $\tilde{\pi}^j(p)$ is identical to the corresponding definition in Chapter 6 with $\tilde{Y}^j$ substituted for $\mathcal{Y}^j$. Because the formal properties of these sets are the same, the profit functions $\tilde{\pi}^j(p)$ have the same properties.

Theorem 10.1 *Assume P.II and P.III. Then $\pi^j(p) \geq 0$ for all $j \in F$, all $p \in \mathbf{R}_+^N$ such that $\pi^j(p)$ is well defined. $\pi^j(p)$ is a continuous function of p in every neighborhood such that $\pi^j(p)$ exists. $\tilde{\pi}^j(p)$ is a well-defined continuous function of p for all $p \in P$, and $\pi^j(p) = \tilde{\pi}^j(p)$ for all p so that $S^j(p)$ is attainable in Y^j; $\pi^j(p) = \tilde{\pi}^j(p)$ for all p so that $S^j(p) = \tilde{S}^j(p)$.*

Proof Exercise 10.2.

Note that in Theorem 10.1 $\pi^j(p)$ may not be well defined (may not exist) for some values of p. This reflects that since $\pi^j(p)$ is defined as the maximum of a real-valued function on the domain Y^j, a well-defined value of $\pi^j(p)$ depends on that maximum existing. Since Y^j is not compact, the maximum may not exist. That is why we depend so heavily on $\tilde{\pi}^j(p)$, defined by the compact domain $\tilde{Y}^j$.

10.3 Household income

Household i's income is defined as

$$M^i(p) = p \cdot r^i + \sum_{j \in F} \alpha^{ij} \pi^j(p).$$

That is, we define household income as the sum of the value of the household endowment plus the value of the household's share of firm profits. For the model with restricted firm supply behavior, household income is

$$\tilde{M}^i(p) = p \cdot r^i + \sum_{j \in F} \alpha^{ij} \tilde{\pi}^j(p).$$

Note that $M^i(p)$ is a continuous, nonnegative, real-valued function of p wherever π^j is well defined for all $j \in F$. $\tilde{M}^i(p)$ is continuous, real-valued, nonnegative, and well defined for all $p \in P$. $M^i(p) = \tilde{M}^i(p)$ whenever $S^j(p) = \tilde{S}^j(p)$ for all $j \in F$, in particular for p so that $S^j(p)$ is attainable in Y^j for all $j \in F$.

10.4 Excess demand and Walras' Law

Definition *The excess demand function at prices $p \in P$ is $Z(p) = D(p) - S(p) - r$.*

As before we denote $\tilde{Z}(p) = \tilde{D}(p) - \tilde{S}(p) - r$. In the present setting, $\tilde{Z}(p)$ is something of an artificial construct, representing the excess demand function of an economy characterized by artificial bounds on the firms' production technology and households' budget sets of the underlying true economy.

Lemma 10.1 *Let $M^i(p)$ and $D^i(p)$ be well defined and assume C.IV, C.V, and C.VII. Then $p \cdot D^i(p) = M^i(p)$.*

Proof Exercise 10.3.

Lemma 10.1 develops one of the principal implications of monotone preferences, C.IV. All budgets will be fully spent. This is an essential point in proving Walras' Law. A naive reading of Lemma 10.1 would suggest that it says there is no saving.

However, in a model with dated goods, saving takes the form of purchasing goods dated for future delivery.

Walras' Law is one of the essential building blocks of the proof of existence of general equilibrium. It says that at any prices where excess demand is well defined, the value of excess demand, evaluated at prevailing prices, is zero. This is not an equilibrium condition. It is true at all price vectors, in and out of equilibrium. The Walras' Law reflects two essential elements of the model: the disbursement of profits to shareholders (embodied in the definition of the budget constraint) and the equality of expenditure to income (Lemma 10.1—deriving from monotonicity). The first of these is essentially an accounting consistency requirement; the profits have to go somewhere. Monotonicity of preferences reflects the idea of scarcity, which is essential to economic analysis. The Walras' Law then embodies the technical implications of these economic assumptions.

Theorem 10.2 (Walras' Law) *Assume C.IV, C.V, and C.VII, and suppose $Z(p)$ is well defined. Then $p \cdot Z(p) = 0$.*

Proof Note that

$$p \cdot Z(p) = p \cdot \sum_{i \in H} D^i(p) - p \cdot \sum_{j \in F} S^j(p) - p \cdot \sum_{i \in H} r^i.$$

By Lemma 10.1, we have

$$p \cdot D^i(p) = M^i(p) = p \cdot r^i + \sum_{j \in F} \alpha^{ij} \pi_j(p)$$

$$= p \cdot r^i + \sum_{j \in F} \alpha^{ij}(p \cdot S^j(p))$$

and

$$\sum_{i \in H} p \cdot D^i(p) = \sum_{i \in H} p \cdot r^i + \sum_{i \in H} \sum_{j \in F} \alpha^{ij}(p \cdot S^j(p)),$$

which can be written as

$$p \cdot \sum_{i \in H} D^i(p) = p \cdot \sum_{i \in H} r^i + p \cdot \sum_{j \in F} \sum_{i \in H} \alpha^{ij} S^j(p).$$

Note the changed order of summation in the last term. Recall that $\sum_{i \in H} \alpha^{ij} = 1$ for each j. We have then

$$p \cdot \sum_{i \in H} D^i(p) = p \cdot r + p \cdot \sum_{j \in F} S^j(p)$$

$$p \cdot \left[\sum_{i \in H} D^i(p) - \sum_{j \in F} S^j(p) - r \right] = p \cdot Z(p) = 0.$$

QED

We showed in Chapter 8 that under P.I–P.III and P.IV the attainable subset of Y^j is bounded. We defined $\tilde{Y}^j$ as a bounded subset of Y^j containing the attainable part of Y^j as a proper subset. Under P.I–P.IV it is then redundant to assume P.VI (boundedness) explicitly since it is implied by P.I–P.IV according to Theorems 8.1 and 8.2. The following results from Chapter 6 were proved using P.I–P.III, and P.V. They are still valid and applicable under the definitions of Chapters 8–10.

Lemma 6.1 *Assume C.I–C.V, C.VII, C.VIII, P.I–P.III, and P.V. The range of $\tilde{Z}(p)$ is bounded. $\tilde{Z}(p)$ is continuous and well defined for all $p \in P$.*

Theorem 6.2 (Weak Walras' Law) *Assume C.I–C.V, C.VII, C.VIII, P.I–P.III, and P.V. For all $p \in P$, $p \cdot \tilde{Z}(p) \leq 0$. For p such that $p \cdot \tilde{Z}(p) < 0$, there is $k = 1, 2, \ldots, N$ so that $\tilde{Z}_k(p) > 0$.*

The Weak Walras' Law tells us that any value of the truncated demand function $\tilde{Z}(p)$ will have one of two characteristics. Either the value of excess demand, evaluated at prevailing prices, is nil (as in the Walras' Law) or the value is negative and there is positive excess demand for some one or several of the N goods. This differs from the usual Walras' Law (Theorem 10.2) since the excess demand function $\tilde{Z}(p)$ here is based on household demand functions $\tilde{D}^i(p)$ and the firm supply functions $\tilde{S}^j(p)$ that include a restriction to keep demand and supply inside a sphere of radius c. The Weak Walras' Law presents the counterpart to Walras' Law we can expect in the truncated version of the model where households may not fully spend income and firms may not fully pursue profitable production if the quantity constraints on expenditure or supply are binding. It is not as elegant as the Walras' Law, referring not to actual excess demands (which are not everywhere well defined) but to their well-defined counterpart. Nevertheless, it serves a similar function in emphasizing the role of scarcity in proving the existence of general equilibrium. We saw this in Theorem 7.1 and we will see it again in Theorem 11.1.

10.5 Bibliographic note

The definition of household income as the value of endowment plus the share of firm profits appears in Arrow and Debreu (1954) and Debreu (1959).

Exercises

10.1   In the economy with excess demand function $Z(p)$, the market for good k is said to clear at prices $p \in P$ if $Z(p) \leq 0$, with $p_k = 0$ for k such that

$Z_k(p) < 0$. Recall the statement of the classic Walras Law

For all $p \in P$, $p \cdot Z(p) = 0$.

A common interpretation of Walras' Law is: *At prices $p \in P$, if there is market clearing in all markets but one (that is, in $N - 1$ markets) then the remaining (N th) market clears as well.* Explain and demonstrate the validity of the common interpretation.

10.2   Prove Theorem 10.1.

10.3   Prove Lemma 10.1. You will find the monotonicity assumption C.IV useful.

11

General equilibrium of the market economy: The unbounded technology case

11.1 General equilibrium

In this chapter we will consider the general equilibrium of an economy with (possibly) unbounded production technologies where demands and supplies are point valued. We will establish the most important single result in this book, Theorem 11.1, the existence of general equilibrium. We know that a sufficient condition for point-valuedness of supply and demand is strict convexity of tastes and technologies, P.V and C.VII. As noted in Chapter 6, homogeneity of degree zero of $D^i(\cdot)$ and $S^j(\cdot)$ in p means that we may, without loss of generality, restrict the price space to be the unit simplex in $\mathbf{R}^N$,

$$P = \left\{ p \mid p \in \mathbf{R}^N, p_k \geq 0, k = 1 \ldots, N, \sum_{k=1}^N p_k = 1 \right\}.$$

From Chapter 10, the market excess demand function is defined as

$$Z(p) = \sum_{i \in H} D^i(p) - \sum_{j \in F} S^j(p) - r.$$

There are some regions of P where $Z(\cdot)$ may not be well defined, since the maximization of profits in determining S^j or utility in determining D^i may not have a well-defined value. This arises in as much as the opportunity sets, Y^j or $B^i(p)$, may be unbounded. Then profit or utility may lack a well-defined maximum.

We are interested in investigating a market clearing equilibrium defined as:

Definition $p^0 \in P$ is said to be an equilibrium price vector if $Z(p^0) \leq 0$ (the inequality applies coordinatewise) with $p_k^0 = 0$ for k such that $Z_k(p^0) < 0$.

That is, an equilibrium is characterized by market clearing for all goods except perhaps free goods, which may be in excess supply in equilibrium.

11.2 An artificially restricted economy

We would like to establish the existence of a general equilibrium where the economy is characterized by the excess demand function $Z(p)$. We are hampered in this quest because there are regions of price space where $Z(p)$ is not well defined. The strategy of proof is to consider the bounded counterpart of the economy, the artificially bounded economy characterized by the excess demand function $\tilde{Z}(p)$. We will establish the existence of equilibrium in this artificially bounded economy. We know we can do so, since this economy fulfills all of the conditions required of an economy in Chapters 4–7, particularly Theorem 7.1. There will be an equilibrium price vector p^* for the artificially bounded economy so that $\tilde{Z}(p^*) \leq 0$. But the equilibrium allocation is attainable. As noted in Lemma 7.1, the quantity constraint on $\tilde{D}^i(p)$ is not binding in equilibrium. By Theorems 8.3(b) and 9.1(b), $S^j(p^*) = \tilde{S}^j(p^*)$ and $D^i(p^*) = \tilde{D}^i(p^*)$. At the equilibrium of the artificially bounded economy, demand and supply coincide with those of the unrestricted economy. Therefore, $\tilde{Z}(p^*) = Z(p^*) \leq 0$. But then the trick is done. We have an equilibrium for the original economy characterized by $Z(p)$.

We will describe the artificially bounded economy by taking the production technology of each firm j to be $\tilde{Y}^j$ rather than Y^j and by taking the demand function of each household i to be $\tilde{D}^i(p)$ rather than $D^i(p)$. In this special restricted case we will refer to the excess demand function of the economy as $\tilde{Z}(p)$. As demonstrated in Chapters 4, 5, and 6, the artificially restricted excess demand function is well defined for all $p \in P$. $\tilde{Z}: P \rightarrow \mathbf{R}^N$. The *unrestricted* economy is defined by Y^j, D^i, and Z. As demonstrated in Chapters 8–10, $Z(p)$ and $\tilde{Z}(p)$ will coincide for p so that each firm and household's plans in the restricted economy, $\tilde{S}^j(p)$ and $\tilde{D}^i(p)$, are attainable.

We have the following observations on $\tilde{Z}(p)$:

Weak Walras' Law (Theorem 6.2): For all $p \in P$, $p \cdot \tilde{Z}(p) \leq 0$. For p such that $p \cdot \tilde{Z}(p) < 0$, there is $k = 1, 2, \ldots, N$, so that $\tilde{Z}_k(p) > 0$.

$\tilde{Z}(p)$ is a continuous function, assuming P.II–P.V, C.I–C.V, C.VII, and C.VIII (Theorem 4.1, Theorem 5.2).

From Chapter 7 we know that there is $p^0 \in P$, so that p^0 is an equilibrium of the artificially restricted economy characterized by $\tilde{Z}(p)$. How do we know this? The economy characterized by $\tilde{Y}^j$ and $\tilde{D}^i(p)$ fulfills all of the assumptions of Theorem 7.1 when we substitute $\tilde{Y}^j$, the bounded subset of Y^j, for $\mathcal{Y}^j$, the bounded technology sets of Chapters 4 through 7. Therefore, by applying Theorem 7.1 we can find $p^0 \in P$ so that $\tilde{Z}(p^0) \leq 0$, with $p_k^0 = 0$ for k so that $\tilde{Z}_k(p^0) < 0$.

11.3 General equilibrium of the unrestricted economy

We now wish to establish the existence of general equilibrium in the unrestricted economy, Theorem 11.1. We start with Lemma 11.1: Consider the restricted economy characterized by $\tilde{Y}^j$, $\tilde{S}^j$, and $\tilde{D}^i$ and show that it has a general equilibrium by Theorem 7.1. This result is in itself of no interest since the economy to which it applies is entirely artificial. We will then show that the equilibrium of the artificially restricted economy is attainable in the actual economy. It then follows that, at the equilibrium prices of the artificially restricted economy, the firm supply functions and household demand functions of the actual economy coincide with those of the restricted economy. This coincidence follows from Theorem 8.3(b) and Theorem 9.1(b). Hence, the equilibrium price vector developed in Lemma 11.1 is also an equilibrium of the unrestricted economy. This proves Theorem 11.1.

Lemma 11.1[1] *Assume P.II–P.V, C.I–C.V, CVII, and C.VIII. There is $p^* \in P$ so that p^* is an equilibrium of the artificially restricted economy. That is $\tilde{Z}(p^*) \leq 0$ and $p_k^* = 0$ for k so that $\tilde{Z}_k(p^*) < 0$.*

Proof Lemma 11.1 is merely a restatement of Theorem 7.1, so the proof is completely redundant. We reproduce the treatment here merely for completeness.

We will show that there is $p^* \in P$ so that $\tilde{Z}(p^*) \leq 0$, with $p_k^* = 0$, for k so that $\tilde{Z}_k(p^*) \leq 0$. p^* is an equilibrium price vector of the artificially bounded economy.

We formulate a price adjustment function, $T: P \to P$. Define $T(p)$ in the following fashion for each coordinate $k = 1, 2, 3, \dots, N$:

$$T_k(p) \equiv \frac{p_k + \max[0, \tilde{Z}_k(p)]}{1 + \sum_{n=1}^{N} \max[0, \tilde{Z}_n(p)]} = \frac{p_k + \max[0, \tilde{Z}_k(p)]}{\sum_{n=1}^{N} \{p_n + \max[0, \tilde{Z}_n(p)]\}}.$$

The price adjustment function T raises the relative price of goods in excess demand and reduces that of goods in excess supply while keeping the price vector on the simplex. The denominator is trivially positive.

By Lemma 6.1, $\tilde{Z}(p)$ is a continuous function. Then $T(p)$ is a continuous function from the simplex into itself since continuity is preserved under the operations of max, addition, and division by a positive-valued continuous function. By the Brouwer Fixed-Point Theorem (Theorem 2.10) there is $p^* \in P$ so that $T(p^*) = p^*$.

---

[1] I acknowledge and thank John Roemer and Li Li for help in formulating the proof.

But then for all $k = 1, \ldots, N$,

$$p_k^* = \frac{p_k^* + \max[0, \tilde{Z}_k(p^*)]}{1 + \sum_{n=1}^{N} \max[0, \tilde{Z}_n(p^*)]}.$$

Thus, either $p_k^* = 0$ or

$$p_k^* = \frac{p_k^* + \max[0, \tilde{Z}_k(p^*)]}{1 + \sum_{n=1}^{N} \max[0, \tilde{Z}_n(p^*)]} > 0.$$

CASE 1 $p_k^* = 0 = \max[0, \tilde{Z}_k(p^*)]$. Hence $\tilde{Z}_k(p^*) \leq 0$.

CASE 2

$$p_k^* = \frac{p_k^* + \max[0, \tilde{Z}_k(p^*)]}{1 + \sum_{n=1}^{N} \max[0, \tilde{Z}_n(p^*)]} > 0.$$

To avoid repeated tedious notation, let

$$0 < \alpha = \frac{1}{1 + \sum_{n=1}^{N} \max[0, \tilde{Z}_n(p^*)]} \leq 1.$$

This case now resolves into two subcases:

CASE 2A $\alpha = 1$ implies $\tilde{Z}_k(p^*) \leq 0, \quad$ all k.

CASE 2B $\alpha < 1$.

We have

$$p_k^* = \alpha p_k^* + \alpha \max[0, \tilde{Z}_k(p^*)]$$

or

$$(1 - \alpha) p_k^* = \alpha \max[0, \tilde{Z}_k(p^*)].$$

Multiplying through by $\tilde{Z}_k(p^*)$, we get

$$(1 - \alpha) p_k^* \tilde{Z}_k(p^*) = \alpha(\max[0, \tilde{Z}_k(p^*)]) \tilde{Z}_k(p^*).$$

We can restate the Weak Walras' Law as

$$0 \geq p^* \cdot \tilde{Z}(p^*) = \sum_{k \in \text{Case } 1} p_k^* \tilde{Z}_k(p^*) + \sum_{k \in \text{Case } 2} p_k^* \tilde{Z}_k(p^*)$$

$$= 0 + \sum_{k \in \text{Case } 2} p_k^* \tilde{Z}_k(p^*) = \sum_{k \in \text{Case } 2} p_k^* \tilde{Z}_k(p^*).$$

Simplifying, multiplying through by $(1 - \alpha)$, and substituting we get

$$0 \geq (1 - \alpha) \sum_{k \in \text{Case 2}} p_k^* \tilde{Z}_k(p^*) = \alpha \sum_{k \in \text{Case 2}} (\max[0, \tilde{Z}_k(p^*)]) \tilde{Z}_k(p^*).$$

But this means that $\tilde{Z}_k(p^*) \leq 0$, for all k in Case 2.

However, then, there is no k, either in case 1 or 2, so that $\tilde{Z}_k(p^*) > 0$. From the Weak Walras' Law it follows that $p^* \cdot \tilde{Z}(p^*) = 0$. Hence for k so that $\tilde{Z}_k(p^*) < 0$, it follows that $p_k^* = 0$. This completes the proof of Lemma 11.1.   QED

Theorem 11.1 *Assume P.II–P.V, C.I–C.V, C.VII, and C.VIII. There is $p^* \in P$ so that p^* is an equilibrium price vector. That is, $Z(p^*) \leq 0$ and $p_k^* = 0$ for k so that $Z_k(p^*) < 0$.*

Proof We note from Lemma 11.1 that there is an equilibrium price vector $p^* \in P$ for the artificially restricted economy. There is $p^* \in P$ so that $\tilde{Z}(p^*) \leq 0$ with $p_k^* = 0$ for k so that $\tilde{Z}_k(p^*) < 0$. Now we must show that the equilibrium of the restricted economy is also an equilibrium of the unrestricted economy. First we note that the production plans at p^* of each firm in the artificially restricted economy, $\tilde{S}^j(p^*)$, are attainable, and similarly for $\tilde{D}^i(p^*)$. This follows simply from the definition of equilibrium, which implies that the equilibrium allocation be attainable. That is, $\tilde{Z}(p^*) = \sum_{i \in H} \tilde{D}^i(p^*) - r - \sum_{j \in F} \tilde{S}^j(p^*) \leq 0$ implies $r + \sum_{j \in F} \tilde{S}^j(p^*) \geq \sum_{i \in H} \tilde{D}^i(p^*) \geq 0$. But then by Theorems 8.3(b) and 9.1(b) we have $\tilde{S}^j(p^*) = S^j(p^*)$ for all $j \in F$. It follows that $\tilde{\pi}^j(p^*) = \pi^j(p^*)$ and hence $\tilde{M}^i(p^*) = M^i(p^*)$ for all $i \in H$. But then by Theorem 9.1(b), $\tilde{D}^i(p^*) = D^i(p^*)$. By definition, $Z(p^*) = \sum_{i \in H} D^i(p^*) - r - \sum_{j \in F} S^j(p^*)$. Therefore, $\tilde{Z}(p^*) = Z(p^*)$. But then $Z(p^*) \leq 0$, with $p_k^* = 0$ for k so that $Z_k(p^*) < 0$, so p^* is an equilibrium price vector.   QED

Theorem 11.1 is the most important single result of this book. It says that the competitive economy, guided only by prices, has a market-clearing equilibrium outcome. The decentralized price-guided economy has a consistent solution. This is the defining result of the general equilibrium theory.

11.4 The Uzawa Equivalence Theorem

The principal mathematical tool we used in proving Lemma 11.1 and hence Theorem 11.1 is the Brouwer Fixed-Point Theorem. There is now a distinctive result that shows that the use of the Brouwer Fixed-Point Theorem is not merely convenient. It is essential. We will demonstrate the mathematical equivalence of two propositions: (i) the existence of equilibrium in an economy characterized by a continuous excess demand function fulfilling Walras' Law and (ii) the Brouwer Fixed-Point Theorem. We already know that the Brouwer Fixed-Point Theorem implies existence of equilibrium. We will now demonstrate the converse: If we are always sure of existence of equilibrium in such an economy, then the Brouwer Fixed-Point Theorem must follow. The Brouwer Fixed-Point Theorem implies existence of general equilibrium; existence of general equilibrium implies the Brouwer Fixed-Point Theorem. Thus, the two apparently distinct results are mathematically equivalent.

We will now demonstrate this equivalence. Just to get terminology and notation straight (and to keep it distinct from the economic model developed above) we will restate some results and introduce some new notation for familiar constructs.

Let S be the unit simplex in $\mathbf{R}^N$. Recall two propositions:

Brouwer Fixed-Point Theorem (BFPT) Let $f : S \to S$, where f is continuous. Then there is $p^* \in S$ so that $p^* = f(p^*)$.

Walrasian Existence of Equilibrium Proposition (WEEP) Let $X : S \to \mathbf{R}^N$ so that

(1) $X(p)$ is continuous for all $p \in S$ and
(2) $p \cdot X(p) = 0$ (Walras' Law) for all $p \in S$.[2]

Then there is $p^* \in S$ so that $X(p^*) \leq 0$ with $p_i^* = 0$ for i so that $X_i(p^*) < 0$.

The observation that these two results are equivalent constitutes Theorem 11.2, below. Mathematical equivalence means that each proposition implies the other. We already know that BFPT implies WEEP; that was Theorem 1.2. It remains to demonstrate that the implication goes the other way as well. The proposition requires that – using WEEP but not BFPT – we prove that for an arbitrary continuous function from the simplex to itself, there is a fixed point. The strategy of proof is to take an arbitrary continuous function $f(p)$ from the simplex into itself. We use $f(p)$ to construct a continuous function mapping from S into $\mathbf{R}^N$ fulfilling Walras' Law. That is, we construct an "excess demand" function (derived from no actual economy but fulfilling the properties required in WEEP). The strategy of proof then is to find the general equilibrium price vector associated with this excess demand function and show that it is also a fixed point for the original function. Obviously, this plan requires clever construction of the excess demand function.

Theorem 11.2 (Uzawa Equivalence Theorem)[3] *WEEP implies BFPT.*

---

[2] We use the strong form of Walras' Law for convenience.
[3] The result is due to Hirofumi Uzawa (1962).

Proof We must demonstrate the following property: Let $f(\cdot)$ be an arbitrary continuous function mapping S into S. Assume WEEP but not BFPT. Then there is $p^* \in S$ so that $f(p^*) = p^*$.

Let $f : S \to S$, where f is continuous. Let

$$\mu(p) \equiv \frac{p \cdot f(p)}{|p|^2}$$

$$\equiv \frac{|p||f(p)|}{|p|^2} \cos(p, f(p)) \leq \frac{|f(p)|}{|p|},$$

where $\cos(p, f(p))$ denotes the cosine of the angle included by p, $f(p)$. Let

$$X(p) \equiv f(p) - \mu(p)p.$$

The function $X(p)$ represents "excess demand." If we have constructed it cleverly enough, the equilibrium price vector of $X(p)$ will also be a fixed point of $f(\cdot)$. The geometry of this construction is illustrated in Figure 11.1. It makes for a compelling visual demonstration that the equilibrium price vector of the excess demand function $X(p)$ is necessarily a fixed point of the function $f(p)$. Note that

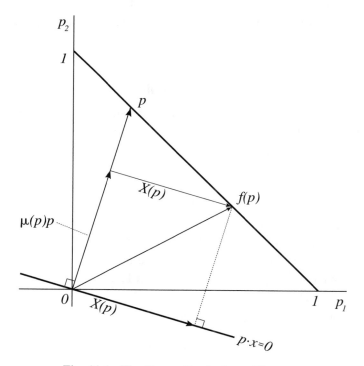

Fig. 11.1. The Uzawa Equivalence Theorem

$X(p)$ fulfills (1) and (2) of WEEP. We have

$$p \cdot X(p) = p \cdot f(p) - \frac{p \cdot f(p)}{|p|^2}|p|^2 = 0;$$

this is Walras' Law (2).

Hence, assuming WEEP, there is $p^* \in S$ so that $X(p^*) \leq 0$. Note that by construction $X(p^*) = 0$. This follows since $p_i^* = 0$ for $X_i(p^*) < 0$. If there were i so that $X_i(p^*) < 0$, it would lead to a contradiction: $p_i^* = 0$, so $0 > X_i(p^*) = f_i(p^*) - \mu(p^*)p_i^* = f_i(p^*) - 0 \geq 0$. Therefore, $X(p^*) = f(p^*) - \mu(p^*)p^* = 0$. Thus $f(p^*) = \mu(p^*)p^*$. But p^* and $f(p^*)$ are both points of the simplex. The only scalar multiple of a point on the simplex that remains on the simplex occurs when the scalar is unity. That is, $f(p^*) \in S$, $p^* \in S$, and $f(p^*) = \mu(p^*)p^*$ implies $\mu(p^*) = 1$, which implies $f(p^*) = p^*$.[4]   QED

What are we to make of the Uzawa Equivalence Theorem? It says that use of the Brouwer Fixed-Point Theorem is not merely one way to prove the existence of equilibrium. In a fundamental sense, it is the only way. Any alternative proof of existence will include, inter alia, an implicit proof of the Brouwer Theorem. Hence this mathematical method is essential; one cannot pursue this branch of economics without the Brouwer Theorem. If Walras failed to provide an adequate proof of existence of equilibrium himself, it was in part because the necessary mathematics was not yet available.

11.5 Bibliographic note

The proof of existence of equilibrium presented here parallels that of Arrow and Debreu (1954). The Uzawa Equivalence Theorem appeared first in Uzawa (1962) and is discussed in Debreu (1982).

Exercises

11.1   Describe the significance of:
    (a) The Uzawa Equivalence Theorem, Theorem 11.2. Does it have an implication for the importance of mathematics in economics?
    (b) The Existence of General Equilibrium Theorem, Theorem 1.2, Theorem 7.1, or Theorem 11.1.

11.2   Consider the following definition:

$$\{p^0, x^{0i}, y^{0j}\}, p^0 \in \mathbf{R}_+^N, i \in H, j \in F,$$

---

[4] My acknowledgment and thanks go to Jin-lung Lin for providing the central idea of this argument.

is said to be a competitive equilibrium if

  (i) $y^{0j} \in Y^j$ and $p^0 \cdot y^{0j} \geq p^0 \cdot y$ for all $y \in Y^j$, for all $j \in F$,
  (ii) $x^{0i} \in X^i$, $p^0 \cdot x^{0i} \leq M^i(p^0) = p^0 \cdot r^i + \sum_{j \in F} \alpha^{ij} p^0 \cdot y^{0j}$ and
      $x^{0i} \succsim_i x$ for all $x \in X^i$ with $p^0 \cdot x \leq M^i(p^0)$ for all $i \in H$, and
  (iii) $0 \geq \sum_{i \in H} x^{0i} - \sum_{j \in F} y^{0i} - \sum_{i \in H} r^i$ with $p_k^0 = 0$ for coordi-
      nates k so that the strict inequality holds.

(a) The concept of competitive equilibrium is supposed to reflect *decentralization* of economic behavior. Explain how this definition embodies the concept of decentralization.

(b) The concept of competitive equilibrium is supposed to reflect market clearing. Explain how this definition includes market clearing.

11.3 Consider the general competitive equilibrium of a production economy with redistributive taxation of income from endowment. Half of each household's income from endowment (based on actual endowment, not net sales) is taxed away. The proceeds of the tax are then distributed equally to all households. We then have,

$$M^i(p) = p \cdot (.5\, r^i) + \sum_{j \in F} \alpha^{ij} p \cdot y^j + T,$$

where T is the transfer of tax revenues to the household,

$$T = (1/\#H) \sum_{h \in H} p \cdot (.5\, r^h).$$

(a) Define a competitive equilibrium in this economy.
(b) State Walras' Law for this economy. Does it hold? Explain.
(c) Does a competitive equilibrium generally exist in this economy? Explain.

11.4 We now consider the economy of Exercise 11.3 with income taxation only on the household's net sales of endowment (rather than on the value of the full endowment as above). Household i's after tax income is now

$$M^i(p) = (1 - \tau)p \cdot (r^i - x^i)_+ + T,$$

where the notation $(\cdot)_+$ indicates the vector consisting of the nonnegative coordinates of $(\cdot)$ with zeros replacing the negative coordinates of $(\cdot)$. We now let $T = (1/H)\tau \sum_{i=1}^{H}(p \cdot (r^i - x^i)_+)$.

(a) Define a competitive equilibrium in this economy.
(b) State Walras' Law for this economy. Does it hold? Explain.
(c) Does a competitive equilibrium generally exist in this economy? Explain.

11.5   The model below is an interpretation of E. Malinvaud's *Theory of Unemployment Reconsidered*.

Consider the general equilibrium of a private ownership production economy. There are $\#H$ households, $i = 1, \ldots, \#H$. Each household i has a continuous monotonic, concave utility function $u^i(\cdot)$ and is endowed with resources $r^i \in \mathbf{R}_+^N$. There is a finite number of firms comprising the set F. Firm j has a compact convex technology set Y^j. Firm supply behavior is guided by simple profit maximization:

$$y^j = \arg\max_{y \in Y^j} p \cdot y,$$

The expression "$y^j = \arg\max_{y \in Y^j} p \cdot y$" defines y^j as the maximizer of $p \cdot y$ in Y^j. i's income is

$$M^i(p) = p \cdot r^i.$$

Note that M^i makes no allowance for the payment of firm profits to owners. i's consumption behavior is

$$(C) \ choose \quad x^{0i} \in \mathbf{R}_+^N, \ p \cdot x^{0i} \leq M^i(p), \ u^i(x^{0i}) \geq u^i(x)$$

$$for \ all \ x \ such \ that \ p \cdot x \leq M^i(p).$$

(a) Is Walras' Law fulfilled in the economy in this case? Explain.
(b) Is the excess demand function continuous in prices? Explain briefly. Feel free to cite known results.
(c) Does a competitive general equilibrium exist in the economy? Always? Never? Explain.

Part D

Welfare economics

Ever since Adam Smith's evocation of an invisible hand, market equilibrium has been supposed not only to clear markets but also to achieve an efficient allocation of resources. This view is embodied below in Chapter 12 in a definition and two major results. We define a very general efficiency concept, Pareto efficiency. We then state and prove the two major results relating market equilibrium to efficient allocation, which are the two most important results in welfare economics.

The First Fundamental Theorem of Welfare Economics agrees with Adam Smith: A market equilibrium allocation is Pareto efficient. This result can be demonstrated in a surprisingly elementary fashion. It requires very little mathematical structure and it does not require any assumption of convexity. If, despite nonconvexity, the economy has a market equilibrium, that equilibrium allocation is Pareto efficient.

The Second Fundamental Theorem of Welfare Economics requires more mathematical structure. It is a more surprising and deeper result. It says – assuming convexity of tastes and technology – that any efficient allocation can be supported as a competitive equilibrium. Find an efficient allocation. Then there are prices and a distribution of resource endowments of goods and share ownership that will allow the efficient allocation to be an equilibrium allocation at those prices and endowments. Market allocation is compatible with any efficient allocation subject to a redistribution of income.

12

Pareto efficiency and competitive equilibrium

12.1 Pareto efficiency

The purpose of economic activity is to allocate scarce resources to promote the welfare of households in their consumption of goods and services. There is a very large number of possible allocations of resources (typically an uncountable infinity), but most of them are wasteful – we can do better. Some wasteful allocations are those that do not make effective use of productive resources (corresponding to points inside the production frontier in the Robinson Crusoe economy). An alternative form of inefficiency occurs in allocations that allocate the mix of outputs among consumers without equating marginal rates of substitution, leaving room for improvement in the mix of consumption across households (wasteful points corresponding to those off the locus of tangencies in the Edgeworth box).

Economic theory does not give us precise guidance as to the desirable distribution of income and wealth across households. The theory is agnostic on the distribution of income between Smith and Jones and between Rockefeller and Micawber. We are led then to posit a criterion of nonwastefulness as a standard for the effective utilization of scarce resources, while avoiding the moral question of the desirable distribution of income. The nonwastefulness criterion is *Pareto efficiency*, and it is fundamentally a simple idea. A (Pareto) improvement in allocation is a reallocation that increases some household's utility (moves higher in the preference quasi-ordering) while reducing no household's utility. An allocation is Pareto efficient if there is no further room among attainable allocations for (Pareto) improvement.

To analyze this concept more fully we start with the definitions needed to formalize these concepts.

Definition *An allocation x^i, $i \in H$, is attainable if there is $y^j \in Y^j$, $j \in F$, so that $0 \leq \sum_{i \in H} x^i \leq \sum_{j \in F} y^j + \sum_{i \in H} r^i$. (The inequalities hold coordinatewise.)*

Definition *Consider two assignments of bundles to consumers, v^i, w^i, $i \in H$. v^i is said to be Pareto superior to w^i if for each $i \in H$, $v^i \succsim_i w^i$, and for some $h \in H$, $v^h \succ_h w^h$.*

Definition *An attainable assignment of bundles to consumers, w^i, $i \in H$, is said to be Pareto efficient (or Pareto optimal) if there is no other attainable assignment v^i so that v^i is Pareto superior to w^i.*

Definition $\{p^0, x^{0i}, y^{0j}\}$, $p^0 \in \mathbf{R}_+^N$, $i \in H$, $j \in F$, $x^{0i} \in \mathbf{R}^N$, $y^{0j} \in \mathbf{R}^N$, *is said to be a competitive equilibrium if*

  (i) $y^{0j} \in Y^j$ and $p^0 \cdot y^{0j} \geq p^0 \cdot y$ *for all $y \in Y^j$, for all $j \in F$,*

 (ii) $x^{0i} \in X^i$, $p^0 \cdot x^{0i} \leq M^i(p^0) = p^0 \cdot r^i + \sum_{j \in F} \alpha^{ij} p^0 \cdot y^{0j}$ *and $x^{0i} \succsim_i x$ for all $x \in X^i$ with $p^0 \cdot x \leq M^i(p^0)$ for all $i \in H$, and*

(iii) $0 \geq \sum_{i \in H} x^{0i} - \sum_{j \in F} y^{0j} - \sum_{i \in H} r^i$ *with $p_k^0 = 0$ for coordinates k so that the strict inequality holds.*

This definition is sufficiently general to include the equilibria developed in Theorems 7.1, 11.1, and 17.7.

12.2 First Fundamental Theorem of Welfare Economics

We are now ready to state and prove the First Fundamental Theorem of Welfare Economics. It says that every equilibrium is an optimum. A competitive equilibrium allocation is always Pareto efficient. The result is remarkable in two ways. First, it requires virtually no assumptions or mathematical structure beyond the definitions of equilibrium and efficiency and an assumption of scarcity (monotonicity). Second, it does not require convexity of tastes or technology. In addition, the proof is disarmingly simple. We start from a competitive equilibrium. That means that households are optimizing utility subject to a budget constraint and that firms are maximizing profits. We use a proof by contradiction. Suppose the theorem were false. That would mean that there is an attainable Pareto preferable allocation. Evaluate the preferable allocation at equilibrium prices. For those households whose consumptions are strictly improved at the alternative allocation, the cost of their consumption bundle must go up as well. If these more expensive bundles are attainable, then they must be more profitable as well. But that leads to a contradiction. If they are more profitable and attainable then the equilibrium allocation cannot be an equilibrium. The contradiction proves the theorem.

To prove the First Fundamental Theorem of Welfare Economics, it is useful to have the budget constraint fulfilled as an equality in equilibrium, as noted in Lemmas 7.1, 10.1, or 17.4.

Theorem 12.1 (First Fundamental Theorem of Welfare Economics) *Assume C.IV and C.V. Let $p^0 \in \mathbf{R}_+^N$ be a competitive equilibrium price vector of the economy. Let w^{0i}, $i \in H$, be the associated individual consumption bundles, and let y^{0j}, $j \in F$, be the associated firm supply vectors. Then w^{0i} is Pareto efficient.*

Proof $w^{0i} \succsim_i x$, for all x so that $p^0 \cdot x \le M^i(p^0)$, for all $i \in H$. This is a property of the equilibrium allocation. Consider an allocation x^i that household $i \in H$ regards as more desirable than w^{0i}. If the allocation x^i is preferable, it must also be more expensive. That is,

$$x^i \succ_i w^{0i} \quad \text{implies} \quad p^0 \cdot x^i > p^0 \cdot w^{0i}.$$

Similarly, profit maximization in equilibrium implies that production plans more profitable than y^{0j} at prices p are not available in Y^j. $p^0 \cdot y > p^0 \cdot y^{0j}$ implies $y \notin Y^j$. Noting that markets clear at the equilibrium allocation, we have

$$\sum_{i \in H} w^{0i} \le \sum_{j \in F} y^{0j} + r.$$

Note that, for each household $i \in H$, by C.IV (as emphasized in Lemmas 7.1, 10.1, and 17.4),

$$p^0 \cdot w^{0i} = M^i(p^0) = p^0 \cdot r^i + \sum_j \alpha^{ij}(p^0 \cdot y^{0j}),$$

and summing over households,

$$\sum_{i \in H} p^0 \cdot w^{0i} = \sum_i M^i(p^0) = \sum_i \left[p^0 \cdot r^i + \sum_j \alpha^{ij}(p^0 \cdot y^{0j}) \right]$$

$$= p^0 \cdot \sum_i r^i + p^0 \cdot \sum_i \sum_j \alpha^{ij} y^{0j}$$

$$= p^0 \cdot \sum_i r^i + p^0 \cdot \sum_j \sum_i \alpha^{ij} y^{0j}$$

$$= p^0 \cdot r + p^0 \cdot \sum_j y^{0j} \quad \left(\text{since for each } j, \sum_i \alpha^{ij} = 1 \right).$$

Suppose, contrary to the theorem, there is an attainable allocation v^i, $i \in H$, so that $v^i \succsim_i w^{0i}$, for all i with $v^h \succ_h w^{0h}$ for some $h \in H$. The allocation v^i must be more expensive than w^{0i} for those households made better off and no less expensive for the others. Then we have

$$\sum_{i \in H} p^0 \cdot v^i > \sum_{i \in H} p^0 \cdot w^{0i} = \sum_{i \in H} M^i(p^0) = p^0 \cdot r + p^0 \cdot \sum_{j \in F} y^{0j}.$$

But if v^i is attainable, then there is $y'^j \in Y^j$ for each $j \in F$, so that

$$\sum_{i \in H} v^i \le \sum_{j \in F} y'^j + r,$$

where the inequality holds coordinatewise. But then, evaluating this production plan at the equilibrium prices, p^0, we have

$$p^0 \cdot r + p^0 \cdot \sum_{j \in F} y^{0j} < p^0 \cdot \sum_{i \in H} v^i \le p^0 \cdot \sum_{j \in F} y'^j + p^0 \cdot r .$$

So $p^0 \cdot \sum_{j \in F} y^{0j} < p^0 \cdot \sum_{j \in F} y'^j$. Therefore, for some $j \in F$, $p^0 \cdot y^{0j} < p^0 \cdot y'^j$. But y^{0j} maximizes $p^0 \cdot y$ for all $y \in Y^j$; there cannot be $y'^j \in Y^j$ so that $p \cdot y'^j > p \cdot y^{0j}$. Hence, $y'^j \notin Y^j$. The contradiction shows that v^i is not attainable.

QED

Note that the First Fundamental Theorem does not require convexity of tastes or technologies. If there is an equilibrium in a nonconvex economy (a possibility since convexity is part of the sufficient, not necessary, conditions for existence of equilibrium), then the equilibrium allocation is Pareto efficient.

Theorem 12.1, the First Fundamental Theorem of Welfare Economics, is a mathematical statement of Adam Smith's notion of the invisible hand leading to an efficient allocation. A competitive equilibrium decentralizes an efficient allocation. Prices provide the incentives so that firms and households guided by prices and self-interest can, acting independently, find an efficient allocation.

12.3 Second Fundamental Theorem of Welfare Economics

The Second Fundamental Theorem of Welfare Economics says that every Pareto efficient allocation of an economy with convex preferences and technology is an equilibrium for a suitably chosen price system, subject to an initial redistribution of endowment and ownership shares. Any desired redistribution of welfare (subject to attainability) can be achieved through a market mechanism subject to a redistribution of endowment and ownership.[1] The strategy of proof is to characterize an efficient allocation as a common point on the boundaries of two convex sets with disjoint interiors: the set of attainable allocations and the set of Pareto preferable allocations. The Separating Hyperplane Theorem tells us that we can run a hyperplane between them. The normal to the hyperplane is the price system that supports the efficient allocation. This is presented in Theorem 12.2. It is then a matter of bookkeeping to attribute endowments to households to allow them to support the

---

[1] Note that this may require an implausible redistribution of labor endowment, that is, redistributing to one household ownership of another's labor.

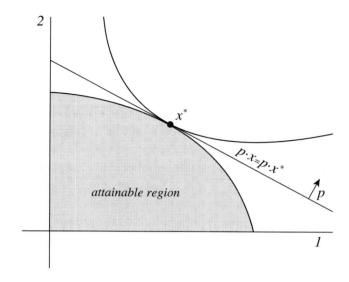

Fig. 12.1. Supporting an efficient allocation (Theorem 12.2).

allocation as an equilibrium. That is the corollary that embodies the Second Fundamental Theorem of Welfare Economics. This is actually a very familiar result from the Robinson Crusoe economy and is illustrated in Figure 12.1.

In proving Theorem 12.2, we will fully utilize the structure of technology and preferences, particularly convexity, developed above. The economy of Theorem 12.2 is characterized by convexity of the aggregate technology set $Y(= \sum_{j \in F} Y^j)$, convexity of preferences and consumption sets X^i, and continuity and monotonicity of preferences.

In order to prove Theorem 12.2, we will use the Separating Hyperplane Theorem. Recall:

Theorem 2.12 (Separating Hyperplane Theorem) *Let A, $B \subset \mathbf{R}^N$; let A and B be non-empty, convex, and disjoint, that is, $A \cap B = \phi$. Then there is $p \in \mathbf{R}^N$, $p \neq 0$, so that $p \cdot x \geq p \cdot y$ for all $x \in A$, $y \in B$.*

In addition, a minor lemma helps with the technical structure of the proof.

Lemma 12.1 *Assume C.I–C.VI. Let $x^0 \in X^i$. Then there is $x^\nu \in X^i$, $\nu = 1, 2, 3, \ldots, x^\nu \succ_i x^0$, so that $x^\nu \to x^0$.*

Proof Under C.II and C.IV, the sequence $x^\nu = x^0 + (1/\nu, 1/\nu, 1/\nu, \ldots, 1/\nu)$ has the property that $x^\nu \in X^i$, $\nu = 1, 2, 3, \ldots, x^\nu \succ_i x^0$. Trivially, $x^\nu \to x^0$.   QED

Recall the definition $A^i(x^i) \equiv \{x \mid x \in X^i, x \succsim_i x^i\}$. Under the assumptions of convexity and continuity of preferences, $A^i(x^i)$ is a closed convex set. Starting from the allocation x^i, $i \in H$, we can take the sum of sets $\sum_{i \in H} A^i(x^i)$; this sum, called A, is also a convex set and represents the set of aggregate consumptions preferred or indifferent to x^i. Consider a subset of A that includes aggregate consumptions strictly preferred to x^i (approximately the interior of A). Let us denote this set by $\mathcal{A}$, which is also a convex set. A point in $\mathcal{A}$ represents an aggregate consumption mix that can provide an allocation Pareto preferable to x^i, $i \in H$. The set of aggregate attainable allocations is the (coordinatewise) nonnegative elements of $Y + \{r\}$. We will denote this set as $B = (Y + \{r\}) \cap \mathbf{R}^N_+$, a convex set. Starting from a Pareto efficient allocation x^i, $i \in H$, under monotonicity, the sets $\mathcal{A}$ and B must be disjoint. If not, there would be an attainable Pareto preferable allocation. But this is precisely the setting where we can employ the Separating Hyperplane Theorem. The normal to the separating hyperplane is the price system that decentralizes the efficient allocation. The existence of such a price system is the import of Theorem 12.2.

Theorem 12.2 *Assume P.I–P.IV and C.I–C.VI. Let x^{*i}, y^{*j}, $i \in H$, $j \in F$, be an attainable Pareto efficient allocation. Then there is $p \in P$ so that*

(i) x^{*i} minimizes $p \cdot x$ on $A^i(x^{*i})$, $i \in H$, and
(ii) y^{*j} maximizes $p \cdot y$ on Y^j, $j \in F$.

Proof Let $x^* = \sum_{i \in H} x^{*i}$, and let $y^* = \sum_{j \in F} y^{*j}$. Note that $x^* \leq y^* + r$ (the inequality applies coordinatewise). Let $A = \sum_{i \in H} A^i(x^{*i})$. Let $B = Y + \{r\}$. A and B are closed convex sets with common points, x^*, $y^* + r$. Let $\mathcal{A} = \sum_{i \in H} \{x \mid x \in X^i, x \succ_i x^{*i}\} = \sum_{i \in H} \{X^i \backslash G^i(x^{*i})\}$, a convex set whose closure is A (by Lemma 12.1). Set $\mathcal{A}$ represents aggregate consumption bundles that can provide an allocation that is a Pareto improvement over x^{*i}, $i \in H$. Note that under C.IV, since x^{*i} is a Pareto efficient allocation, $\mathcal{A}$ and B are disjoint. x^* is an element of A and of B, but x^* is not interior to A or B. By the Separating Hyperplane Theorem, there is a normal p, so that

$$p \cdot x \geq p \cdot v \quad \text{for all } x \in \mathcal{A} \text{ and all } v \in B.$$

By continuity of preferences and continuity of the dot product we have also $p \cdot x \geq p \cdot v$ for all $x \in A$ and all $v \in B$. This has a distinctive implication for points common to A and B: x^*, $(y^* + r) \in A \cap B$, so x^* and $(y^* + r)$ minimize $p \cdot x$ on A and maximize $p \cdot x$ on B.

By C.IV, p will be nonnegative, coordinatewise. We may without loss of generality choose $p \in P$. Since x^* and $(y^* + r)$ are common points of A and B, we have that x^* and $(y^* + r)$ minimize $p \cdot x$ on A and maximize $p \cdot v$ on B. That is, the value of the dot product $p \cdot x^*$ is the largest of any such dot product for an element of B and the smallest of any for an element of A. However, x^* is the sum of many elements, one for each of $A^i(x^{*i})$, $i \in H$, and y^* is the sum of many elements, one for each Y^j, $j \in F$. Then the additive structure of A and B implies that x^{*i} minimizes $p \cdot x$ on $A^i(x^{*i})$ and y^{*j} maximizes $p \cdot y$ on Y^j. That is,

$$p \cdot x^* = \min_{x \in A} p \cdot x = \min_{x^i \in A^i(x^{*i})} p \cdot \sum_{i \in H} x^i = \sum_{i \in H} \left(\min_{x \in A^i(x^{*i})} p \cdot x \right),$$

and

$$p \cdot (r + y^*) = \max_{v \in B} p \cdot v = p \cdot r + \sum_{j \in F} \left(\max_{y^j \in Y^j} p \cdot y^j \right).$$

So x^{*i} minimizes $p \cdot x$ for all $x \in A_i(x^{*i})$ and y^{*j} maximizes $p \cdot y$ for all $y \in Y^j$.

QED

Theorem 12.2 presents the mathematical structure we need. It says that the separation theorem can be used to find prices that support any efficient allocation. The corollary below constitutes the Second Fundamental Theorem of Welfare Economics. It says that the supporting prices introduced in Theorem 12.2 can be used, along with a suitably chosen redistribution of endowment, to support any chosen efficient allocation as an equilibrium.

For full generality, the corollary presents two possible cases of household incomes. This represents the complexity of corner solutions again. Case 1 (presumably the most common) occurs when the household expenditure at the efficient allocation exceeds the minimum level in the consumption set. Then the household is a utility maximizer subject to budget constraint. Case 2 occurs when the efficient allocation attributes expenditure to the household equal the minimum in its consumption set. In that case the household is an expenditure minimizer subject to utility constraint. Restricting attention to interior allocations would eliminate this complexity by confining attention to Case 1.

Corollary 12.1 (Second Fundamental Theorem of Welfare Economics) *Assume P.I–P.IV and C.I–C.VI. Let x^{*i}, y^{*j} be an attainable Pareto efficient allocation. Then there is $p \in P$ and $\hat{r}^i \in \mathbf{R}^N$, $\hat{r}^i \geq 0$, $\hat{\alpha}^{ij} \geq 0$, so that*

$$\sum_{i \in H} \hat{r}^i = r,$$

$$\sum_{i \in H} \hat{\alpha}^{ij} = 1 \quad \text{for each } j,$$

$$p \cdot y^{*j} \text{ maximizes } p \cdot y \quad \text{for } y \in Y^j,$$

and

$$p \cdot x^{*i} = p \cdot \hat{r}^i + \sum_{j \in F} \hat{\alpha}^{ij}(p \cdot y^{*j}).$$

Further, for each $i \in H$, one of the following properties holds:

CASE 1 $(p \cdot x^{*i} > \min_{x \in X^i} p \cdot x) : x^{*i} \succsim_i x$ *for all $x \in X^i$ so that*

$$p \cdot x \le p \cdot \hat{r}^i + \sum_{j \in F} \hat{\alpha}^{ij}(p \cdot y^{*j}), \quad or$$

CASE 2 $(p \cdot x^{*i} = \min_{x \in X^i} p \cdot x) : x^{*i}$ *minimizes $p \cdot x$ for all x so that $x \succsim_i x^{*i}$.*

Proof Applying Theorem 12.2, we have $p \in P$ so that y^{*j} maximizes $p \cdot y$ for all $y \in Y^j$ and so that x^{*i} minimizes $p \cdot x$ for all $x \in A^i(x^{*i})$. We must show two properties, (1) that $\hat{r}^i$, $\hat{\alpha}^{ij}$ can be found fulfilling the above equations and inequalities, and (2) that household behavior can be characterized as utility optimization subject to budget constraint in Case 1 and as cost minimization subject to utility level in Case 2.

By attainability of the allocation, we have

$$\sum_{i \in H} x^{*i} \le \sum_{j \in F} y^{*j} + r.$$

By Pareto efficiency of the allocation, we know that the strict inequality applies here only in redundant goods k that are desirable to no household so $p_k = 0$. Further, by weak monotonicity, C.IV, there is at least one good that is desirable and hence supports a positive price. Multiplying through by p, with the recognition of free goods, we have

$$\sum_{i \in H} p \cdot x^{*i} = \sum_{j \in F} p \cdot y^{*j} + p \cdot r.$$

But then it is merely simple arithmetic to find suitable $\hat{r}^i$, $\hat{\alpha}^{ij}$. A simple choice (one of many possible) is to let

$$\lambda_i = \frac{p \cdot x^{*i}}{\sum_{h \in H} p \cdot x^{*h}},$$

and set $\hat{r}^i = \lambda_i r$, $\hat{\alpha}^{ij} = \lambda_i$, for all $i \in H$, $j \in F$.

On the consumer side now, we wish to show that cost minimization subject to a utility constraint is equivalent to utility maximization subject to a budget constraint in Case 1. This follows from continuity of preferences. Suppose, on the contrary, there is x'^i so that $p \cdot x'^i = p \cdot x^{*i}$ and $x'^i \succ_i x^{*i}$. We will show that this leads to a contradiction. By continuity of preferences, C.V, there is an ε neighborhood about x'^i so that all points in the neighborhood are superior or indifferent, $\succsim_i$, to x^{*i}. But then some points of the neighborhood are less expensive at p than x^{*i}, and x^{*i} is no longer a cost minimizer for $A_i(x^{*i})$. This is a contradiction, and hence there can be no such $x^{\prime i}$. The assertion for Case 2 is merely a restatement of the property shown in Theorem 12.2. QED

The Second Fundamental Theorem of Welfare Economics represents a significant defense of the market economy's resource allocation mechanism. It says (assuming convexity of tastes and technology) that any efficient allocation of resources can be decentralized using the price mechanism, subject to an initial redistribution of endowment. This is the basis of the common prescription in public finance that any attainable distribution of welfare can be achieved using a market mechanism and lump-sum taxes (corresponding to the redistribution of endowment). On this basis, public authority intervention in the market through direct provision of services (housing, education, medical care, child care etc.) is an unnecessary escape from market allocation mechanisms with their efficiency properties. Public authority redistribution of income should be sufficient to achieve the desired reallocation of welfare while retaining the market discipline for efficient resource utilization.

12.4 Bibliographic note

The notion that competitive equilibrium and efficient allocation are closely related concepts dates back at least to Adam Smith (1776). The mathematical treatment here, emphasizing the use of separating hyperplanes rather than the differential calculus, is attributed to Arrow (1951) and is fully expounded in Koopmans (1957) and in Debreu (1959).

Exercises

12.1   Consult Exercises 2 and 3 of Chapter 7. In each of those problems, when a competitive equilibrium exists, is the resulting allocation Pareto efficient?

12.2   Consider the general equilibrium of a pure exchange economy with redistributive income taxation. Net income taxation is not on endowment, but rather on that portion of endowment (net) sold. There is a finite number of households in the set $H, i = 1, 2, 3, \ldots, \#H$. Each household i has continuous monotone convex preferences $\succsim_i$ and is endowed with resources $r^i \in \mathbf{R}_+^N$. There is an income tax at rate $\tau, 0 < \tau < 1$, with rebate in the amount T. Household i's after-tax income is

$$M^i(p) = p \cdot \hat{r}^i - \tau p \cdot (r^i - x^i)_+ + T,$$

where $T = (1/\#H)\tau \sum_{i \in H}[(p \cdot (r^i - x^i)_+]$. The notation $(\cdot)_+$ denotes the vector consisting of the positive coordinates of $(\cdot)$. Household i chooses consumption $x^i \in \mathbf{R}_+^N$ to optimize $\succsim_i$ subject to

$$p \cdot x^i \leq M^i(p).$$

(a) Define a competitive equilibrium in this economy.

(b) Proving existence of competitive equilibrium is a bit tricky. When a competitive equilibrium exists, is the allocation Pareto efficient? Explain.

12.3 A well-recognized problem in industrial organization and welfare economics is allocative efficiency with a natural monopoly. A natural monopoly is a firm characterized by a large nonconvexity in the production technology, hence displaying (weakly) declining marginal costs throughout the relevant range of output levels. An efficient allocation will typically include only one firm active in this market (hence it has a monopoly). Marginal cost pricing (generally characterizing an efficient market allocation) is incompatible with a market equilibrium (marginal cost is below average cost, so marginal cost pricing leads the firm to run losses). A conventional proposal to deal with this problem is as follows:

Government should provide a subsidy to the firm (financed by nondistortionary taxation) to repay its losses. The firm should price at marginal cost. The resulting allocation is (thought to be) Pareto efficient.

(a) Why is this proposal thought to achieve a Pareto efficient allocation?

(b) Diagram a simple Robinson Crusoe two-commodity case where it will achieve an efficient allocation.

  (i) Diagram the production frontier in the case of declining marginal cost.

  (ii) Diagram an interior optimum.

  (iii) Diagram the budget line (and the lump-sum tax) supporting the efficient allocation.

(c) Show that the proposal may also support an inefficient allocation as a marginal cost pricing equilibrium.

  (i) Diagram the production frontier in the case of declining marginal cost.

  (ii) Diagram a corner optimum.

  (iii) Diagram the budget line (and the lump-sum tax) supporting an inefficient interior allocation.

(d) Discuss. How does this relate to the Fundamental Theorems of Welfare Economics? Can local conditions (marginal equivalences, $MRS = MRT$) fully characterize efficient allocations in this problem? Why or why not?

12.4   The usual U-shaped cost curve model of undergraduate intermediate economics includes a small nonconvexity (diminishing marginal cost at low
output levels). This is a violation of our usual convexity assumptions on
production (P.I or PV). Consider the general equilibrium of an economy
displaying U-shaped cost curves. It is possible that a general equilibrium
exists despite the small violation of convexity. After all, P.I and P.V are
sufficient, not necessary, conditions. If a general equilibrium does exist despite the small nonconvexity, will the allocation be Pareto efficient? Does
the First Fundamental Theorem of Welfare Economics apply? Explain.

12.5   One of the assumptions used in proving the First Fundamental Theorem of
Welfare Economics, Theorem 12.1, is weak monotonicity of preferences,
C.IV. Show that the theorem is false without this assumption.

12.6   External effects (e.g., air pollution, water pollution, annoyance due to
neighboring noise, traffic congestion) occur in economic analysis when
one firm or household's actions affect the tastes or technology of another
through nonmarket means. That is, in an external effect, the interaction
between two firms does not take the form of supply of output or demand
for input going through the market (and hence showing up in price). It
would be characterized rather as the shape of one firm's available technology set depending on the output or input level of another firm. Or it
might be characterized as one firm's inputs (like clean air at a tourist resort)
being nonmarketed but their availability being affected by the production
decisions of another firm.

   Does the model of Chapter 12 treat external effects? Explain your
answer. How does the treatment of externalities (or lack of treatment)
show up in the specification of the model?

12.7   Describe the significance of:
   (a) The First Fundamental Theorem of Welfare Economics (Theorem 12.1).
   (b) The Second Fundamental Theorem of Welfare Economics (Theorem
       12.2 and Corollary 12.1).

12.8   Consider an economy with two consumption goods, x and y, and one input
to production L, which is inelastically supplied. Let a and k be positive
constants. Production of x is by simple constant returns,

$$x = kL^x,$$

where L^x is the amount of L used as an input to x. Production of y involves
a set-up cost, $S \geq 0$ (a nonconvexity),

$$y = 0 \qquad \text{if } L^y \leq S$$
$$y \leq a(L^y - S) \quad \text{if } L^y > S$$

where L^y is the amount of labor used as an input to y. The total labor input supplied is

$$L^x + L^y = L^0.$$

(a) Set $S = 0$. Will a Pareto efficient allocation typically be supported as a profit-maximizing competitive equilibrium (subject to a possible redistribution of household endowments)? Explain. If the answer is "no," are there special cases where an efficient allocation can nevertheless be sustained as a competitive equilibrium? Explain. A diagram may be useful.

(b) Set $S > 0$. Will a Pareto efficient allocation typically be supported as a profit-maximizing competitive equilibrium (subject to a possible redistribution of household endowments)? Explain. If the answer is "no," are there special cases where an efficient allocation can nevertheless be sustained as a competitive equilibrium? Explain. A diagram may be useful.

Part E

Bargaining and equilibrium: The core

One of the ideas presented repeatedly to students of economics is the link between large numbers of economic agents and competitive, price-taking, behavior. The notion is that in a large economy individual agents are strategically powerless and hence price-taking behavior makes sense. We can now give a formal proof of this argument. It is presented in Chapters 13 and 14. We define the core of a market economy as a generalization of the idea of the Edgeworth box. There will be many different kinds of traders and the usual N commodities. We will take a limit as the economy becomes large in a stylized fashion. The striking result is that the family of solutions to a bargaining problem corresponding to the contract curve in the Edgeworth box shrinks to the set of competitive allocations. In a large economy strategic bargaining merely gets you to the competitive equilibrium. We will prove that in a large economy, individual traders really do lack strategic power. Hence, competitive price-taking is the appropriate model of behavior.

13

The core of a market economy

13.1 Bargaining and competition

The model we have been using so far is competitive in a rather refined sense. All agents act as price-takers. They treat prices parametrically, as variables that they cannot control and to which they must adapt. The prices themselves are set by an impersonal market mechanism (idealized as the Walrasian auctioneer). The assumption that individual buyers and sellers are powerless to affect market prices reflects one idea of the notion of competition, that the market is so large that individual actions have no impact. But that makes up only half of what we mean by competition. In ordinary usage, we say competition occurs when each economic agent tries to do as well as possible by making the most advantageous deals he can. This is the idea of competition as conflict. One of the major achievements of modern general equilibrium theory is that we can demonstrate formally that these two notions of competition are equivalent. We can show mathematically that a model of bargaining and deal making where each buyer and seller tries to get the best deal possible leads to a price-taking equilibrium in a large economy. Hence, we can demonstrate the soundness of the informal notion that large economies leave individuals strategically powerless. We will present a concept of the outcome of strategic bargaining known as the *core* of the market economy. The core appeared in Chapter 1 as the contract curve. We will develop it more fully in this chapter. In Chapter 14 we will show that in a large economy the core and competitive equilibrium are identical. Thus, the strategic outcome in a large economy is equivalent to nonstrategic price-taking.

In order to define the core we start by summarizing the model of the economy, particularly of consumers, that we developed in Chapter 5. We will develop the model of the core for a pure exchange economy. That is, we will consider an economy without production, where the only economic activity is trade of endowment among consumers. This is obviously a special case, but the traditional and most interesting issues can successfully be treated here. Generalization to a linear production economy is straightforward (Debreu and Scarf (1963)).

Households are characterized by their endowments and preferences. There is a finite set of households H. Each $h \in H$ has an endowment $r^h \in \mathbf{R}_+^N$ and a preference quasi-ordering $\succsim_h$ defined on $\mathbf{R}_+^N$ (we take $X^h = \mathbf{R}_+^N$). An allocation is an assignment of $x^h \in \mathbf{R}_+^N$ for each $h \in H$. A typical allocation, $x^h \in \mathbf{R}_+^N$ for each $h \in H$, will be denoted $\{x^h, h \in H\}$. An allocation, $\{x^h, h \in H\}$, is feasible if $\sum_{h \in H} x^h \leq \sum_{h \in H} r^h$, where the inequality holds coordinatewise. We assume preferences fulfill weak monotonicity (C.IV), continuity (C.V), and strict convexity (C.VII).

13.2 The core of a pure exchange economy

The primitive concepts for bargaining in the core are ownership and preferences. Each household (trader) owns its endowment and can dispose of it at will. Consider the entire set of feasible allocations. Any one of them can be proposed as a possible allocation for the economy. The concept of bargaining that defines the core is that groups of households (known as coalitions) form to see how satisfactory an allocation they can achieve by trading their endowment among themselves. If any trader or group of traders, a coalition, can achieve an allocation on its own that it prefers to one proposed, the coalition will withdraw from the proposed allocation and trade on its own. The strategic threat available to any coalition is to withdraw from a proposed allocation. The threat is credible when the withdrawal will allow it to move to an alternative allocation that according to its preferences is superior for its members. The idea of bargaining here is that any proposed allocation must pass the test of whether a coalition can improve its own situation by withdrawing from the proposed allocation. If so, then the allocation will not be sustained in the core. It will be *blocked*. If not, then the proposal remains. With $\#H$ households, there are $2^{\#H}$ possible coalitions, so this becomes quite an exacting test in a large economy. We now formalize this notion of bargaining.

Definition *A **coalition** is any subset $S \subseteq H$. Note that every individual comprises a (singleton) coalition.*

Definition *An allocation $\{x^h, h \in H\}$ is **blocked** if there is a coalition $S \subseteq H$ and an assignment $\{y^h, h \in S\}$ so that:*

(i) $\sum_{h \in S} y^h \leq \sum_{h \in S} r^h$ *(where the inequality holds coordinatewise),*
(ii) $y^h \succsim_h x^h$,   *for all $h \in S$, and*
(iii) $y^{h'} \succ_{h'} x^{h'}$,   *for some $h' \in S$*

The idea of **blocking** is that a coalition S blocks a proposed allocation x^h if, using only the resources available to S, it can achieve an allocation to the members of S that is a Pareto improvement over x^h for the members of S. When the coalition S considers blocking, it considers only its own resources and tastes. S takes no account of the situation of the remaining traders, $H \setminus S$.

Definition *The **core** of the economy is the set of feasible allocations that are not blocked by any coalition $S \subseteq H$.*

The core is a generalization of Edgeworth's concept of the contract curve. The definition of the core tells us a fair amount about core allocations:

- Any allocation in the core must be individually rational. That is, if $\{x^h, h \in H\}$ is a core allocation then we must have $x^h \succsim_h r^h$, for all $h \in H$. If not, then the proposed core allocation would be blocked by a single-member coalition (singleton) for whom x^h was inferior to endowment. That is, the proposed allocation was not individually rational.
- Any allocation in the core must be Pareto efficient. This follows since if $\{x_h, h \in H\}$ were not Pareto efficient, the coalition of all agents could improve upon the allocation merely by redistributing consumption. That is, if $\{x^h, h \in H\}$ is a core allocation then we must have that for all alternative feasible assignments y^h, $x^h \succsim_h y^h$, for all $h \in H$ or $x^h \succ_h y^h$ for some $h \in H$. This holds for all alternative feasible assignments $\{y^h, h \in H\}$. If not, then the proposed core allocation would be blocked by a coalition $S = H$, consisting of all of the traders.

Merely defining the core does not mean that it is an interesting concept. For example, the set of core allocations could be empty. If that happened then there would be very little to discuss. However, this is happily not the case. We can show several results:

(i) The competitive equilibrium is always in the core (Theorem 13.1). The conditions under which the competitive equilibrium exists are well developed (Theorems 7.1, 11.1, and 17.7 applied to a pure exchange economy). Hence, whenever the conditions for those theorems are fulfilled (principally continuity and convexity of preferences), we can be sure that the core is nonempty.

Most interesting is the behavior of the core for economies where the number of traders is large. This model will be developed in Chapter 14. The principal result there (Theorem 14.2) is that

(ii) For a large economy, the set of competitive equilibria and the core are virtually identical. All core allocations are (nearly) competitive equilibria. Hence our two concepts of competition coincide for a large economy. Price-taking behavior in equilibrium is the natural outcome of the bargaining process in a large economy.

13.3 The competitive equilibrium allocation is in the core

We will now state and prove the principal result of this chapter: inclusion of the competitive equilibrium in the core. It is useful to restate the definition of competitive equilibrium for this pure exchange economy.

Definition $p \in \mathbf{R}_+^N$, $x^h \in \mathbf{R}_+^N$, *for each* $h \in H$, *constitutes a competitive equilibrium if*

(i) $p \cdot x^h \leq p \cdot r^h$, *for each* $h \in H$,

(ii) $x^h \succsim_h y$, *for all* $y \in R_+^N$, *such that* $p \cdot y \leq p \cdot r^h$, *and*

(iii) $\sum_{h \in H} x^h \leq \sum_{h \in H} r^h$ *(the inequality holds coordinatewise) with* $p_k = 0$ *for any* $k = 1, 2, \ldots, N$ *so that the strict inequality holds.*

Theorem 13.1 here states that any competitive equilibrium (if it exists) is included in the core. In proving the theorem we use the same logic that we used in proving the First Fundamental Theorem of Welfare Economics. Starting from a competitive equilibrium allocation, along with its price vector, we note that any preferable allocation must be more expensive evaluated at equilibrium prices than the competitive allocation. This leads to a contradiction.

Theorem 13.1 *Let the economy fulfill C.IV and C.V. Let* p, x^h, $h \in H$, *be a competitive equilibrium. Then* $\{x^h, h \in H\}$ *is in the core of the economy.*

Proof We will present a proof by contradiction. Suppose the theorem were false. Then there would be a blocking coalition $S \subseteq H$ and a blocking assignment y^h, $h \in S$. We have

$$\sum_{h \in S} y^h \leq \sum_{h \in S} r^h \quad \text{(attainability, the inequality holds coordinatewise)}$$

$$y^h \succsim_h x^h, \qquad \text{for all } h \in S, \text{ and}$$

$$y^{h'} \succ_{h'} x^{h'}, \qquad \text{some } h' \in S.$$

But x^h is a competitive equilibrium allocation. That is, for all $h \in H$, $p \cdot x^h = p \cdot r^h$, and $x^h \succsim_h y$, for all $y \in R_+^N$ such that $p \cdot y \leq p \cdot r^h$.

Note that $\sum_{h \in S} p \cdot x^h = \sum_{h \in S} p \cdot r^h$. Then for all $h \in S$, $p \cdot y^h \geq p \cdot r^h$. That is, x^h represents h's most desirable consumption subject to budget constraint. y^h is at least as good under preferences $\succsim_h$ fulfilling monotonicity (C.IV). Therefore, y^h

must be at least as expensive. Furthermore, for h', we must have $p \cdot y^{h'} > p \cdot r^{h'}$. Therefore, we have

$$\sum_{h \in S} p \cdot y^h > \sum_{h \in S} p \cdot r^h.$$

Note that this is a strict inequality. However, for coalitional feasibility we must have

$$\sum_{h \in S} y^h \leq \sum_{h \in S} r^h.$$

But since $p \geq 0$, $p \neq 0$, we have $\sum_{h \in S} p \cdot y^h \leq \sum_{h \in S} p \cdot r^h$. This is a contradiction. The allocation $\{y^h, h \in S\}$ cannot simultaneously be smaller or equal to the sum of endowments r^h coordinatewise and be more expensive at prices p. The contradiction proves the theorem. **QED**

13.4 Bibliographic note

The notion of rational bargaining solutions and their relation to competitive equilibrium goes back at least to Edgeworth's (1881) pioneering work. The core concept is attributed to Gillies (1953) and its application in economics begins with Shubik (1959). The treatment of the core of a market economy here parallels that of Debreu and Scarf (1963).

Exercise

13.1 Consider a two-person (1 and 2) two-commodity (x and y) economy. Both households have the utility function $u(x, y) = (x + 1)^{1/2}(y + 1)^{1/2}$. Let $r^1 = (99, 0)$ and $r^2 = (0, 99)$. Describe the core of this economy.

14

Convergence of the core of a large economy

14.1 Replication; a large economy

There is a long-standing tradition in economic theory emphasizing the importance of large ("thick") markets in maintaining competition. The underlying idea is that if the number of agents in the market is large enough then no single agent can have monopoly power. Consequently, a competitive price-taking equilibrium will be maintained. Our task in this chapter is to present a rigorous statement and proof of this result in the model of the core of a market economy. We will show that in a large economy, the core allocations are nearly identical to the competitive equilibrium allocation. That is, in a large economy, there is virtually no incremental return to the monopolistic strategic behavior associated with coalition formation (the strategic behavior assumed in the core). Hence in a large economy, there is no point in behaving strategically. The best an agent can do is to follow price-taking competitive behavior. This result is actually quite general in models where no single trader is large relative to the size of the market. The version of the theorem we will present here depends on the idealization that the economy becomes large (and hence each trader becomes strategically negligible) through successive replication of the set of traders. The economy keeps cloning itself. As the growth goes from duplicate to triplicate, ..., to Q-tuplicate, and so on, the set of core allocations keeps getting smaller, although it always includes the set of competitive equilibria (per Theorem 13.1). We will show that it eventually shrinks to the point where only the competitive equilibria are left. This is the core convergence result. In a large economy, the core converges to the competitive equilibrium. This treatment, allowing the economy to become large through replication, is the simplest version of the theorem to prove, and that is why we present it here. Alternative treatments include using more complicated techniques to let the economy become large without requiring replication. Alternatively, more advanced mathematical techniques (nonatomic measure theory) can be used to treat economies that start out with infinitely many agents rather than approach the large size as a limit.

162

We will treat a Q-fold replica economy, denoted Q-H. Q will be a positive integer; $Q = 1, 2, \ldots$. In a Q-fold replica economy we take an economy consisting of households $h \in H$, with endowments r^h and preferences $\succsim_h$, and create a similar larger economy with Q times as many agents in it, totaling $\#H \times Q$ agents. There will be Q agents with preferences $\succsim_1$ and endowment r^1, Q agents with preferences $\succsim_2$ and endowment $r^2, \ldots,$ and Q agents with preferences $\succsim_{\#H}$ and endowment $r^{\#H}$. Each household $h \in H$ now corresponds to a household *type*. There are Q individual households of type h in the replica economy Q-H. Note that the competitive equilibrium prices in the original H economy will be equilibrium prices of the Q-H economy. Household h's competitive equilibrium allocation x^h in the original H economy will be a competitive equilibrium allocation to all type h households in the Q-H replica economy. Agents in the Q-H replica economy will be denoted by their type and a serial number. Thus, the agent denoted h, q will be the qth agent of type h, for each $h \in H, q = 1, 2, \ldots, Q$.

14.2 Equal treatment

We will now prove a very useful technical result, the equal treatment property. The power of the replication approach is that it simplifies the idea of a large economy. There will be Q agents of type h, for each $h \in H$. We can show that for each h, all Q of them are treated identically so that we do not need to consider the allocation to any individual but rather need to analyze only the allocation to his type. This is particularly straightforward to demonstrate if we assume strict convexity of preferences (C.VII). Denote the allocation (in $\mathbf{R}_+^N$) to the agent h, q as $x^{h,q}$.

Theorem 14.1 (Equal treatment in the core) *Assume C.IV, C.V, and C.VII. Let $\{x^{h,q}, h \in H, q = 1, \ldots, Q\}$ be in the core of Q-H, the Q-fold replica of economy H. Then for each h, $x^{h,q}$ is the same for all q. That is, $x^{h,q} = x^{h,q'}$ for each $h \in H, q \neq q'$.*

The proof of Theorem 14.1 will be by contradiction. The strategy of proof is to note that if the theorem fails there will be individuals of a single type who have differing consumptions and then to show that this will allow construction of a blocking coalition. If, contrary to the theorem, consumptions differ within type, then for each type of household we can identify one individual who, according to the preferences of that type, has the least desirable allocation (there may be a tie). We then form a coalition consisting of one member of each type, the member with the least desirable core allocation. We then show that this coalition of the least well-off can achieve with their own endowments a better (strictly better for some types, no worse for others) allocation to each trader than the proposed core allocation. This constitutes a blocking coalition to the proposed core allocation, and hence a contradiction. What allocation can they achieve? For each type h, we will show that the coalition of the worst off can achieve the average type h core allocation. Thus, each member of this coalition moves from being the worst off of its type to being average – a definite improvement and one we will demonstrate to be attainable.

Proof of Theorem 14.1 Recall that the core allocation must be feasible. That is,

$$\sum_{h \in H} \sum_{q=1}^{Q} x^{h,q} = \sum_{h \in H} \sum_{q=1}^{Q} r^h.$$

Equivalently,

$$\frac{1}{Q} \sum_{h \in H} \sum_{q=1}^{Q} x^{h,q} = \sum_{h \in H} r^h.$$

Suppose the theorem to be false. Consider a type h so that $x^{h,q} \neq x^{h,q'}$. First we note that for type h, these consumptions have different utility levels, that is, either $x^{h,q} \succ_h x^{h,q'}$ or $x^{h,q'} \succ_h x^{h,q}$. This follows from Pareto efficiency of the core combined with strict convexity of preferences. If $x^{h,q} \sim_h x^{h,q'}$ (that is, if $x^{h,q}$ and $x^{h,q'}$ were indifferent to one another) then by strict convexity of preferences (C.VII) we have that $[(x^{h,q} + x^{h,q'})/2] \succ_h x^{h,q} \sim_h x^{h,q'}$. This would mean that the allocation $\{x^{h,q}, h \in H, q = 1, \ldots, Q\}$ was not Pareto efficient and hence not in the core. The contradiction shows that we must have $x^{h,q} \succ_h x^{h,q'}$ or $x^{h,q'} \succ_h x^{h,q}$. Hence, for each type h, we can rank the consumptions attributed to type h according to $\succsim_h$.

For each h, let x^{h^*} denote the least preferred of the core allocations to type h, $x^{h,q}, q = 1, \ldots, Q$. For some types h, all individuals of the type will have the same consumption and x^{h^*} will be this expression. For those in which the consumption differs, x^{h^*} will be the least desirable of the consumptions of the type. We now form a coalition consisting of one member of each type: the individual from each type carrying the worst core allocation, x^{h^*}. The strategy of proof is to show that this coalition blocks the proposed core allocation and hence to demonstrate that the proposed allocation cannot truly be in the core.

Consider the average core allocation to type h, to be denoted $\bar{x}^h$. $\bar{x}^h = \frac{1}{Q} \sum_{q=1}^{Q} x^{h,q}$. We have, by strict convexity of preferences (C.VII),

$$\bar{x}^h = \frac{1}{Q} \sum_{q=1}^{Q} x^{h,q} \succ_h x^{h^*} \text{ for those types } h \text{ so that } x^{h,q} \text{ are not identical,}$$

and

$$x^{h,q} = \bar{x}^h = \frac{1}{Q}\sum_{q=1}^{Q} x^{h,q} \sim_h x^{h^*} \text{ for those types } h \text{ so that } x^{h,q} \text{ are identical.}$$

From feasibility, above, we have that

$$\sum_{h \in H} \bar{x}^h = \sum_{h \in H} \frac{1}{Q}\sum_{q=1}^{Q} x^{h,q} = \frac{1}{Q}\sum_{h \in H}\sum_{q=1}^{Q} x^{h,q} = \sum_{h \in H} r^h.$$

In other words, a coalition composed of one of each type (the worst off of each) can achieve the allocation $\bar{x}^h$. However, for each agent in the coalition, $\bar{x}^h \succsim_h x^{h^*}$ for all h and $\bar{x}^h \succ_h x^{h^*}$ for some h. Therefore, the coalition of the worst off individual of each type blocks the allocation $x^{h,q}$. The contradiction proves the theorem. QED

The equal treatment property, Theorem 14.1, greatly simplifies the notation characterizing core allocations as the economy grows. Since the allocation within type is identical in the core, we can characterize the core by the allocation attributed to each type. $\text{Core}(Q) = \{x^h, h \in H\}$ where $x^{h,q} = x^h, q = 1, 2, \ldots, Q$, and the allocation $x^{h,q}$ is unblocked.

14.3 Core convergence in a large economy

The next result, Theorem 14.2, is the principal result in the study of the core. We will show that as the economy becomes large through an increasing number of replications, the core shrinks[1] until it converges to the set of competitive equilibria. Thus, in a large economy, the core outcomes (based on strategic behavior) are equivalent to the price-taking (nonstrategic) solutions. The mathematical foundation of this result, given by the Bounding Hyperplane Theorem, is that a convex set is supported by a hyperplane. The normal to the hyperplane will serve as the supporting price vector for the equilibrium.

Why does the core shrink as the economy becomes large? The individual agents are indivisible. Increasing the size of the economy through replication overcomes the indivisibility, allowing coalitions to form with arbitrary proportional composition of types. In a small economy ($Q = 1$), each individual agent is unique and has some bargaining power. As the economy becomes large ($Q = 2, 3, 4, \ldots$), no individual is unique. The presence of many others reduces any one individual's

---

[1] In most examples, the set of core allocations really does shrink, becoming much smaller as the number of agents increases. There are examples, however, in which little or no shrinkage occurs; these will typically be examples in which the core of a small economy is equivalent to the set of competitive equilibria, so it has no room to contract further.

bargaining power. The large number of replications helps to overcome the indivisibility of the agents. The logic of the shrinking core is simple: As Q grows there
are more blocking coalitions, and they are more varied. Any coalition that blocks
an allocation in Q-H still blocks the allocation in $(Q + 1)$-H, but there are new
blocking coalitions and allocations newly blocked in $(Q + 1)$-H.

Recall the Bounding Hyperplane Theorem:

Theorem 2.11, Bounding Hyperplane Theorem (Minkowski) *Let K be convex,
$K \subseteq \mathbf{R}^N$. There is a hyperplane H through z and bounding for K if z is not interior
to K. That is, there is $p \in \mathbf{R}^N$, $p \neq 0$, so that for each $x \in K$, $p \cdot x \geq p \cdot z$.*

To avoid the usual difficulties of possible discontinuity at the boundary with minimal
income we will assume strong sufficient conditions to assure that the core allocation
is bounded away from positions of minimal imputed income. We introduce

(C.IX) $r^h \in interior\ (X^h)$, for all $h \in H$. If $X^h = \mathbf{R}^N_+$, then $r^h \gg 0\ (r^h_k > 0$, for
      all $k = 1, 2, 3, \ldots, N)$.

Theorem 2.14 (Debreu-Scarf) *Assume C.IV, C.V, C.VII, and CIX. Let
$\{x^{oh}, h \in H\} \in core(Q)$ for all $Q = 1, 2, 3, 4, \ldots$. Then $\{x^{oh}, h \in H\}$ is a
competitive equilibrium allocation for Q-H, for all Q.*

Proof We must show that there is a price vector p so that for each household type
h, $p \cdot x^{oh} \leq p \cdot r^h$ and that x^{oh} optimizes preferences $\succsim_h$ subject to this budget.
The strategy of proof is to create a set of net trades preferred to those that achieve
$\{x^{oh}, h \in H\}$. We will show that it is a convex set with a supporting hyperplane.
The normal to the supporting hyperplane will be designated p. We will then argue
that p is a competitive equilibrium price vector supporting $\{x^{oh}, h \in H\}$.

For each $i \in H$, let $\Gamma^i = \{z \mid z \in \mathbf{R}^N, z + r^i \succ_i x^{oi}\}$. What is this set
of vectors Γ^i? Γ^i is defined as the set of net trades from endowment r^i so that
an agent of type i strictly prefers these net trades to the trade $x^{oi} - r^i$, the trade
that gives him the core allocation. We now define the convex hull (set of convex
combinations) of the family of sets $\Gamma^i, i \in H$. Let $\Gamma = \{\sum_{i \in H} a_i z^i \mid z^i \in \Gamma^i,
a_i \geq 0, \sum a_i = 1\}$, the set of convex combinations of preferred net trades. The
set Γ is the convex hull of the union of the sets Γ^i. (See Figure 14.1.) Note that
$(x^{oh} - r^h) \in boundary(\Gamma^h)$, $(x^{oh} - r^h) \in \overline{\Gamma}^h$, and $(x^{oh} - r^h) \in boundary(\Gamma)$ for
all h.

The strategy of proof now is to show that Γ and the constituent sets Γ^i are arrayed
strictly above a hyperplane through the origin. The normal to the hyperplane will
be the proposed equilibrium price vector.

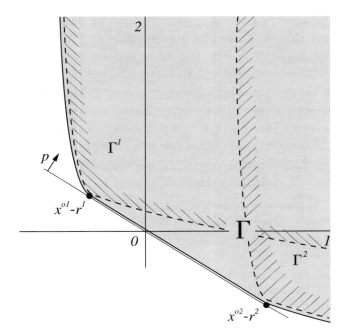

Fig. 14.1. Core convergence (Theorem 14.2).

We wish to show that $0 \notin \Gamma$. We will show that the possibility that $0 \in \Gamma$ corresponds to the possibility of forming a blocking coalition against the core allocation x^{oi}, a contradiction. Suppose that $0 \in \Gamma$. By C.V (continuity of preferences), Γ^i is open for each i, so Γ is open as well (We ignore for convenience regions where Γ^i may coincide with a boundary derived from X^i). If $0 \in \Gamma$, then there is an ε-neighborhood about 0 ($\varepsilon > 0$) contained in Γ. The typical element of Γ can be represented as $\sum a_i z^i$, where $z^i \in \Gamma^i$. Let $\mathbf{R}^N_-$ denote the nonpositive quadrant of $\mathbf{R}^N$. Take the intersection $\Gamma \cap \mathbf{R}^N_-$, that is, the nonpositive quadrant of Γ. Choose $z \in \Gamma \cap \mathbf{R}^N_-$ so that $z = \sum a_i z^i$ with a_i rational for all i. This is possible since $\varepsilon > 0$ and any real a_i can be approximated arbitrarily closely by a sequence of rationals. Find a common denominator for the a_i. Consider Q equal to the common denominator of the a_i (this is how replication with large Q overcomes the indivisibility of the individual agents). We have $\sum a_i z^i \leq 0$ (coordinatewise). We wish to show that this implies the presence of a blocking coalition against the allocation x^{oi} in H-Q, where Q is the common denominator of the a_i. Form the coalition S, consisting of Qa_i (an integer) of type i agents, $i \in H$. Consider the allocation $x'^i = r^i + z^i$ to agents in S. Note that $x'^i \succ_i x^{oi}$ (by definition of Γ^i). We have $\sum a_i z^i \leq 0$. Thus $\sum (Qa_i) z^i \leq 0$. But then we have $\sum (Qa_i)(x'^i - r^i) \leq 0$ or, equivalently, $\sum (Qa_i) x'^i \leq \sum (Qa_i) r^i$, which means x'^i is attainable by S. But x'^i improves upon x^{oi} according to the preferences of $i \in S$. Thus S blocks x^{oi}, which is a contradiction. Hence, as claimed, $0 \notin \Gamma$.

Having established that 0 is not an element of Γ, we should recognize that 0 is nevertheless very close to Γ. Indeed $0 \in$ boundary of Γ. This occurs inasmuch as $0 = (1/\#H) \sum_{h \in H} (x^{oh} - r^h)$, and the right-hand side of this expression is an element of $\overline{\Gamma}$, the closure of Γ. Thus 0 represents just the sort of boundary point through which a supporting hyperplane may go in the Bounding Hyperplane Theorem. The set Γ is trivially convex. Hence we can invoke the Bounding Hyperplane Theorem. There is $p \in \mathbf{R}^N$, $p \neq 0$, so that for all $v \in \Gamma$, $p \cdot v \geq p \cdot 0 = 0$. Noting C.IV (monotonicity), we know that $p \geq 0$. Now $(x^{oh} - r^h) \in \overline{\Gamma}$ for each h, so $p \cdot (x^{oh} - r^h) \geq 0$. But $\sum_{h \in H} (x^{oh} - r^h) = 0$, so $p \cdot \sum_{h \in H} (x^{oh} - r^h) = 0$. Hence $p \cdot (x^{oh} - r^h) = 0$ each h. Equivalently, $p \cdot x^{oh} = p \cdot r^h$. This gives us

$$p \cdot 0 = p \cdot \sum_{h \in H} \frac{1}{\#H} (x^{oh} - r^h) = \inf_{x \in \Gamma} p \cdot x = \sum_{h \in H} \frac{1}{\#H} \left[\inf_{z^h \in \Gamma^h} p \cdot z^h \right],$$

so

$$p \cdot (x^{oh} - r^h) = \inf_{z^h \in \Gamma^h} p \cdot z^h.$$

We have then for each h, that $p \cdot (x^{oh} - r^h) = \inf p \cdot y$ for $y \in \Gamma^h$. Equivalently, x^{oh} minimizes $p \cdot (x - r^h)$ subject to $x \succsim_h x^{oh}$. In addition, $p \cdot x^{oh} = p \cdot r^h$. Further, by C.IX, there is an ε-neighborhood of x^{oh} contained in X^h. By C.IV, C.V, and C.IX, expenditure minimization subject to a utility constraint is equivalent to utility maximization subject to budget constraint. Hence $x^{oh}, h \in H$, is a competitive equilibrium allocation.   QED

The method of proof here is to allow replication to overcome the indivisibility of the individual households. This shows up as we take a common denominator on the fractions a_i. The common denominator represents the number of replications needed to achieve the proportion a_i of type i, for all $i \in H$, in the economy. Because the rationals are dense in the reals, any irrational proportion can be achieved arbitrarily closely by a sufficiently large number of replications.

14.4 Interpreting the core convergence result

The principal interpretation of the core convergence result is to confirm the idea that large economies are competitive. Price-taking behavior is a good model of rational behavior in a large economy. The convergence result shows that, in a large economy, bargaining will not improve upon the competitive equilibrium. Any advantage one coalition can achieve by banding together for strategic trade will be lost as another coalition blocks the new allocation.

We can interpret the coalitions of the core convergence story as monopolies, or attempts to form monopoly cartels. It is a misinterpretation of the result to say that in a large economy monopolies don't matter. They matter terribly if they are allowed to persist. The result is that monopolies cannot persist in a regime of freely forming counter-cartels; freely forming cartels and counter-cartels give rise to the core. The process of bargaining in the core lets individual agents outside the attempted monopoly form countervailing coalitions with members of the monopoly cartel. They thus try to dilute the monopoly profits by inducing individual members of the cartel to defect. The result in the core is that the cartel is broken and a near-competitive core allocation is reestablished. Note that this scenario supposes that individual members of a proposed cartel can bargain freely to improve their individual situations by making side deals (or threatening to do so) with agents outside the cartel. In actual economies, cartels recognize this problem and strictly enforce rules against side deals.

An essential element of the bargaining process in the core model is the ease of forming countervailing coalitions. The model takes no account of the difficulty of forming coalitions and hence has nothing to say about differences in the ease with which coalitions may form. In actual economies, of course, forming a coalition (making a deal) is a resource-using process in itself and there are differences among (potential) coalitions in the costs of coalition formation. Adam Smith (1776) warned us that any meeting of the members of a particular business could result in a (monopolistic) agreement contrary to the interests of the general public. In the core model this remains true, but it is countered by the possible meeting of any member of that business with members of the general public to form an agreement contrary to the interests of the business group. Which of these coalitions seems more likely to form? In a model where coalition formation is costless, as above, they will both form effortlessly to move the economy to the core allocation. In a model where coalition formation is costly, we may guess that forming a coalition of members of the same business is an easier operation than one that mixes business and public members. Hence we see the power of Smith's prediction.

14.5 Bibliographic note

The treatment of core convergence here follows that of Debreu and Scarf (1963). They introduce the powerful simplification of replica economies. Cornwall (1979) provides an excellent expository treatment. A more general treatment, allowing the economy to become large without replication but with some uniformity requirement on the addition of households, relies on the Shapley-Folkman theorem (introduced in Starr (1969)). That treatment is presented in Arrow and Hahn (1972) and Anderson (1978). An excellent elucidation of this more general treatment appears in Ichiishi (1983).

Exercises

14.1   Consider core convergence in a pure exchange economy with two goods, (x, y), two household types, and (integer) Q of each type.
Type 1: endowment $(99, 1)$
   utility function $u^1(x, y) = x^{(1/2)} y^{(1/2)}$
Type 2: endowment $(1, 99)$
   utility function $u^2(x, y) = x^{(1/2)} y^{(1/2)}$
(a) Consider the allocation
    type 1: $(10, 10)$
    type 2: $(90, 90)$.
    Show that this allocation is in the core for $Q = 1$.
(b) Show that the allocation in part a is blocked for $Q = 2$. Discuss.
(c) Find an allocation in the core for arbitrarily large Q. Explain.

14.2   Consider a pure exchange economy composed of households in the set H, where the economy becomes large through Q-fold replication.
(a) Let p^0 be an equilibrium price vector for the original economy. Show that p^0 is also an equilibrium price vector for the (larger) economy replicated Q times.

   Now consider the special case where there are two commodities, x and y, and two trader types. Type 1 is characterized as

$$u^1(x, y) = x \cdot y$$
$$r^1 = (10, 0).$$

Type 2 is characterized as

$$u^2(x, y) = x^{1/2} y^{1/2}$$
$$r^2 = (0, 10).$$

(b) Show that the following allocation, a^1 to type 1 and a^2 to type 2, is in the core for all levels of replication Q:

$$a^1 = a^2 = (5, 5)$$

(c) Show that the following allocation, a^1 to type 1 and a^2 to type 2, is in the core for the original economy with one of each type and is not in the core for a replica economy with $Q \geq 2$:

$$a^1 = (9, 9); a^2 = (1, 1).$$

Discuss.

14.3   (with acknowledgment to Richard Cornwall). Four examples are given
       below of a pure exchange economy and of a proposed allocation for this
       economy. For each, show whether or not the proposed allocation is:
       (i) Pareto efficient,
       (ii) in the core,
       (iii) obtainable as a competitive equilibrium with respect to some price
            vector. In each example, explain your reasoning for each of (i), (ii),
            and (iii).

Example 14.1 This example has two goods denoted a and b and four
traders, each having the same utility function

$$u(a, b) = ab.$$

The endowment vectors are:

$$r^1 = r^2 = (10, 10)$$

and

$$r^3 = r^4 = (10, 30).$$

In this example, allocation is

$$x^1 = x^2 = (7.5, 15)$$

and

$$x^3 = x^4 = (12.5, 25).$$

Example 14.2 This example is the same as Example 1 except that the
allocation is

$$x^1 = x^2 = \left(\sqrt{50}, 2\sqrt{50}\right)$$

and

$$x^3 = x^4 = \left(20 - \sqrt{50}, 40 - 2\sqrt{50}\right).$$

Example 14.3 This example is the same as Example 1 except that the
allocation is

$$x^1 = \left(\sqrt{50}, 2\sqrt{50}\right), x^2 = (7.5, 15)$$

and

$$x^3 = x^4 = (12.5, 25).$$

Example 14.4 This example is the same as Example 1 except that the allocation is

$$x^1 = (8, 12), x^2 = (9, 11)$$

and

$$x^3 = (12, 23), x^4 = (11, 29).$$

14.4   Consider a sequence of pure exchange economies. Each economy has an equal number of traders of the following types:

	Type 1	Type 2
Utility function	$u^1(x, y) = x^{1/2}y^{1/2}$	$u^2(x, y) = x^{1/2}y^{1/2}$
Endowment	$r^1 = (0, 5)$	$r^2 = (5, 0)$

Economy E-1 consists of one trader of each type; economy E-2 consists of two traders of each type. Economy E-K consists of K traders of each type.

(a) Find the core of E-1.

(b) Show that the allocation $a^1 = (1, 1), a^2 = (4, 4)$ is in the core of E-1.

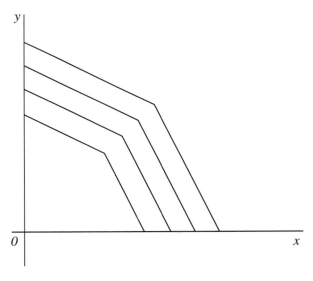

Fig. 14.2. Nonconvex preferences (Exercise 14.5).

(c) Show that the allocation in which both traders of type 1 get a^1 and both traders of type 2 get a^2 is *not* in the core of E-2.

(d) Find an allocation that is in the core of E-K for all K. Explain.

14.5 Consider the core of a pure exchange economy composed of three identical agents, 1, 2, 3. There are two goods, x and y. For each of the agents $i = 1, 2, 3$, i's utility function is

$$u^i(x^i, y^i) = x^i + y^i + \max[x^i, y^i],$$

where x^i and y^i are i's consumption of x and y, respectively. This utility function results in an indifference map that looks like Figure 14.2. The preferences are nonconvex, violating C.VII.

Let each agent's endowment be $e^i = (2, 2)$, two units of x and y each. Assume the equal treatment property:

(E) at any core allocation, all agents i have equal utility.

Demonstrate the following points:

(a) At any Pareto efficient allocation, at most one agent will have positive holdings of both goods.

(b) The core is empty.

Part F

The scope of markets

The models above can be interpreted to treat allocation over time and under uncertainty. In order to do so the space of commodities traded needs to be interpreted to include intertemporal trade and trade in insurance or event-contingent goods. These are the notions of futures markets and contingent commodity markets. The concept of complete markets available over time and uncertainty is sometimes described as "a full set of Arrow-Debreu futures markets."

15

Time and uncertainty: Futures markets

15.1 Introduction

We have already demonstrated the existence and efficiency of general equilibrium in an economy of N goods with active markets for trading them. But what are these N goods? The answer is that they could be anything. This generality reflects the distinctive power of mathematical modeling. The model and its interpretation are separate. We have a mathematical model that provides a general family of results based on mathematical relations among the variables. How we label the variables and interpret the results is now up to us. The model could apply to trading mineral samples at annual meetings of an amateur gemologists society. It can apply to the trading and production of a small closed economy. It can apply to trading and production of an entire world economy. In each case, of course, it applies only if the assumptions of the model are fulfilled. What we know in each instance is that if the assumptions of the model are fulfilled then the conclusions follow: There will be market clearing prices that lead to a Pareto efficient allocation. This is true whether the prices and allocations are for rock samples, the goods available in a small economy, or those available throughout the world. We have left until now a more complete discussion of the range of goods to be allocated by the market mechanism.

The simplest economic models take no explicit account of time. Thus, the model of Chapters 3–14 covers a simple one-period model where all allocation is at a single date. Equivalently, it covers a static, steady-state economy with no intertemporal trade.

Is the general equilibrium model timeless then? Does it have nothing to say about allocation over time? On the contrary, it has a great deal to say about time, allocation over time, and the institutions required for a market economy to achieve efficient intertemporal allocation. It says simply:

Make the markets for goods over time look just like those in the general equilibrium model and the same formal results will follow. You'll be able to establish an intertemporal equilibrium and intertemporally efficient allocation. All that remains is to interpret what economic institutions it requires for intertemporal goods allocation to look like the general equilibrium model.

That's actually quite a tall order – one that we undertake in the next section.

The simplest economic models take no explicit account of uncertainty. The general equilibrium model covers a simple economic model where all allocation is in a given certain environment. Is the general equilibrium model then without uncertainty? Does it have nothing to say about allocation under uncertainty? On the contrary, it has a great deal to say about uncertainty, allocation over uncertain events, and the institutions required for a market economy to achieve efficient allocation of goods and risk under uncertainty. It says simply:

Make the markets for goods under uncertainty look just like those in the general equilibrium model and the same formal results will follow. You'll be able to establish an equilibrium for goods across uncertain events and an efficient allocation of risk bearing. All that remains is to interpret what economic institutions it requires for goods allocation under uncertainty to look like suitable goods in the general equilibrium model.

This too is quite a tall order, which we undertake in Section 15.3.

We can outline the character of the economic model's requirements on the space of commodities and firm and household relations to them.

For the market:

- All economically significant scarce resources are traded in the market; goods distinct from one another in production or consumption are distinct coordinates in N-dimensional commodity space.
- There is a single market date at which all supplies and demands are expressed and equated. Budget constraints and firm profits are expressed effective with this date.

For the firm:

- There is a single scalar maximand, profit.
- All economically relevant production possibilities are fully expressed in the firm technology set.

For the household:

- There is a single maximand, $\succsim_i$ or, equivalently, the scalar $u^i(\,\cdot\,)$.
- There is a single scalar budget constraint.

For the economy:

- Firm profits are distributed to households. Walras' Law holds.

Our task now is to see how a model of allocation over time and uncertainty can fulfill this outline.

15.2 Time: Futures markets

We can now reinterpret the model above as a model of allocation and economic activity over time. The way we do that is to reinterpret the concept of commodity. Otherwise identical goods deliverable at different dates are to be different commodities. Since firms and households will make their allocation decisions about commodities, they are also making intertemporal allocation decisions.

The idea of a commodity is a primitive concept in the model developed above. The definition of a commodity is implicit in how the notion of *commodity* enters the model. Two goods are different commodities if they enter separately in the production or consumption decisions of households and firms. If they require different resources to produce them or differ in their consumption desirability, then they are different goods.

In a timeless model with differing geographic locations a commodity is defined:

by *what* it is (its description), and
by *where* it is available (its location).

The same good available in two different locations represents two different commodities. After all, a New York driver is not interested in gasoline available in California, and it is a resource-using process (transportation) to convert a gallon of California gasoline to a gallon of New York gasoline. Hence, for the purposes of the model developed in Chapters 3–14, it is perfectly reasonable to interpret deliverable location as a defining characteristic of a commodity. In a one-period model or a stationary equilibrium model then, we distinguish commodities by their delivery location. The model would then be perfectly consistent with differing equilibrium prices of otherwise identical orange juice deliverable in Florida or in Alaska.

Can we apply this same notion to goods separated by time rather than by distance? There are many examples in actual economies of goods distinguished by delivery date. The most prominent is the organized futures markets such as the Chicago Board of Trade, Chicago Mercantile Exchange, or the New York Commodities Exchange. In these markets there is active trade in grains, metals, fibers, petroleum, and foods, specified by description, quality, place of delivery, and by date of delivery. Contracts for goods otherwise identical in description and location may trade at prices differing substantially by date of delivery. It is a resource-using production activity (storage) to convert goods deliverable at one date into goods deliverable at a succeeding date. Goods deliverable in the distant future may trade at prices far different from those in the present. Prices for future delivery may be lower than current delivery (spot) prices, reflecting the anticipated availability of additional new harvests or other supplies be coming available. Alternatively, current prices for future delivery may be higher, reflecting storage costs. Prices payable currently for future delivery may be lower than for spot delivery, reflecting time discounting. That is, prices are in the nature of present discounted values, discounted from the delivery date back to the market date.

We can take this notion of futures prices and discuss our general equilibrium model where there is a full set of futures markets. A commodity is characterized

by *what* it is (its description),
by *where* it is available (its location), and
by *when* it is available (its date).

There are actively traded goods for all dates: If a good will be available at a particular date in the future, futures contracts for the good deliverable at that date are traded in the market at the market date. The formal mathematical model of production and consumption remains completely unchanged by this change in interpretation. However, to understand the implications of this augmented model of futures markets requires some economic interpretation.

Let's start with N, the number of commodities. We take N to be finite. The number N includes as a separate count every good, at every location where it is deliverable, and at every date at which it is deliverable. N is clearly a large finite number. Assuming N is finite amounts to assuming that there is a finite number of locations at which goods can be delivered and that there is no significant spatial difference within each location. More importantly, assuming N is finite means that in terms of economic time there is an ending date, and so we are using a finite horizon model. The finite horizon may be very far away (e.g., 10,000 years is a finite number), but this artificial construct is unfortunately mathematically essential. We could interpret this as indicating a true determinate predictable end to economic activity. Alternatively, we could interpret the finite horizon as a time so distant that prospects beyond the horizon can have no effect on supply and demand on futures markets meeting in the present.

The trickiest issue involves interpreting the prices of goods, $p \in P$, $p = (p_1, p_2, \ldots, p_N)$. There is only a single meeting of the market. The market mechanism – personified as a Walrasian auctioneer – simultaneously balances supply and demand for all dated goods. Each household has only a single budget constraint, representing receipts and expenditures at all dates from the present to the finite horizon. Firms have only a single calculation of profit, representing the net return on receipts for outputs and expenditures for inputs over all dates from the present to the finite horizon. All receipts and expenditures for spot (current) goods and future deliveries are evaluated at the single market date. Hence we can interpret p_i, the price of commodity i (where the description of commodity i includes i's delivery date), as a present discounted value of commodity i discounted from the delivery date to the market date. This model is usually described as including futures markets for all goods at all future dates.

The convention on payment for futures contracts bought and sold is institutionally a bit different here from those in operation in actual economies. Our model requires payment at the market date, far in advance of delivery. In contrast, at the Chicago Board of Trade, agreements to buy or sell commodities may be undertaken years in advance; full payment is made only at delivery. In the present model, all of the financial elements of economic activity take place at the single market date prior to the rest of economic activity. Costs are incurred, revenues received, accounts debited and credited at the market date, long prior to delivery. This reflects an assumption of full reliability of the agents without possibility of default on the promised deliveries.

How do we interpret the household endowment $r^h \equiv (r_1^h, r_2^h, \ldots, r_N^h)$? The household is endowed with present and future goods. The household typically is endowed with its own labor deliverable in the present and in each of the next several periods, up until the date of its death. In addition the household may own other dated goods. If it owns land, its rights to the use of the land are time dated from the present up until a finite horizon. A similar situation occurs for other real goods with which the household is endowed (we deal with share ownership α^{hj} in a moment).

How can we describe household consumption $x^h \equiv (x_1^h, x_2^h, \ldots, x_N^h)$ in this economy with complete futures markets? Each coordinate in x^h represents dated planned consumption of a particular good. Hence the vector x^h comprises a list at each of the dates in the present and the future of planned consumption at that date. It represents a lifetime consumption plan for household h.

Similarly, firm j's production $y^j \in Y^j$ represents a dated plan for inputs and outputs at a sequence of dates. Thus, seeds, labor, and the use of land in the spring result in a harvest in the fall. Grapes, barrels, and a cellar in 1995 result in good wine in 1996 and excellent wine in 1997. Capital in 1995, 1996, ... combined with labor and intermediate inputs create output in 1995, 1996, ... The set Y^j then represents an array of technically possible plans of mixing dated inputs to produce dated outputs from the present through the finite horizon for firm j. Among the production possibilities, of course, is $0 \in Y^j$, the possibility of not operating firm j actively at all.

Input and output prices are discounted values, discounted to the market date. At prevailing prices $p \in P$, firm j's profit is

$$\pi^j(p) = \max_{y \in Y^j} p \cdot y = p \cdot S^j(p).$$

That is, $\pi^j(p)$ is the sum evaluated at the market date, over all dates from the present through the time horizon of the (present discounted) value of outputs less the (present discounted) value of inputs. Firm j's supply behavior $S^j(p)$ is then characterized as choosing a production plan in the present and for all future dates to maximize the present discounted value of the flows of outputs less inputs of the firm. The profit $\pi^j(p)$ is the value of firm profits discounted to the market date or, equivalently, a present discounted value of the flow of firm profits. Maximizing firm (discounted) profit and maximizing firm (stock market) value are identical.

In actual economies, markets meet at each date, and receipts and expenditures take place at each date. In this model, receipts and expenditures take place only at the market date though delivery of goods takes place throughout time. The presence of the complete futures markets allows all of the receipts and expenditures of the firm representing current and future deliveries to be collapsed into a single number representing the present discounted value of the firm's profits. Hence $\pi^j(p)$ represents the (stock market) value of the firm. The presence of the complete futures market eliminates the distinction between the value of the firm and it's stream of profits by collapsing the future into the single market date. The complete futures market eliminates the stock-flow distinction between income and wealth.

The preferences of household h, $\succsim_h$, represent preferences on time-dated streams of consumption from the present through the future until the horizon. The preferences $\succsim_h$ include h's attitude toward consumption timing (impatience) as well as desires for variety and consistency in consumption over time. Household h's preferences into the distant future are taken to be fully predictable (since this is a subjective certainty model).

The value of endowment and goods prices are discounted values, discounted to the market date. As before, household h's income is characterized as $M^h(p) = p \cdot r^h + \sum_{j \in F} \alpha^{hj} \pi^j(p)$. Its consumption behavior is characterized as before. Household h chooses $x^h \in X^h$ to optimize $\succsim_h$ subject to $p \cdot x^h \leq M^h(p)$. That is, h chooses a consumption plan for the present through the horizon to optimize a planned program of consumption evaluated by h's preferences for consumption across goods and time. It does so subject to the budget constraint that the present discounted value of the consumption plan is bounded above by the present discounted value of endowment plus the value of firm ownership (this latter equals the discounted value of the flow of outputs less inputs from the firms).

Market equilibrium is characterized as prices $p \in P$, a price for each dated good representing a present discounted value, so that all markets clear. That is, for each good at each date the futures market demand for the dated good is equated to the futures market supply with the possibility of free goods in oversupply.

Here is what the economic activity looks like in this model. The market takes place at a time prior to all economic activity. Prices are quoted for all goods at all current and future dates up to a finite horizon. Prices of future goods may be conceived as present values discounted to the market date. At those prices firms formulate a production/supply plan that maximizes the value of the firm. This is equivalent to maximizing the discounted value of the dated stream of firm profits earned through sales and purchases deliverable at the succession of dates. Household budgets are formulated as the value of endowment (equivalently, the discounted value of the dated stream of endowed goods) plus the value of firm ownership, both evaluated at the market date. The household then chooses a consumption plan to satisfy preferences subject to the budget. The value of the consumption plan (discounted value of the dated stream of goods consumption) is constrained by the budget. Equilibrium is characterized as a price vector for the array of goods that equates supply and demand for all dated goods. The household comes to market with a dated endowment stream and delivers the endowment to the market. It leaves the market with contracts for a consumption plan for the present through the horizon. That is the only meeting of the market. Because markets are complete and there is no uncertainty, reopening the market would serve no function – there would be no transactions. The balance of economic activity from the market date to the horizon consists in fulfillment of the contracts undertaken on the futures market. As usual, equilibrium is efficient. There is no reallocation of goods or factors across firms, households, or over time that would create a Pareto-improving reallocation. Household well-being here is judged not at a single point in time but rather over the lifetime up to the horizon, according to household intertemporal preferences.

The notion of a household becomes a bit more complex in this setting since the household is active in the market at the market date and the model extends through a finite horizon. How can we deal with the unborn? The model is of course silent on this, but it gives scope for interpretation. All households are represented in the market. How can we interpret the unborn? Someone who is unborn at date 1 merely means that they have no endowment dated 1 and prefer to avoid consumption until some later date, b, their birthdate. Who represents their preferences at the market? Although the model tells us nothing, it is clear that for the allocation to be an equilibrium and efficient, they will require representation. An alternative interpretation is that though there are individuals unborn at the market date, there are no unborn households. Unborn individuals' interests are represented by their parents or other ancestors. These are admittedly unsatisfactory replies.

The futures markets here perform the functions both of goods markets and of capital markets. Thus the household budget constraint is in the nature of a lifetime budget constraint. The present discounted value of the household lifetime consumption plan is bounded by household wealth, the present discounted value of endowment plus firm ownership (the household's share of the present discounted value of firm profits). In a model without futures markets this value would be comparable to the value of wealth plus the discounted value of future income streams. The complete futures markets eliminate the distinction between income and wealth. The complete futures markets imply a perfect capital market: There is no effective borrowing constraint on current consumption other than eventual ability to repay. There is no effective constraint on firm investment other than the eventual profitability of the business undertaken. All trade takes place prior to consumption or production. Consumption in one period can be financed by delivery of endowment dated before the consumption takes place (corresponding to saving by the household in a model without futures markets) or after the consumption (corresponding to borrowing). Firms finance their purchase of inputs through the sale of outputs. The outputs may be dated later than the inputs. That is precisely the function of capital markets – the forward sale of outputs finances the prior acquisition of productive inputs.

15.2.1 A sequence economy

The futures market model can seem a bit daunting. It requires so many markets to be available and active at the market date. And it requires that all market activity stop after the single active market date. It seems painfully unrealistic.

There is an alternative, one that carries most of the same structure without the requirement of so many active markets at a single date and that allows markets to reopen. That is the model of a sequence economy, which is equivalent to the futures market model.

The sequence economy is characterized in the following way: At each date there are spot markets for active trade in goods deliverable at that date. There are financial markets in debt instruments – borrowing and lending into the future. Firms and households have perfect foresight concerning the prices prevailing in the future. At each date, firms and households buy and sell spot goods. They face a budget constraint at each date: Sales of goods and debt (borrowing) must finance purchases. To the extent that their purchases on the current market exceed their receipts, they borrow. To the extent that their receipts exceed their expenditures, they lend. At the finite horizon they must fulfill a lifetime budget constraint: No one can be a net debtor at the end of the finite horizon. Equilibrium occurs when all markets clear at each date, both spot good markets and the debt markets. With perfect foresight regarding future spot prices, it is easy to show that the sequence economy model is equivalent to the complete futures market model. Foreseen spot market prices (correctly foreseen to be equivalent to the futures market prices) replace futures prices. Debt markets replace futures markets in redistributing purchasing power over time. Essentially, a simple reinterpretation of the futures market model with the addition of debt instruments allows us to model intertemporal allocation without explicitly resorting to futures markets. This certainly appears more realistic. Of course, it relies on the unrealistic assumption of perfect foresight on spot market prices to replace the unrealistic model of complete markets. The sequence economy model with complete debt markets corresponds to the concept of a perfect capital market.

15.3 Uncertainty – Arrow-Debreu contingent commodity markets

Time is not the only complication in designating the commodities of economic activity. There is also uncertainty. Economically important events that we cannot clearly foresee include the weather, our health, and technical change. It is formally possible fully to take account of uncertainty again through a very clever reinterpretation of the model we already have in place.

We have heretofore defined a commodity by description, location, and date. We now go a step further. Uncertainty means that we don't know what's going to happen in the future. But we do know what might happen. Assume that we can make an exhaustive list of all the uncertain events that might take place in the future. We describe this array of possible events by an event tree (see Figure 15.1). At each date there is assumed to be a finite list of events that describes the condition of the economy in terms of all the economically relevant uncertain events that may occur. The path of events in the economy is framed as transit down one of the branches of the event tree. A *state of the world* will be defined by the current condition (in terms of uncertain events) of the economy and the history of past realizations of uncertain events that leads to it.

In Section 15.2, we reinterpreted our basic model to accommodate time by defining the idea of a *commodity* to include specification of a delivery date. We

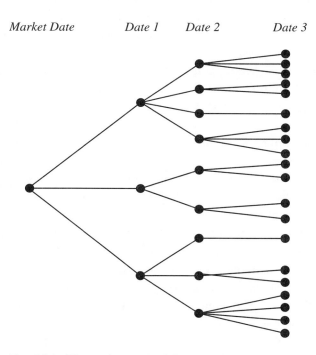

Fig. 15.1. Uncertain states of the world: An event tree.

now perform the same reinterpretation to accommodate uncertainty by defining a commodity to include specification of a state of the world. A commodity is now characterized

by *what* it is (its description),
by *where* it is available (its location),
by *when* it is available (its date), and
by it's *state of the world* (the uncertain event in which it is deliverable).

The number of commodities N has grown again. Again we take N to be finite. That means we are assuming that the number of possible uncertain events is finite at every date (in addition to the previous assumption that the number of time periods is finite).

What is a commodity in this setting? It's not really something you can use or consume. Rather, it is a promise of delivery of a particular good or service at a particular date if an uncertain event actually occurs. The term for that is a *contingent commodity*. This sounds a bit bizarre, but we have all experienced contingent commodities. An HMO (health maintenance organization) medical plan is a contingent commodity (or a bundle of contingent commodities). It is a contingent commodity providing medical care in the uncertain event that you are ill or injured. An auto club membership is also a contingent commodity. It provides towing and emergency repair service in the uncertain event that your car malfunctions. An insurance contract is a closely related concept. Insurance usually provides a payment of money in case a specified uncertain event occurs – that's not precisely the same as a contingent commodity, but it's similar if the payment is chosen to cover the cost of a particular purchase you want to make in the event. We discuss this further in Section 15.4.

The price of good i will not generally be the price of a definite consumption. It is the price of a contingent commodity, the price of a specific good *deliverable if a specified event occurs*.

What is the meaning of y^j, firm j's production plan, in this setting? Prior to the start of economic activity, j's management considers the production possibilities along each branch of the event tree. For a farming enterprise, the production possibilities might look something like this: Inputs of land, labor, and seed in the spring produce an uncertain output. There are three events to deal with: drought, normal rain, and flood. In each event there will be an output, but the quantity will differ by the event. Thus, the production possibilities of j are well specified though uncertain only because of the uncertainty of the weather. Firm j then consults its technology Y^j and the prevailing prices of contingent inputs and outputs. It will choose a plan y^j that specifies the inputs it needs and the outputs it expects in each event and date. It makes a plan for each branch of the event tree – actual events will take it only along one branch of the tree. It may buy inputs and sell outputs along each branch of the tree, wherever the currently prevailing prices make this purchase and sale of contingent commodities profitable. Consequently, most of its planning will never be implemented. Most of the contingent commodities it buys and sells will not be delivered, since the events in which they are deliverable may not take place. The plan is chosen to maximize the value of $p \cdot y$ for y in Y^j. In order to make this choice of profit-maximizing contingent production plan, the firm does not need to forecast which states are more likely nor does it need an attitude toward risk. Its production opportunities are fully specified by Y^j; the profitability of any plan is fully implied by p. Implicit in this formulation is the concept that the firm's supply decisions are default free. Even if the firm (or its managers) believes the probability of an event occurring to be nil, it will sell output in that event only to the extent that it purchases contingent inputs that will allow production of the projected output in the unlikely situation that the event actually takes place.

At prevailing prices $p \in P$, firm j's profit is

$$\pi^j(p) = \max_{y \in Y^j} p \cdot y = p \cdot S^j(p).$$

That is, $\pi^j(p)$ is the sum evaluated at the market date, over all dates and events of the (present discounted) value of contingent outputs less the (present discounted) value of contingent inputs. Firm j's supply behavior $S^j(p)$ is then characterized as choosing a production plan in the present and for all future uncertain events to maximize the present discounted value of the flows of contingent outputs less contingent inputs of the firm. Maximizing firm profit and maximizing firm (stock market) value are identical.

A household h's endowment vector r^h is an N-dimensional vector listing the endowed contingent commodities of the household: 24 hours a day of labor/leisure in the event the household is alive and well, 0 in the event the household is dead, and so forth. As before, household h's income is characterized as $M^h(p) = p \cdot r^h + \sum_{j \in F} \alpha^{hj} \pi^j(p)$. The household sells all its endowment r^h. The endowment consists of contingent commodities, most of which will never actually be delivered (since their events may not take place). Nevertheless, the full endowment of contingent commodities is sold forward and the proceeds enter h's budget.

Household h's consumption vector x^h represents a state-contingent dated list of projected consumptions. Each coordinate in x^h represents a dated contingent consumption of a particular good in its specified state of the world. The vector x^h is a list, at each date and state, of planned consumption at that date/state pair. It represents a lifetime event-contingent consumption plan for household h. The preferences of household h, $\succsim_h$, represent preferences on time-dated, state-contingent commodities from the present through the future until the horizon. Household h

considers the prospect of each possible mix of contingent commodities, and $\succsim_h$ represents h's preferences among them. Since the contingent commodities are not precisely consumptions, it is not precisely accurate to say that $\succsim_h$ represents h's consumption preferences. Rather, $\succsim_h$ represents h's preferences among contingent commodity consumption programs, preferences that reflect the result of h's consumption preferences on actual goods when delivered, h's personal judgments on the likelihood that the individual uncertain events will actually take place, and h's attitude toward risk (unpredictable variation in consumption). Vector x^h represents a portfolio of risky assets. The preference ordering $\succsim_h$ then represents h's preferences among those portfolios.

One way to think of the formulation of $\succsim_h$ is to regard the preference ordering on contingent commodities as representing an expected utility. This is the most easily interpretable formulation. Nevertheless, assuming expected utility optimizing behavior is not necessary to pursue the model. Any transitive continuous preference ordering on portfolios of contingent commodities will do the job. The assumption of convex preferences, C.VI or C.VII, will typically be maintained; that implies risk-averse behavior. A risk lover will concentrate his portfolio on consumption deliverable in a single event – he doesn't want to hedge his bets. However, convex preferences on the portfolio imply that given the choice of two equally desirable portfolios, each with its payoff concentrated in a different single event, the midpoint of the two portfolios will be preferred to either extreme. The midpoint represents hedging – not putting all your eggs in one basket. That's risk aversion.

In this model of contingent commodities, household h's demand behavior is characterized just as before. Household h chooses $x^h \in X^h$ to optimize $\succsim_h$ subject to $p \cdot x^h \leq M^h(p)$. That is, h chooses a state-contingent dated consumption plan for the present through the horizon to optimize the consumption plan evaluated by h's portfolio preferences for contingent commodities subject to a wealth constraint. A portfolio will imply a dated consumption plan across time along each branch of the event tree. Risk takes the form of possible variation in consumption across events. The way for the household to assure a steady consumption is to choose contingent commodities that deliver the same consumption plan independent of events. Alternatively, at the market date, the household can adjust its contingent consumption plans to vary with the market's price differentials. Market prices for each commodity will reflect the differing scarcities of goods across events, household state-varying tastes for the goods (desirability of the good *an umbrella in the rain* will differ from that of *an umbrella in dry weather*), household attitudes toward risk, and household probability judgments on the likelihood of the states of the world. Household h chooses its optimal portfolio subject to the budget constraint. The budget constraint says that the value of the portfolio of contingent commodities chosen is bounded by the value of the contingent commodity endowment plus the value of the household endowment of firm shares (whose value is also determined on the contingent commodity market).

Equilibrium in this contingent commodity economy occurs just as in the certainty economy with futures markets. The market prices all of the contingent commodities. Supplies and demands are announced by firms and consumers. Prices adjust until supply equals demand. Households come to the market with their endowed contingent commodities and sell the endowment. They acquire a portfolio of contingent commodities that represents their most desirable portfolio subject to budget constraint. Payment takes place at the market date. The profits of firms, the value of household endowments, and the value of household budget constraints and of household consumption plans are all computed in terms of the prices of these plans at the contingent commodity prices. The household budget constraint applies at the single market date. All contingent commodities are bought, sold, and paid for at the market date. Payment is made for the contingent commodity contract, not for actual delivery (which may never take place).

Since most of the possible states of the world do not take place, most contingent commodity contracts expire without being executed by delivery. In the absence of any learning or change in subjective probabilities or tastes, there is no need for markets to reopen. If they did reopen there would be no active trade on them. Once the equilibrium is established, remaining economic activity in the economy consists merely in the execution of the contracted plans. At each date households and firms discover the state of the world. They discard as worthless all of their contracts for contingent commodities deliverable in other states at that date and contracts for future delivery in branches of the event tree that they now know will not take place. They then deliver and take delivery on the contracts for the date-state pair that pertains. The balance of economic activity through the horizon consists of fulfilling their previously contracted plans.

The equilibrium allocation of risky assets is Pareto efficient relative to $\succsim_h$, that is, relative to household preferences on contingent commodity portfolios. Given the endowments r^h and available technologies Y^j, there is no attainable reallocation of inputs to firms j or of contingent commodity outputs to households h that would move some household h higher in its ranking of portfolios, $\succsim_h$, without moving some other household h' lower in its ranking of portfolios, $\succsim_{h'}$. This means that the allocation of risk bearing among households is Pareto efficient. There is no rearrangement of the risky assets, the contingent commodities, among households that would be Pareto improving in terms of household portfolio preferences.

We should recognize as well what Pareto efficiency of the allocation of contingent commodities does not mean. The concept of efficiency here takes the probability judgments of households as both exogenous and given. It is perfectly consistent with our concept of efficiency that we could improve the allocation of goods actually delivered by improving household foresight of the future. All the market does is to efficiently implement the allocation of contingent commodities subject to prevailing expectations. Efficiency of the allocation of contingent commodities does not assure us that there will be no regrets. After the state of the world is revealed, many agents will discover that their expectations were mistaken and they will wish that they had arranged their portfolios differently. Indeed, their mistaken expectations may cause a real misallocation of resources. Widely held expectations may raise contingent commodity prices for goods deliverable in an expected event. Those high prices for the expected event then may lead to input reallocations that skew output toward the expected event away from other events. For example, if most households expect flooding then market prices of output deliverable in the event of flooding will be higher (than they would otherwise be) as well. Farms wishing to produce output deliverable in that event to take advantage of the high prices will reallocate planting to forms that will deliver in the event of flooding (e.g., planting on high ground at additional expense of resources). These additional resources will turn out to have been wasted if the flooding does not take place. The markets efficiently allocate resources, consumption, and risk for a given state of expectations of the future. They provide no substitute for foresight.

15.4 Uncertainty – Arrow securities markets

Contingent commodity markets provide in equilibrium for an efficient allocation of risk bearing. Within each date-event pair, they provide an efficient allocation of goods. They do so at potentially great cost either to realism or to the operating costs of the markets, for this model requires a great many markets to be active at the market date, and none to be active thereafter. This model requires that each good be traded at the market date before the start of economic activity in a multitude of different contracts. There will be a different contingent commodity for each good, date, and event combination. Since each node on the event tree constitutes a different event at the date represented, the proliferation of date-event pairs is immense. And the model requires that each good be traded in a separate contract for each such pair! This is an overwhelming proliferation of contingent commodities! The model calls for many more active markets at the market date than we ever see actually in reality – and it calls for far fewer at most dates in real time than we actually see in market economies. How can we escape this bind? Can we retain the essential elements of this model – market allocation of goods and risk – while moving to greater realism, fewer active markets for risky goods, and more active spot markets?

It is possible to restate the model of the contingent commodity general equi-librium in a way that retains all of the results but lets us significantly reduce the number of markets in active use at each date and allows trade to reopen at each date, adding a touch of realism to the model. We define an *Arrow insurance contract* in the following way: Suppose there is a "money" or numeraire in which we can describe a payment of generalized purchasing power. For each date-event pair, t, s, the contract $c(t, s)$ pays one unit of purchasing power if event s occurs at date t and nil otherwise. Then, instead of a full set of contingent commodity markets, we can use a mix of insurance contracts and spot markets (markets for actual goods deliverable in the current period) to achieve the same allocation as available in the contingent commodity equilibrium.

In designating a commodity i, we have not thus far needed to distinguish i by the date or event in which it is deliverable. It is time to do that now. Using a somewhat imprecise notation, let us write $i \in (t, s)$ if good i is deliverable at date t, state s, and of course $i \notin (t, s)$, if not. Now consider the value of h's spending on contingent commodities deliverable in (t, s), $\sum_{i \in (t,s)} p_i x_i^h$. That is the amount at currently prevailing contingent commodity prices that household h spends on the contingent commodity market for goods deliverable at date t, state s. Suppose we then reopen the spot markets for goods in (t, s). Denote the spot price of good $i \in (t, s)$ on the spot market at t as q_i. Finally, let the price of an Arrow insurance contract payable in (t, s) be $\theta_{t,s}$. Let household h buy $S_{t,s}^h$ units of Arrow insurance contract $c(t, s)$, where

$$S_{t,s}^h = \sum_{i \in (t,s)} q_i x_i^h.$$

For $i \in (t, s)$, set $p_i = \theta_{t,s} q_i$. Then the household budget constraint can be restated as $\sum_{t,s} \theta_{t,s} S_{t,s}^h \leq M^h(p) = M^h(\theta, q)$. Here θ and q denote the vectors of $\theta_{t,s} \cdot q_i$. Thus the household budget (and hence the entire household optimization problem) can be restated in terms of the prices of Arrow insurance contracts $\theta_{t,s}$ and the spot prices q_i without any direct reference to the contingent commodity markets or their prices p_i.

A firm's policy in this economy is to formulate its profit-maximizing production plan, just as it did in the full contingent commodity model. The firm needs no attitude toward risk. Like households, it does need to have correct state-contingent price foresight. That is, the firm correctly foresees that if event s occurs at date t, then the price of good i will be p_i. The firm then maximizes its value (the present discounted value of the stream of state-contingent outputs less the cost of inputs it plans) based on its technology and the correctly foreseen state-contingent prices and Arrow securities prices. It announces its planned profits to its shareholders who incorporate the announced values in their budget constraints. In each date-event pair, the firm may have a deficit or surplus of receipts less disbursements attributable to that date-event should it occur. The firm finances its production plan by trading on the Arrow securities markets and distributing profits to shareholders. The value of the firm profits (its stock market valuation entering the owners' budgets) equals the value of its securities sales less its purchases. The demands of price foresight here are significant (and implausible), but so is the reduction in the volume of transactions and corresponding increase in verisimilitude. Indeed, in actual market economies with well-developed financial markets, firm stock market values do indeed enter owners' budget constraints and represent a present discounted value under uncertainty of future profit streams.

What we have just argued is that a family of simple accounting identities can create a formal equivalence between two quite different models. The first (Model I) is the model of the contingent commodity markets:

The market meets once for all time and a very large number of contingent commodities are traded; most do not result in delivery of actual goods.

The second (Model II) is a model of securities markets for securities (Arrow insurance contracts) payable in abstract purchasing power:

The securities market meets once; goods markets reopen at each date for spot trade. Most securities do not result in actual payment.

We claim that Models I and II are equivalent. The key to this equivalence is simply that in Model II spot relative prices for goods in each state should be the same as their relative prices in Model I and that the securities positions assumed by traders in Model II be sufficient at the resultant spot market prices to support their consumption plans from Model I.

What can we conclude? We can replace the full set of contingent commodity markets discussed in Section 15.3 with a much smaller number of markets. Instead of a market for each good deliverable in each date and event, we can use a securities market that distributes purchasing power across dates and events. In those events where a firm is profitable or a household has a large endowment, the model replaces the remuneration for those real goods with the value of securities payable in money for the date-event pair. In each date and event, once the event that actually pertains is clear, spot markets for factors of production and for consumption goods open to distribute the actual goods for consumption and factors to use. Instead of maintaining a full set of contingent commodity markets for all goods deliverable in all events, the only goods markets actually in use are those for events that actually take place. There are active securities (or insurance) markets, one for each possible date-event combination. The capital market function of the contingent commodity markets is fulfilled by the securities markets: To finance activity in one date-event from the anticipated proceeds of another, sell securities from the second and spend the proceeds on securities payable in the first.

To demonstrate this equivalence, firms and households need perfect price foresight for each date-event pair in the future. How else will they know the value of securities to buy and sell? At the market date all of the firms and households must know what the spot market prices q_i are going to be. The N commodity markets do not all need to meet, but the economy needs to use the information that they would generate. However, generating the equilibrium prices is a prime responsibility of the markets. We may argue that this is too much foresight for the model to require; how can market prices be known even before the markets meet? Alternatively, we can argue that the requirements of the model are plausible; households may reasonably be expected to have a good forecast of market prices under well-specified events (for example, they would expect agricultural prices to be higher in the event of bad weather than in good). Further, it is not necessary for all agents to foresee all prices. They need only know the value of firms and of the budgets they need in each date-state. These are summaries, not individual prices. Nevertheless, the notion of perfect price foresight is troubling. It is particularly hard to defend in the case of multiple equilibria, where even the Walrasian auctioneer with full information cannot predict which of several possible equilibria will prevail.

15.5 Conclusion – the missing markets

The use of futures markets, contingent commodity markets, and Arrow insurance markets (with perfect date-state price foresight) allows the market mechanism to overcome the confusion generated by time and uncertainty. Markets can work successfully when there are enough of them. We need a sufficient variety of commodity and financial instruments traded in the market to allow the market allocation mechanism to do its job. Unfortunately, this model appears to require many more active markets than are actually in use in real economies. The financial markets of a modern economy, including stock exchanges, futures exchanges, option exchanges, and the (dealer) market for insurance instruments not sold on exchanges, provide an array of markets for intertemporal allocation and exchange of risk that is rich and complex. Nevertheless, they are sparse compared to the array of possible uncertainties and dates facing economic agents.

The message of this family of models is that a rich enough array of active markets can result in a successful allocation over time and uncertainty. Conversely, one source of allocative failures in actual economies is the absence of a sufficiently large array of future and contingent commodities actively traded. A persistent objection to the class of models is that they require far too many active markets – many more than will be found in an actual economy. The reasons for these mismatches between theory and practice are not to be found in the theory; they reflect issues omitted from the model: the costs of operating markets themselves, and the difficulty or cost of verifying the state of the world.

The major results articulated in Chapters 3–14 for an applied economist or policy maker are a restatement of the laissez-faire doctrine: The market will perform allocation decisions and do it right. The discussion in this chapter points out a strength and a weakness in that message. We have demonstrated the power of that formal result by showing that it persists over time and across uncertainty. We have demonstrated its fragility by showing that it requires many more active markets than actual economies contain. When a laissez-faire advocate insists that the market makes the best allocation decisions, he or she is using the fundamental theorems of welfare economics. The advocate doesn't typically stop to qualify such claims for the market by noting that the proposed economy lacks sufficient insurance markets fully to handle uncertainty or capital markets perfect enough fully to deal with intertemporal allocation.[1]

15.6 Bibliographic note

The brilliantly simple notion of dated commodities first appears in Hicks (1939). The notion of contingent commodities and of Arrow insurance contracts appears in Arrow (1953, 1964) and is well expounded in Debreu (1959).

Exercises

15.1   Consider the economy with a finite time horizon and a nonrenewable natural resource (e.g., coal or oil). In each of the following cases describe the process of decision making with regard to use of the nonrenewable resource and state whether the allocation may be expected to be Pareto efficient. Will the economy run out of coal or oil because of excessively rapid use? Why or why not? Explain.

CASE 1 A full set of futures markets. There are active futures markets for the resource and its products available for delivery at all present and future dates.

CASE 2 No futures markets, perfect foresight, and perfect capital markets. There are no active futures markets but there is perfect price foresight regarding the resource, its outputs, and all other goods. All agents have access to a perfect capital market that allows them to borrow and lend, and spend and save, at common equilibrium interest rates, subject only to a lifetime budget constraint.

---

[1] The bridge between theory and application requires luck and interpretation. All theories in the sciences are abstract, but they give predictions about concrete results. That's true in physics and chemistry as well as in economics. No theory perfectly fits application. The theory is a guide to application. It's a judgment call when the omissions of the theory are sufficiently great and relevant to cause a failure in application.

CASE 3 No futures markets, no active capital markets, perfect price fore-sight. Saving and investment decisions are taken but they are autarkic – households have no access to a market for borrowing and lending.

15.2 Consider an economy in general equilibrium with a full set of Arrow-Debreu contingent commodity markets. Explain how the economy deals with medical insurance. How does it work? Is medical insurance just another contingent commodity? Is there a moral hazard problem (over-spending when the insured event occurs since insurance will cover the bill)? Will every household be insured for every illness or injury?

15.3 Consider a firm planning to start operations in an intertemporal certainty economy with a full set of futures contracts. There are profitable oppor-tunities to produce widgets for supply at $t + 2$; this production requires inputs at t. The firm is inactive prior to t. How does the firm finance its production plan?

15.4 Consider a firm deciding the production and sale of output in an uncertainty economy with a full set of Arrow-Debreu contingent commodity contracts. Let there be two dates, 0 and 1. There is one state in date 0 and three states in date 1 (denoted 1.1, 1.2, and 1.3).

  (i) Describe the decision making of the firm.
  (ii) Explain the trade-off's as the firm chooses among producing for each of the alternative contingencies 1.1, 1.2, and 1.3.
  (iii) If production is intertemporal (requiring inputs at one date to produce output at a succeeding date), explain how it is financed.
  (iv) Does risk aversion of the firm's management or owners enter the pro-duction decision? Explain.

15.5 Consider education as a private investment good. Explain the following observations:

  (a) In the Arrow-Debreu Walrasian model with a full set of futures markets, efficient allocation of resources does not require government provision of education. The market will provide and distribute education in a Pareto efficient fashion.
  (b) In actual economies, market imperfections may prevent private markets from financing efficient levels of education. This may create a role for nonmarket provision or explicit subsidy.

Part G

An economy with supply and demand correspondences

In Chapters 4–11, we developed the theory of firm and household behavior, concentrating on the case of strictly convex preferences and strictly convex production technology sets. Using strict convexity allowed us to use point-valued supply and demand functions. There are many settings, however, where this mathematically simple formulation seems inappropriate economically, for example, when there are perfect substitutes in consumption or when production technologies are linear. In these cases, where weak rather than strict convexity holds, supply and demand relations appear to be set valued. Figure G.1 presents the example of a firm with a linear production technology and the resulting set-valued supply function. Figure G.2 shows the case of a consumer choosing between perfect substitutes with the resulting set-valued demand behavior. It is important in these examples that preferences and technology be convex, even though they are not strictly convex. That assures us that a household demand or a firm supply at given prices can be characterized as a convex set. Figure G.3 depicts, in partial equilibrium, typical resulting supply and demand curves and possible market equilibria.

We need a mathematical treatment that will allow us to deal with this additional complexity. Fortunately, there is an available theory of continuous point-to-set mappings that fully parallels the theory of continuous functions. We will develop concepts of continuity and a fixed-point theorem that will allow us to duplicate, in the more general setting of set-valued supply and demand, the results on existence of equilibrium we developed for point-valued supply and demand in Chapters 4 through 11. Chapter 12's results on the efficiency of equilibrium and supportability of efficient allocation do not depend on point-valuedness of demand and supply and are hence unaffected by whether strict or weak convexity is used.

Our modeling plan for an economy characterized by set-valued supply and demand functions (to be denoted *correspondences*) will closely parallel the model developed for point-valued supply and demand functions in Chapters 4 to 11. The model we developed there focused on the notion of continuous supply and

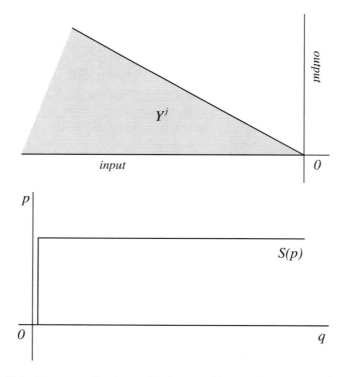

Fig. G.1. Linear production technology and its supply correspondence.

demand behavior as a function of prices; combined with the Walras' Law, continuity led to existence of general competitive equilibrium. We develop in Chapter 16 a concept of continuity of correspondences, called upper hemicontinuity. We will describe – under the assumptions of weak rather than strict convexity – supply and demand correspondences as upper hemicontinuous correspondences in prices. We further show that each supply and demand correspondence evaluated at a given price vector will be a convex set. We will show in Chapters 16 and 17 that essentially the same results we found in Chapters 4 to 11 are true of an economy where the set-valued demand and supply are upper hemicontinuous and convex valued. That is, the property "upper hemicontinuous convex-valued correspondence" will play the same role in this more general setting that "continuous function" played in the treatment of Chapters 4 to 11. Thus we substitute the Kakutani Fixed-Point Theorem (on upper hemicontinuous convex-valued correspondences) for the Brouwer Fixed-Point Theorem and corresponding results follow.

Recall how the argument for existence of competitive equilibrium goes in Chapters 8 to 11:

We consider an artificially bounded economy. A price adjustment process continuous in excess demand (which is itself continuous in prices) is posited. Hence price adjustment

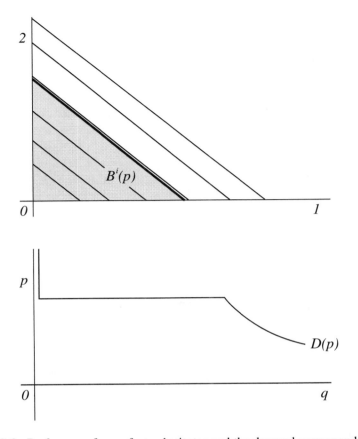

Fig. G.2. Preferences for perfect substitutes and the demand correspondence.

can be characterized as a continuous function from price space into itself. Price adjustment is then shown to lead to a fixed point of the price adjustment process as the result of a fixed-point theorem. This fixed point is then shown to be an equilibrium of the artificially bounded economy.

The artificial bound on the economy is then shown not to be a binding constraint in equilibrium. Hence the household and firm optimizations at the equilibrium prices of the artificially bounded economy are still optimizing when the artificial bounds are removed. Markets still clear. The equilibrium of the artificially bounded economy is an equilibrium of the true unbounded economy.

We will develop a treatment of the economy with set-valued excess demand and supply that parallels the summary above. The market excess demand correspondence at given prices will be simply the set summation of household demand correspondences minus the summation of firm supply correspondences minus endowment. Excess demand will be upper hemicontinuous and convex valued whenever all of the individual firm and household demands and supplies are upper

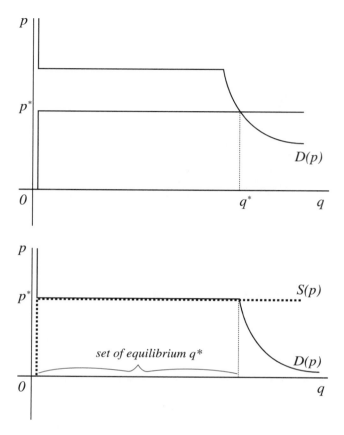

Fig. G.3. Equilibrium in a market with supply and demand correspondences.

hemicontinuous and convex valued. We develop a fixed-point theorem (Kakutani Fixed-Point Theorem) for upper hemicontinuous convex-valued correspondences. Then we will find a price adjustment function for a Walrasian auctioneer in this set-valued economy that is also upper hemicontinuous and convex valued. We will then describe the set of possible excess demands (suitably bounded to include all "attainable" supply and demand values as a proper subset) as a compact convex set. Finally, we will characterize the state of the economy as a point in the Cartesian product of the price simplex with the space of possible excess demands. Price and excess demand adjustments will be represented as an upper hemicontinuous convex-valued mapping from this space into itself. There is a fixed point that will be shown to be a competitive equilibrium for an artificially bounded economy, and by extension, to the actual economy.

16

Mathematics: Analysis of point to set mappings

16.1 Correspondences

We will call a point-to-set mapping a *correspondence*. A function maps points into points. A correspondence (or point-to-set mapping) maps points into sets of points. Let A and B be sets. We would like to describe a correspondence from A to B. For each $x \in A$ we associate a *nonempty* set $\beta \subset B$ by a rule φ. Then we say $\beta = \varphi(x)$ and φ is a correspondence. The notation to designate this mapping is $\varphi : A \to B$. For example, suppose A and B are both the set of human population. Then we could let φ be the cousin correspondence $\varphi(x) = \{y \mid y \text{ is } x\text{'s cousin}\}$. Note that if $x \in A$ and $y \in B$ it is meaningless or false to say $y = \varphi(x)$, rather we say $y \in \varphi(x)$. The *graph* of the correspondence is a subset of $A \times B : \{(x, y) \mid x \in A, y \in B \text{ and } y \in \varphi(x)\}$.

For example, let $A = B = \mathbf{R}$. We might consider $\varphi(x) = \{y \mid x - 1 \le y \le x + 1\}$. The graph of $\varphi(\cdot)$ appears in Figure 16.1.

16.2 Upper hemicontinuity (also known as upper semicontinuity)

In the balance of this chapter and the next, we concentrate on mappings from one real Euclidean space into another, from $\mathbf{R}^N$ into $\mathbf{R}^K$, for $N \ge 1$ and $K \ge 1$. The continuity concept for correspondences will parallel that for functions – a correspondence is continuous when nearby points in the domain are mapped into sets nearby in the range. "Nearby" becomes a bit more complicated. We introduce two independent concepts of continuity of correspondences: upper and lower hemicontinuity. For functions (point-valued correspondences) they are equivalent to one another and equivalent to continuity.

Definition *Let $\varphi : S \to T$, φ be a correspondence, and S and T be closed subsets of $\mathbf{R}^N$ and $\mathbf{R}^K$, respectively. Let $x^v, x^0 \in S$, $v = 1, 2, 3, \ldots$; let $x^v \to x^0$,*

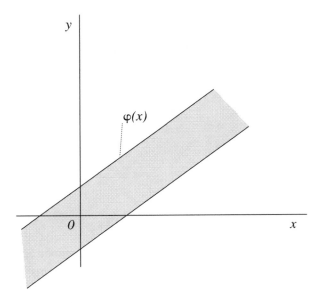

Fig. 16.1. A typical correspondence, $\varphi(x) = \{y \mid x - 1 \le y \le x + 1\}$.

$y^v \in \varphi(x^v)$, *for all $v = 1, 2, 3, \ldots$, and $y^v \to y^0$. Then φ is said to be **upper hemi-continuous** (also known as upper semicontinuous) at x^0 if and only if $y^0 \in \varphi(x^0)$. Upper hemicontinuity asserts the presence of a point in the correspondence evaluated at a specific point.*

Intuitively, φ is upper hemicontinuous at x^0 if whenever φ is sneaking up on a value y^0 in the range as it approaches x^0 in the domain, the correspondence can catch that value y^0 in $\varphi(x^0)$. If you can sneak up on a value, you can catch it. That is upper hemicontinuity. Let's consider a few examples:

Example 16.1 *An upper hemicontinuous correspondence.* Let $\varphi(x)$ be defined as follows. $\varphi : \mathbf{R} \to \mathbf{R}$. For

$$x < 0, \quad \varphi(x) = \{y \mid x - 4 \le y \le x - 2\}$$

$$x = 0, \quad \varphi(x) = \{y \mid -4 \le y \le +4\}$$

$$x > 0, \quad \varphi(x) = \{y \mid x + 2 \le y \le x + 4\}.$$

Note that $\varphi(\cdot)$ is convex valued. For each $x \in \mathbf{R}$, $\varphi(x)$ is a convex set. The graph of $\varphi(\cdot)$ is shown in Figure 16.2. For all $x^0 \in \mathbf{R}$, $\varphi(\cdot)$ is upper hemicontinuous at x^0. This may be obvious from inspection, but we should demonstrate it more

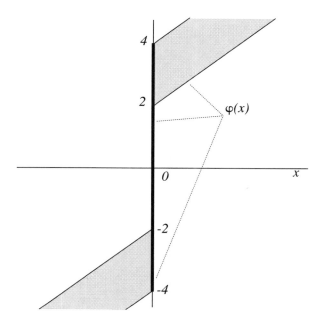

Fig. 16.2. Example 16.1 – An upper hemicontinuous correspondence.

formally. Consider the sequence $y^\nu \in \varphi(x^\nu)$, where $x^\nu \in \mathbf{R}$, $x^\nu \to x^0$. Without loss of generality let $x^0 \le 0$ (note the weak inequality). If $y^\nu \to y^0$, then $x^0 - 4 \le y^0 \le x^0 - 2$. Then $y^0 \in \varphi(x^0)$. The tricky point appears to be at $x = 0$. But the essential notion is that $\varphi(0)$ contains all of the limit points of $\varphi(\cdot)$ evaluated in the neighborhood of $x = 0$. That is the property that defines upper hemicontinuity. In contrast, consider Example 16.2.

Example 16.2 *A correspondence not upper hemicontinuous at 0.* Let $\varphi(x)$ be defined much as in Example 16.1 but with a discontinuity at 0. $\varphi : \mathbf{R} \to \mathbf{R}$. For

$$x < 0, \quad \varphi(x) = \{y \mid x - 4 \le y \le x - 2\}$$
$$x = 0, \quad \varphi(0) = \{0\}$$
$$x > 0, \quad \varphi(x) = \{y \mid x + 2 \le y \le x + 4\}.$$

Note that $\varphi(\cdot)$ is convex valued. For each $x \in \mathbf{R}$, $\varphi(x)$ is a convex set. The graph of $\varphi(\cdot)$ is shown in Figure 16.3. At x^0 different from 0, the behavior is just as in Example 16.1, so the correspondence is upper hemicontinuous at those values. At $x^0 = 0$ we have the following problem. Without loss of generality consider a sequence $x^\nu > 0$, $x^\nu \to 0$. Consider the sequence $y^\nu \in \varphi(x^\nu)$. $y^\nu \to y^0$. Then $y^0 \ge 2$. But then $y^0 \notin \varphi(0) = \{0\}$. Hence, $\varphi(\cdot)$ is not upper hemicontinuous at 0.

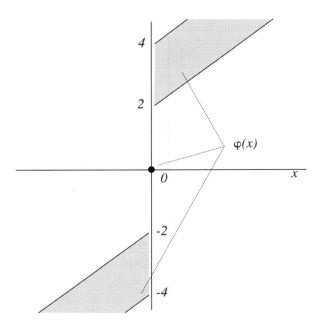

Fig. 16.3. Example 16.2 – A correspondence that is not upper hemicontinuous at 0.

Theorem 16.1 φ *is upper hemicontinuous if and only if its graph is closed in* $S \times T$.

Proof Exercise 16.7

16.3 Lower hemicontinuity (also known as lower semicontinuity)

We now introduce a second, related, concept of continuity for correspondences, lower hemicontinuity. We described, loosely, the notion of *upper* hemicontinuity as the property that if the correspondence approaches a value as a limit, that value is in the correspondence. Conversely, lower hemicontinuity is the property that if a value is in the correspondence, then that value can be approached as the limit of a sequence of values in the correspondence.

Definition *Let* $\varphi : S \to T$, *where S and T are closed subsets of* $\mathbf{R}^N$ *and* $\mathbf{R}^K$, *respectively. Let* $x^\nu \in S$, $x^\nu \to x^0$, $y^0 \in \varphi(x^0)$, $q = 1, 2, 3, \ldots$. *Then* φ *is said to be lower hemicontinuous (also know as lower semicontinuous) at* x^0 *if and only if there is* $y^\nu \in \varphi(x^\nu)$, $y^\nu \to y^0$. *Lower hemicontinuity asserts the presence of a sequence of points in the correspondence evaluated at a convergent sequence of points in the domain.*

Intuitively, φ is lower hemicontinuous at x^0 if whenever $\varphi(x^0)$ includes a value y^0, and x^0 is characterized as the limit of a sequence in the domain, then there is a sequence of values in the correspondence evaluated at that sequence in the domain that is sneaking up on y^0. If you've caught a value, you must be able to sneak up on it. Consider a few examples:

Example 16.3 *A lower hemicontinuous correspondence.* Let $\varphi(x)$ be defined as follows. $\varphi : \mathbf{R} \to \mathbf{R}$. For

$$x \neq 0, \quad \varphi(x) = \{y \mid x - 4 \leq y \leq x\}$$
$$x = 0, \quad \varphi(x) = \{y \mid -3 \leq y \leq -1\}.$$

The graph of $\varphi(\cdot)$ is shown in Figure 16.4. Note that $\varphi(\cdot)$ is convex valued. For each $x \in \mathbf{R}$, $\varphi(x)$ is a convex set. For all $x^0 \in \mathbf{R}$, $\varphi(\cdot)$ is lower hemicontinuous at x^0. The only point where this requires some care is at $x^0 = 0$. Let $x^\nu \to 0$, $y^0 \in \varphi(0)$. To demonstrate lower hemicontinuity, we must show that there is $y^\nu \in \varphi(x^\nu)$ so that $y^\nu \to y^0$. Note that $-3 \leq y^0 \leq -1$. But for ν large, there is $y^\nu \in \varphi(x^\nu)$, so that $y^\nu = y^0$. Hence, trivially, $y^\nu \to y^0$. Note that $\varphi(\cdot)$ is not upper hemicontinuous at $x^0 = 0$. This follows simply because $y = -4$ is the limit of a sequence of values in $\varphi(x^\nu)$ but $-4 \notin \varphi(0)$.

Example 16.4 *An upper hemicontinuous correspondence that is not lower hemicontinuous.* This example is merely Examples 16.1 and 16.2 revisited. $\varphi(\cdot)$ in both

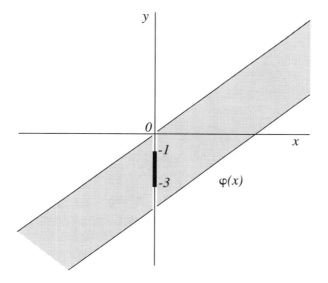

Fig. 16.4. Example 16.3 – A lower hemicontinuous correspondence.

Examples 16.1 and 16.2 is not lower hemicontinuous at $x^0 = 0$. In both cases $0 \in \varphi(0)$ but for a typical sequence $x^\nu \to 0$, there is no $y^\nu \in \varphi(x^\nu)$ so that $y^\nu \to 0$.

16.4 Continuous correspondence

We have presented examples above of upper hemicontinuous correspondences that are not lower hemicontinuous and vice versa. It is certainly possible for a correspondence to be both. A correspondence that is both upper and lower hemicontinuous will be known simply as a continuous correspondence.

Definition *Let $\varphi : A \to B$, with φ a correspondence. $\varphi(\cdot)$ is said to be continuous at x^0 if $\varphi(\cdot)$ is both upper and lower hemicontinuous at x^0.*

Example 16.5 *A continuous correspondence.* The following correspondence, $\varphi(\cdot)$, is both upper and lower hemicontinuous throughout its range and hence is a continuous correspondence. For

$$x < 0, \quad \varphi(x) = \{y \mid 2x \le y \le -x\}$$

$$x = 0, \quad \varphi(x) = \{0\}$$

$$x > 0, \quad \varphi(x) = \{y \mid -2x \le y \le -x\} \cup \{y \mid 3x \le y \le 4x\}.$$

$\varphi(\cdot)$ is illustrated in Figure 16.5. To demonstrate that it is upper hemicontinuous, note that it contains all its limit points. That is, for any convergent sequence in the

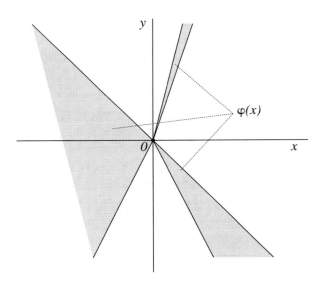

Fig. 16.5. Example 16.5 – A continuous correspondence.

domain and a corresponding convergent sequence of correspondence values in the range, the limit of the sequence of correspondence values is in the correspondence evaluated at the limiting value in the domain. To demonstrate lower hemicontinuity, note that any point in the correspondence evaluated at a point can be approached as the limit of points in the correspondence evaluated at a corresponding convergent sequence in the domain.

Unlike Examples 16.1 through 16.4, $\varphi(\cdot)$ in this example is not convex valued. For $x > 0$, $\varphi(x)$ is a nonconvex set, composed of two noncontiguous segments.

Note that if φ is point valued (i.e., a function) then upper hemicontinuity, continuity (in the sense of a function), and lower hemicontinuity are equivalent.

16.5 Cartesian product of correspondences

Theorem 16.2 *Let $\varphi : S \to T$ and $\mu : S \to U$. Let $\times$ denote the Cartesian product. Then $\varphi \times \mu : S \to T \times U$. Further, if φ and μ are upper hemicontinuous at $x^0 \in S$, then so is $\varphi \times \mu$.*

Proof Exercise 16.8

16.6 Optimization subject to constraint: Composition of correspondences; the Maximum Theorem

We can now use the structure of upper and lower hemicontinuity of correspondences to demonstrate a powerful result: continuity of optimizing behavior. We commonly think of household demand as the result of maximizing utility (a continuous real-valued function of consumption) subject to a budget constraint. This is the stuff of economic analysis every day. We would like to develop sufficient conditions for demand to be an upper hemicontinuous correspondence in prices. The mathematical basis for this result is the Maximum Theorem. This theorem gives us sufficient conditions for optimizing choice behavior to be continuous as a function of variation in constraint.

Suppose the budget constraint set is a continuous (both upper and lower hemicontinuous) correspondence in prices. Prices are an argument that determines the household budget constraint. The constraint set and optimization determine demand. Demand is then characterized as a function of prices (which directly determine the budget constraint set). How will the optimizing demand of the household vary with prices? The Maximum Theorem gives us a clear definite result. Demand will be an upper hemicontinuous correspondence in prices. The Maximum Theorem will tell us that all we need to assert this result is the continuity of the budget

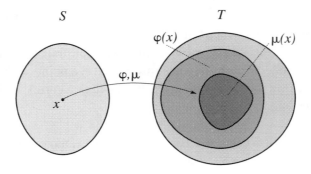

Fig. 16.6. The Maximum Problem.

constraint in prices and the continuity of utility in commodities. However, first we need to state and prove the theorem.

We formalize this notion in the following way. Let $f(\cdot)$ be a real-valued function, and let $\varphi(\cdot)$ be a correspondence intended to represent an opportunity set. Then we let $\mu(\cdot)$ represent the correspondence consisting of the maximizers of $f(\cdot)$ subject to choosing the maximizer in the opportunity set $\varphi(\cdot)$. Formally, we state

The Maximum Problem *Let* $T \subseteq \mathbf{R}^N$, $S \subseteq \mathbf{R}^M$, $f : T \to \mathbf{R}$, *and* $\varphi : S \to T$, *where* φ *is a correspondence, and let* $\mu : S \to T$, *where* $\mu(x) \equiv \{y^0 \mid y^0$ *maximizes* $f(y)$ *for* $y \in \varphi(x)\}$.

This situation is depicted in Figure 16.6. We treat $\mu(\cdot)$ as a correspondence since maximization subject to constraint need not result in a unique maximizer; there may be a set of several or an infinite number of maximizers. Nevertheless, the Maximum Theorem lets us treat this set of maximizers as a well-behaved continuous correspondence, whenever the opportunity set and maximand are continuous.

To prove the theorem we make use of a trivial result.

Lemma 16.1 *Let* x^i *and* y^i *be sequences in* $\mathbf{R}$ *such that* $x^i \geq y^i$ *for all* $i > N^*$. *Let* $x^i \to x^0$ *and* $y^i \to y^0$. *Then* $x^0 \geq y^0$.

Proof Suppose $x^0 \geq y^0$ is not true. Then $y^0 > x^0$ and $y^0 - x^0 > 0$. Thus, there is N_ε and $\varepsilon > 0$ so that for all $i > N_\varepsilon$, $|y^0 - y^i| < \varepsilon$, $|x^0 - x^i| < \varepsilon$, and $\varepsilon < \frac{1}{3}(y^0 - x^0)$. But then $y^i > y^0 - \varepsilon > x^0 + \varepsilon > x^i$. This contradiction proves the lemma. QED

Theorem 16.3 (The Maximum Theorem) *Let* $f(\cdot)$, $\varphi(\cdot)$, *and* $\mu(\cdot)$ *be as defined in the Maximum Problem. Let* f *be continuous on* T *and* φ *be continuous (both upper and lower hemicontinuous) and compact valued at* x^0. *Then* μ *is upper hemicontinuous at* x^0.

Proof We seek to show that if $x^i \in S$, $x^i \to x^0$, $y^i \in \mu(x^i)$, $i = 1, 2, 3, \ldots$, and $y^i \to y^*$ then $y^* \in \mu(x^0)$.

Here's the situation. We have a convergent sequence of constraint parameters (e.g., prices) $x^i \in S$. The sequence converges to a limit point $x^i \to x^0 \in S$. There is a corresponding convergent sequence of optimizing choices $y^i \in \mu(x^i)$ and $y^i \to y^*$. We must show that the limit of that sequence, y^*, is the optimizing choice in the opportunity set defined at x^0, the limit of the sequence in the domain S, $x^i \to x^0$. There are two parts to demonstrating this result. First we must show that y^* is in the opportunity set, that is, that $y^* \in \varphi(x^0)$. Then we must show that y^* is the optimizing choice in $\varphi(x^0)$, that is, that $y^* \in \mu(x^0)$.

We seek to show that if $x^i \in S$, $x^i \to x^0$, $y^i \in \mu(x^i)$, and $y^i \to y^*$ then $y^* \in \mu(x^0)$. By construction $y^i \in \varphi(x^i)$. Recall that φ being continuous means that φ is both upper and lower hemicontinuous. By upper hemicontinuity of φ, $y^* \in \varphi(x^0)$. It remains to show that y^* maximizes $f(y)$ for $y \in \varphi(x^0)$. We must demonstrate that $f(y^*) \geq f(z^*)$ for all $z^* \in \varphi(x^0)$. By lower hemicontinuity of φ there is $z^i \in \varphi(x^i)$ so that $z^i \to z^*$. But recall that $y^i \in \mu(x^i)$ all i so that $f(y^i) \geq f(z^i)$ for all i. Taking the limit as i becomes large, using Lemma 16.1 and continuity of f, we get $f(y^*) \geq f(z^*)$. Thus, $y^* \in \mu(x^0)$.   QED

Example 16.6 *Applying the Maximum Theorem.* Let $S = T = \mathbf{R}$. Let $f(y) = y^2$. Let

$$\varphi(x) = \{y \mid -x \leq y \leq x\} \quad \text{for } x \geq 0$$
$$\varphi(x) = \{y \mid x \leq y \leq -x\} \quad \text{for } x < 0.$$

Then $\mu(x) = \{x, -x\}$, since $\mu(x)$ is the set of maximizers of y^2 for $y \in \varphi(x)$. Note that $\varphi(x)$ is both upper and lower hemicontinuous throughout $\mathbf{R}$ and is convex valued. $\mu(x)$ is upper hemicontinuous by the Maximum Theorem. It is not, however, convex valued.

16.7 Kakutani Fixed-Point Theorem

We now need an extension of the Brouwer Fixed-Point Theorem to the context of correspondences. It is clear that upper hemicontinuity of a correspondence is not a sufficient condition for a mapping from a compact convex set into itself to have a fixed point. (See Figure 16.7.) The condition that does the job is upper hemicontinuity plus the requirement that the correspondence evaluated at each point of the domain be a convex set. This can be illustrated convincingly in mapping the 1-simplex (line segment) into itself. (See Figure 16.8.) This result is the Kakutani Fixed-Point Theorem.

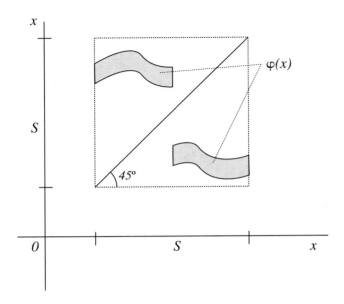

Fig. 16.7. An upper hemicontinuous mapping from an interval (1-simplex) into itself without a fixed point.

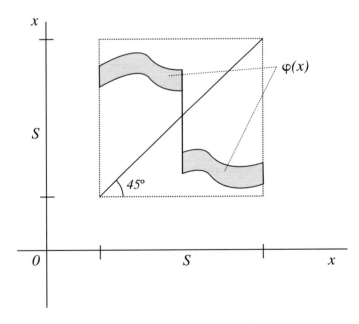

Fig. 16.8. An upper hemicontinuous convex-valued mapping from an interval (1-simplex) into itself with a fixed point.

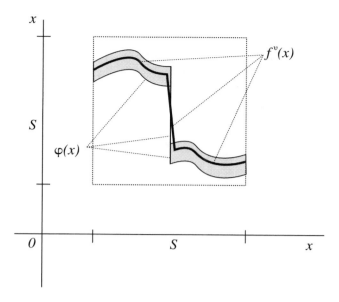

Fig. 16.9. Lemma 16.2 – Approximating an upper hemicontinuous convex-valued correspondence by a continuous function.

We will prove the Kakutani Fixed-Point Theorem as a limiting result of the Brouwer Fixed-Point Theorem. It will help to have a technical lemma.

Lemma 16.2 *Let S be an N-simplex. Let $\varphi : S \to S$ be a correspondence upper hemicontinuous everywhere on S. Further, let $\varphi(x)$ be a convex set for all $x \in S$. Let $v = 1, 2, 3, \ldots$. For each v, there is a continuous function $f^v(\cdot)$ from S into S so that $\min_{y \in \varphi(x)} |f^v(x) - y| < 1/v$ for all x in S.*

Proof The proof is a bit technical so we omit it here. It is presented in Hildenbrand and Kirman (1976). QED

The notion of the lemma is illustrated in Figure 16.9. Note that the lemma, the ability to approximate an upper hemicontinuous correspondence by a sequence of continuous functions, clearly depends on the convex valuedness of $\varphi(\cdot)$.

Theorem 16.4 (Kakutani Fixed-Point Theorem) *Let S be an N-simplex. Let $\varphi : S \to S$ be a correspondence that is upper hemicontinuous everywhere on S. Further, let $\varphi(x)$ be a convex set for all $x \in S$. Then there is $x^* \in S$ so that $x^* \in \varphi(x^*)$.*

Proof Here is the strategy of proof: We will present a limiting argument based on the Brouwer Theorem. Lemma 16.2 says we can find a sequence of continuous functions $f^\nu(\cdot)$ from S into S approximating $\varphi(\cdot)$. By the Brouwer Fixed-Point Theorem, we know that each of the functions $f^\nu(\cdot)$ has a fixed point. The sequence $f^\nu(\cdot)$ is constructed so that it converges to limiting values in $\varphi(\cdot)$. Then the sequence of fixed points of $f^\nu(\cdot)$ will converge to a fixed point of $\varphi(\cdot)$.

Let $\nu = 1, 2, 3, \ldots$. Lemma 16.2 says that there is a sequence of continuous functions $f^\nu(\cdot)$ from S into S so that

$$\min_{y \in \varphi(x)} |f^\nu(x) - y| < \frac{1}{\nu} \quad \text{for all } x \text{ in } S.$$

By the Brouwer Theorem we know that $f^\nu(\cdot)$ has a fixed point; call it x^ν. $x^\nu, \nu = 1, 2, 3, \ldots$, is a sequence on a compact set, S, so – without loss of generality – taking a subsequence, we find its limit point, $x^\nu \to x^0$. We will show that x^0 is a fixed point of $\varphi(\cdot)$.

We have $f^\nu(x^\nu) = x^\nu$. Recall that there is $y^\nu \in \varphi(x^\nu)$ so that $|y^\nu - x^\nu| < \frac{1}{\nu}$. Then $y^\nu \to x^0$. But by upper hemicontinuity of $\varphi(\cdot)$, the properties $x^\nu \to x^0$, $y^\nu \in \varphi(x^\nu)$, and $y^\nu \to x^0$ imply $x^0 \in \varphi(x^0)$. Hence, choose $x^* = x^0$ and we have $x^* \in \varphi(x^*)$. 					QED

Example 16.7 *Applying the Kakutani Fixed-Point Theorem.* Let $\varphi : [0, 1] \to [0, 1]$. Let

$$\varphi(x) = \{1 - x/2\} \quad \text{for } 0 \leq x < .5$$
$$\varphi(0.5) = [.25, .75]$$
$$\varphi(x) = \{x/2\} \quad\quad \text{for } 1 \geq x > .5,$$

where φ is upper hemicontinuous and convex valued. The fixed point is $x^0 = 0.5$. (See Figure 16.10.)

The Kakutani Fixed-Point Theorem is stated (and proved traditionally) on the simplex. We will use a slightly stronger version, the corollary below.

Corollary 16.1 *Let $K \subseteq \mathbf{R}^M$ be compact and convex. Let $\Psi : K \to K$, with $\Psi(x)$ upper hemicontinuous and convex valued for all $x \in K$. Then there is $x^* \in K$ so that $x^* \in \Psi(x^*)$.*

Proof We omit the full proof. The proof depends on the topological equivalence of K and S. We state without proof the following property. Let K be a nonempty, compact, convex set in $\mathbf{R}^M$. Then there is an N-simplex S and $g : K \to S$, so that g is continuous, 1-1, onto, and the inverse of g, g^{-1}, is continuous. This is the topological equivalence of K and S. Because K and S are equivalent, a fixed point in a correspondence in one can be shown to be a fixed point of the

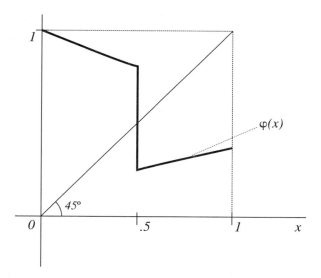

Fig. 16.10. Example 16.7 – Applying the Kakutani Fixed-Point Theorem.

image of the correspondence in the other. The actual proof is a bit more complex, since convexity is not topologically invariant (though a related property, contractibility, is). QED

We will find that the combined property of upper hemicontinuity and convex valuedness of a correspondence plays essentially the same role in the model of set-valued supply and demand behavior that continuity of demand and supply functions plays in the point-valued model. Of course, a continuous (point-valued) function, viewed as a correspondence, is upper hemicontinuous and convex valued.

16.8 Bibliographic note

The exposition of upper and lower hemicontinuous point-to-set mappings is presented in Debreu (1959). The Maximum Theorem is sometimes attributed to Berge (1959). The Kakutani Fixed-Point Theorem first appeared as Kakutani (1941).

Exercises

16.1 Find two correspondences that are upper hemicontinuous but not lower hemicontinuous.

16.2 Find two correspondences that are lower hemicontinuous but not upper hemicontinuous.

16.3   Let $\varphi : \mathbf{R} \to \mathbf{R}$, $\varphi(x) = \{y \mid x - 1 \leq y \leq x + 1\}$. Prove that φ is upper hemicontinuous and prove that φ is lower semicontinuous.

16.4   Give a specific example (complete with sets, functions, etc.) of the Maximum Theorem.

16.5   Let $I = [-1000, 1000]$, $\varphi : I \to I$, $\varphi(x) \equiv [-1, 1]$. Prove that φ is upper hemicontinuous and lower hemicontinuous at $x = 1$.

16.6   Let $I = [-1000, 1000]$, $\varphi : [-998, 997] \to I$. Define φ as follows:

$$\varphi(x) = [x - 2, x - 1] \quad \text{for } -998 < x < 1$$
$$\varphi(x) = [x + 2, x + 3] \quad \text{for } 1 < x < 997$$
$$\varphi(x) = [-1, 0] \cup [3, 4] \quad \text{for } x = 1.$$

Prove that $\varphi(x)$ is upper hemicontinuous at $x = 1$.

16.7   Prove Theorem 16.1: φ is upper hemicontinuous if and only if its graph is closed in $S \times T$.

16.8   Prove Theorem 16.2: Let $\varphi : S \to T$, $\mu : S \to U$. Let $\times$ denote Cartesian product. Then $\varphi \times \mu : S \to T \times U$. Further, if φ and μ are upper hemicontinuous at $x^0 \in S$, then so is $\varphi \times \mu$.

17

General equilibrium of the market economy with an excess demand correspondence

17.1 General equilibrium with set-valued supply and demand

Our plan in this chapter is to take the model of production, consumption, the economy, and market equilibrium of Chapters 8–11[1] and restate it for the case of set-valued demand and supply behavior. Formally this means that we dispense with assumptions of strict convexity of tastes and production technology, C.VII and P.V. We rely rather on weak convexity, C.VI and P.I. Under the remaining assumptions on consumption and production behavior, this will allow us to characterize demand and supply behavior as upper hemicontinuous, convex-valued correspondences. In turn, excess demand will then be characterized as upper hemicontinuous and convex valued. A model of price adjustment that is also upper hemicontinuous and convex valued completes the picture: Applying the Kakutani Fixed-Point Theorem allows us to find a fixed point in price space that achieves a market equilibrium.

Just as we did in Chapters 8–11, we treat the economy in two formats: an artificially restricted bounded economy denoted by the superscript tilde notation ($\sim$) and an unrestricted economy (representing the true model we are really interested in). The artificially restricted economy is a purely technical construct, designed to allow us to develop the properties of the underlying unrestricted economy in a more tractable setting. The technique of the proof is to note that the restricted budget, demand, supply, and profit behavior is always well defined, since it represents optimizing behavior on a compact set. Unrestricted demand and supply correspondences and profit functions may not be everywhere well defined. When the demand and supply correspondences of the restricted economy designate attainable allocations, then they coincide with their counterparts of the unrestricted economy. An equilibrium allocation is necessarily attainable. Hence when we find an equilibrium of the artificially restricted economy (something that is possible for us to do since its behavior is everywhere upper hemicontinuous, convex valued,

---

[1] Note that the model of these chapters includes as a special case the bounded economy model of Chapters 4–7.

and well defined), the equilibrium price vector and allocation is also an equilibrium of the unrestricted (true) economy.

17.2 Production with a (weakly) convex production technology

We will show that supply behavior of the firm is convex and set valued when the production technology is convex but not strictly convex. This includes the cases of constant returns to scale, linear production technology, and perfect substitutes among inputs to production. In each of these cases there may be a (linear) range of equally profitable production plans differing by scale of output or by the input mix. The purpose of developing a theory of set-valued supply behavior is to accommodate this range of indeterminacy.

Supply correspondence with a weakly convex production technology: We now omit P.V and use P.I–P.IV only. In this case the policy of profit maximization for firm j may not yield a unique solution.

Let $S^j(p) = \{y^* \mid y^* \in Y^j, p \cdot y^* \geq p \cdot y \text{ for all } y \in Y^j\}$ be the *supply correspondence* of the firm.

Example 17.1 An upper hemicontinuous, convex-valued supply correspondence. Let firm j's production technology be described as follows.

Let $Y^j = \{(x, y) \mid y \leq -x; x \leq 0, K \geq y \geq 0\}$. That is, output y is produced by a constant returns technology using input x, each unit of x producing one unit of y, up to a limit of K of y. Let the price vector p be an element of the price space $\mathbf{R}_+^2 = \{(p_x, p_y) \mid p_x, p_y > 0\}$. Then for each $p \in \mathbf{R}_+^2$, we have the supply correspondence

$$
\begin{aligned}
S^j(p) &= \{(0, 0)\} \quad \text{for } p_x > p_y, \\
&= \{(-y, y) \mid y \in [0, K]\} \quad \text{for } p_x = p_y, \\
&= \{(-K, K)\} \quad \text{for } p_x < p_y.
\end{aligned}
$$

Note that starting with the convex technology set Y^j, the resulting supply correspondence $S^j(p)$ is also convex valued. The correspondence is upper hemicontinuous (it has a closed graph). $S^j(p)$ is depicted in Figure 17.1. Note that with upper hemicontinuity and convex valuedness, a continuous downward-sloping demand curve will intersect the supply correspondence. The importance of the convexity of Y^j is demonstrated by comparison to Example 17.2, below.

Example 17.2 *An upper hemicontinuous supply correspondence that is not convex valued.* We consider here the supply behavior of a firm situated similarly to

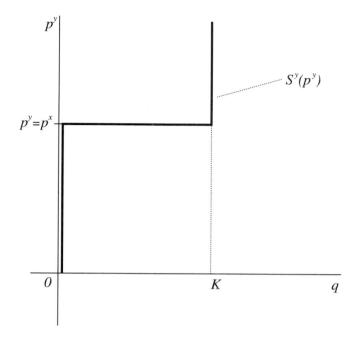

Fig. 17.1. Example 17.1 – An upper hemicontinuous, convex-valued supply correspondence.

Example 17.1 with a minimum efficient scale of output,

$$Y^j = \{(x, y) \mid y \le -x; \ K \ge y \ge 0 \quad \text{for } x \le -k; \ y = 0 \quad \text{for } 0 \ge x > -k\}$$

Y^j is a nonconvex set, representing the scale economy. Minimum efficient scale of output is k; inputs insufficient to support output of k result in a zero output. This technology set gives us a supply correspondence that is upper hemicontinuous, but not convex valued:

$$S^j(p) = \{(0, 0)\} \quad \text{for } p_x > p_y,$$
$$= \{(-y, y) \mid y = 0 \text{ or } y \in [k, K]\} \quad \text{for } p_x = p_y,$$
$$= \{(-K, K)\} \quad \text{for } p_x < p_y.$$

$S^j(p)$ is depicted in Figure 17.2. Note the jump in the supply correspondence at $p_x = p_y$. This jump is sometimes loosely described as a discontinuity. That description is imprecise, since the correspondence is actually upper hemicontinuous. Rather, the correspondence is nonconvex-valued at $p_x = p_y$. The example demonstrates the importance of convex valuedness for the existence of market equilibrium. A continuous downward-sloping demand curve may have no intersection

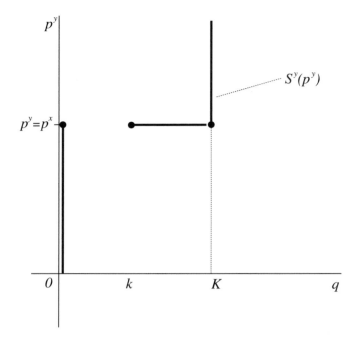

Fig. 17.2. Example 17.2 – an upper hemicontinuous supply correspondence that is not convex-valued.

with $S^j(p)$, hence implying no market equilibrium. Upper hemicontinuity of demand and supply is insufficient to assure a market equilibrium. Convex valuedness of the correspondence may be needed as well.

Taking price vector $p \in \mathbf{R}_+^N$ as given, each firm j "chooses" y^j in Y^j. Profit maximization guides the choice of y^j. Firm j chooses y^j to maximize $p \cdot y$ subject to $y \in Y^j$. We will consider two cases:

- a restricted supply correspondence where the supply behavior of firm j is required to be in a compact convex set $\tilde{Y}^j \subseteq Y^j$, which includes the plans attainable in Y^j as a proper subset, and
- an unrestricted supply correspondence where the only requirement is that the chosen supply behavior lie in Y^j. Of course, Y^j need not be compact. Hence, in this case, profit-maximizing supply behavior may not be well defined. Further, Y^j may include unattainable production plans. When the profit-maximizing production plan is unattainable, it cannot, of course, be fulfilled and cannot represent a market equilibrium.

The restricted supply correspondence will be denoted $\tilde{S}^j(p) \subset \tilde{Y}^j$, and the unrestricted supply correspondence will be $S^j(p) \subset Y^j$.

Recall Theorems 8.1 and 8.2. They demonstrated that under assumptions P.I, P.II, P.III, and P.IV the set of attainable production plans for the economy and for firm j were bounded. We then defined $\tilde{Y}^j$ as the bounded subset of Y^j containing production plans of Euclidean length c or less, where c was chosen as a strict upper bound on all attainable plans in Y^j. That is, choose c such that $|y^j| < c$ (a strict inequality) for y^j attainable in Y^j. Let $\tilde{Y}^j = Y^j \cap \{y \mid |y| \leq c\}$. Note the weak inequality in the definition of $\tilde{Y}^j$. Restricting attention to $\tilde{Y}^j$ in describing firm j's production plans allows us to remain in a bounded set so that profit maximization will be well defined. Note that $\tilde{Y}^j$ is closed, bounded (hence compact), and convex.

Define the restricted supply correspondence of firm j as

$$\tilde{S}^j(p) = \{y^{*j} \mid p \cdot y^{*j} \geq p \cdot y^j \quad \text{for all } y^j \in \tilde{Y}^j, y^{*j} \in \tilde{Y}^j\}.$$

The (unrestricted) supply correspondence of firm j was defined above as

$$S^j(p) = \{y^* \mid y^* \in Y^j, p \cdot y^* \geq p \cdot y \quad \text{for all } y \in Y^j\}.$$

Then we have:

Lemma 17.1 *Under P.I–P.IV, $\tilde{S}^j(p)$ is convex.*

Proof Let $y^1 \in \tilde{S}^j(p)$ and $y^2 \in \tilde{S}^j(p)$. For fixed p, $p \cdot y^1 = p \cdot y^2 \geq p \cdot y$ for all $y \in Y^j$. For $0 \leq \lambda \leq 1$, consider

$$p \cdot [\lambda y^1 + (1 - \lambda)y^2] = \lambda p \cdot y^1 + (1 - \lambda)p \cdot y^2 = p \cdot y^2 \geq p \cdot y$$

for all $y \in Y^j$.

But $(\lambda y^1 + (1 - \lambda)y^2) \in Y^j$ by P.I. QED

Lemma 17.2 *Under P.I–P.IV, $\tilde{S}^j(p)$ is nonempty and upper hemicontinuous for all $p \in \mathbf{R}^N_+, p \neq 0$.*

Proof The set $\tilde{S}^j(p)$ consists of the maximizers of a continuous real-valued function on a compact set. The maximum is hence well defined and the set is nonempty.

To demonstrate upper hemicontinuity, let $p^\nu \to p^0$; $p^\nu, p^0 \in \mathbf{R}^N_+$; $p^\nu, p^0 \neq 0$; $\nu = 1, 2, \ldots$; and $y^\nu \in \tilde{S}^j(p^\nu), y^\nu \to y^0$.
We must show that $y^0 \in \tilde{S}^j(p^0)$. Suppose not. Then there is $y' \in \tilde{Y}^j$ so that $p^0 \cdot y' > p^0 \cdot y^0$. The dot product is a continuous function:

$$p^\nu \cdot y' \to p^0 \cdot y'$$

$$p^\nu \cdot y^\nu \to p^0 \cdot y^0.$$

Therefore, for ν sufficiently large, $p^\nu \cdot y' > p^\nu \cdot y^\nu$. But this contradicts the definition of $\tilde{S}(p^\nu)$. The contradiction proves the lemma. QED

Theorem 17.1 *Assume P.I, P.II, P.III, and P.IV. Then*

(a) $\tilde{S}^j(p)$ *is an upper hemicontinuous correspondence. For each p, $\tilde{S}^j(p)$ is closed, convex, bounded, and nonnull, and*

(b) *if y^j is attainable and $y^j \in \tilde{S}^j(p)$, then $y^j \in S^j(p)$.*

Proof Part (a). Upper hemicontinuity and nonemptiness are established in Lemma 17.2. $\tilde{S}^j(p)$ is bounded since $\tilde{Y}^j$ is bounded. Closedness follows from upper hemicontinuity. Convexity is established in Lemma 17.1.

Part (b): Suppose y^j attainable and $y^j \in \tilde{S}^j(p)$ but $y^j \notin S^j(p)$. Then there is $\hat{y}^j \in Y^j$ so that $p \cdot \hat{y}^j > p \cdot y^j$. Furthermore,

$$p \cdot [\alpha \hat{y}^j + (1 - \alpha)y^j] > p \cdot y^j \quad \text{for any } \alpha, 0 < \alpha \leq 1.$$

But for α sufficiently small,

$$|\alpha \hat{y}^j + (1 - \alpha)y^j| \leq c,$$

so that

$$\alpha \hat{y}^j + (1 - \alpha)y^j \in \tilde{Y}^j.$$

But then $p \cdot (\alpha \hat{y}^j + (1 - \alpha)y^j) > p \cdot y^j$ and $\alpha \hat{y}^j + (1 - \alpha)y^j \in \tilde{Y}^j$; thus y^j is not the maximizer of $p \cdot y$ in $\tilde{Y}^j$ and $y^j \notin \tilde{S}^j(p)$ as was assumed. The contradiction proves the theorem.   QED

Lemma 17.3 (homogeneity of degree 0) *Assume P.I–P.IV. Let $\lambda > 0$, $p \in \mathbf{R}^N_+$. Then $\tilde{S}^j(\lambda p) = \tilde{S}^j(p)$ and $S^j(\lambda p) = S^j(p)$.*

Proof Exercise 17.1.

17.3 Households

We now develop a theory of the household with set-valued demand behavior paralleling the theory of the household developed in Chapter 9. We use all of the structure and assumptions developed there with the exception of the assumption of strict convexity of preferences, C.VII. We use weak convexity, C.VI, which admits the possibility of set-valued linear segments in demand behavior, occurring, for example, in the case of perfect substitutes in consumption. To see how this might arise, consider Example 17.3.

Example 17.3 *Convex set-valued household demand.* Let household i's possible consumption set X^i be $\mathbf{R}^2_+$, the nonnegative quadrant in $\mathbf{R}^2$. Let the household endowment be $(1, 1)$ with no ownership of shares of firms. At prices $p \in \mathbf{R}_+^2$, the household income is $p \cdot (1, 1) = p_x + p_y$. Let household preferences be described by the utility function $u(x, y) = \max[ax, by]$. Then household demand can be characterized as

$$D^i(p) = \begin{cases} ([p_x + p_y]/p_x, 0) & \text{for } \dfrac{p_x}{p_y} < \dfrac{a}{b} \\[2mm] (0, [p_x + p_y]/p_y) & \text{for } \dfrac{p_x}{p_y} > \dfrac{a}{b} \\[2mm] \{(x, [p_x + p_y - p_x x]/p_y) \mid x \in [0, (p_x + p_y)/p_x]\} & \text{for } \dfrac{p_x}{p_y} = \dfrac{a}{b} \\[2mm] \text{undefined for} \quad p_x = 0 \quad \text{or } p_y = 0. \end{cases}$$

Note that $D^i(p)$ is convex set valued for $p_x/p_y = a/b$. This simply reflects the idea that if goods x and y are perfect substitutes at the ratio a/b then, when their prices occur in this ratio, the household will be indifferent among a whole set of linear combinations of x and y in the inverse of this ratio. After all, if the goods x and y are perfect substitutes then it really doesn't matter in what proportion they are used. The demand behavior, $D^i(p)$, is described as upper hemicontinuous and convex valued for all p so that $p_x \neq 0$ and $p_y \neq 0$.

We now define the household's budget set and demand correspondences. The household budget set is precisely as defined in Chapter 9:

$$B^i(p) \equiv \{x \mid x \in \mathbf{R}^N, p \cdot x \leq M^i(p)\}.$$

The definition of demand behavior for household i is here just as it was in Chapter 9, but since we are using C.VI (convexity of preferences) rather than C.VII (strict convexity of preferences) we will be dealing with a demand correspondence rather than a demand function. We have

$$D^i : \mathbf{R}_+^N \to \mathbf{R}^N,$$

$$D^i(p) \equiv \{y \mid y \in B^i(p) \cap X_i, y \succsim_i x \quad \text{for all } x \in B^i(p) \cap X^i\}$$

$$\equiv \{y \mid y \in B^i(p) \cap X^i, u^i(y) \geq u^i(x) \quad \text{for all } x \in B^i(p) \cap X^i\}.$$

We now define the artificially bounded budget and demand sets much as we did in Chapter 9. Choose c so that $|x| < c$ (a strict inequality) for all attainable consumptions x. The artificially restricted budget set is then defined as

$$\tilde{B}^i(p) = \{x \mid x \in \mathbf{R}^N, p \cdot x \leq \tilde{M}^i(p), |x| \leq c\}.$$

Note that $\tilde{B}^i(p)$ is just as defined in Chapters 5 and 9. $\tilde{B}^i(\cdot)$ is homogeneous of degree 0, just as is $B^i(\cdot)$. We now define the artificially restricted demand correspondence,

$$\tilde{D}^i(p) \equiv \{x \mid x \in \tilde{B}^i(p) \cap X^i, x \succsim_i y \quad \text{for all } y \in \tilde{B}^i(p) \cap X^i\}.$$

Note that $\tilde{D}^i(p)$ is just as defined in Chapters 5 and 9, but under weak convexity (C.VI) $\tilde{D}^i(p)$ may be set valued.

Just as in Chapters 6 and 10, firm j's profit function is $\pi^j(p) = \max_{y \in Y^j} p \cdot y$. Since Y^j need not be compact, $\pi^j(p)$ may not be well defined. Firm j's profit function in the artificially restricted firm technology set $\tilde{Y}^j$ is $\tilde{\pi}^j(p) = \max_{y \in \tilde{Y}^j} p \cdot y$. The function $\tilde{\pi}^j(p)$ is always well defined, since $\tilde{Y}^j$ is compact by definition and P.III.

Just as in Chapters 6 and 10, household i's income is defined as

$$M^i(p) = p \cdot r^i + \sum_{j \in F} \alpha^{ij} \pi^j(p).$$

For the model with restricted firm supply behavior, household income is

$$\tilde{M}^i(p) = p \cdot r^i + \sum_{j \in F} \alpha^{ij} \tilde{\pi}^j(p).$$

Note that $M^i(p)$ may not be everywhere well defined since $\pi^j(p)$ is not well defined for some j, p. Conversely, $\tilde{M}^i(p)$ is continuous, real valued, nonnegative, and well defined for all $p \in \mathbf{R}_+^N$. By the same argument as in Chapters 5 and 9, $\tilde{B}^i(p)$ and $\tilde{D}^i(p)$ are homogeneous of degree 0 in p. This allows us to confine attention in prices to the unit simplex in $\mathbf{R}^N$, denoted P.

As in Chapter 9, in order to avoid discontinuities in demand behavior at the boundary of X^i we will continue to assume C.VIII, positivity and sufficiency of income,

$$\tilde{M}^i(p) \gg \min_{x \in X^i \cap \{y \mid y \in \mathbf{R}^N, c \geq |y|\}} p \cdot x \geq 0 \quad \text{for all } p \in P.$$

We want to show that the (artificially restricted) demand correspondence of household i, $\tilde{D}^i(p)$, is upper hemicontinuous and convex valued. To demonstrate upper hemicontinuity, we will use the Theorem of the Maximum, Theorem 16.3. That theorem requires that the opportunity set, in this case $\tilde{B}^i(p) \cap X^i$, be continuous, both upper and lower hemicontinuous. Continuity of $\tilde{B}^i(p) \cap X^i$ is the message of Theorem 17.2.

Theorem 17.2 *Assume P.II, P.III, C.I, C.III, and C.VIII. Then $\tilde{B}^i(p) \cap X^i$ is continuous (lower and upper hemicontinuous), compact valued, and nonnull for all $p \in P$.*

Proof Continuity of $\tilde{B}^i(p) \cap X^i$ depends on continuity of $\tilde{M}^i(p)$. This follows from definition and Theorem 17.1 (upper hemicontinuity of $\tilde{S}^j(p)$). Upper hemicontinuity is left as an exercise. Nonnullness follows directly from C.VIII. Compactness follows from closedness and the restriction to $\{x \mid |x| \leq c\}$. To demonstrate lower hemicontinuity, we will use positivity of income, C.VIII, and the convexity of $\tilde{B}^i(p) \cap X^i$. Consider a sequence $p^v \in P$, $p^v \to p^0$, $y^0 \in \tilde{B}^i(p^0) \cap X^i$. To establish lower hemicontinuity we need to show that there is a sequence y^v, so that $y^v \in \tilde{B}^i(p^v) \cap X^i$ and $y^v \to y^0$. We will consider two cases depending on the cost of y^0 at price vector p^0.

CASE 1 $p^0 \cdot y^0 > 0$ and

$$p^0 \cdot y^0 > \min_{x \in X^i \cap \{y \mid y \in \mathbf{R}^N, c \geq |y|\}} p^0 \cdot x.$$

The strategy of proof in this case is to create the required sequence y^v in the following way. Find a minimum expenditure point, x^0 in $X^i \cap \{x \mid |x| \leq c\}$. We extend a ray from x^0 through y^0. We then take a sequence of points on the ray chosen to fulfill the budget constraint at p^v and to converge to y^0. That sequence is y^v. This construction is depicted in Figure 17.3.

For v large, we have

$$p^v \cdot y^0 > \min_{x \in X^i \cap \{y \mid y \in \mathbf{R}^N, c \geq |y|\}} p^0 \cdot x.$$

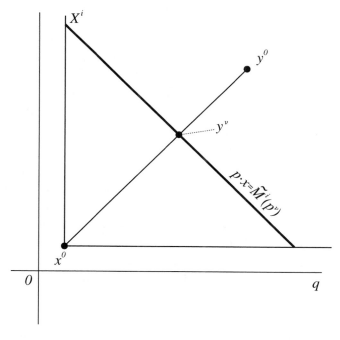

Fig. 17.3. Theorem 17.2 – continuity of the budget set showing the construction of y^v.

We choose x^0 as a cost-minimizing element of $X^i \cap \{x \mid |x| \le c\}$ at prices p^0. Let $x^0 \in X^i \cap \{x \mid |x| \le c\}$ and

$$p^0 \cdot x^0 = \min_{x \in X^i \cap \{y \mid y \in \mathbf{R}^N, c \ge |y|\}} p^0 \cdot x.$$

We now construct y^ν as a convex combination of x^0 and y^0, fulfilling budget constraint at p^ν.

$$\text{Let} \quad \alpha^\nu = \min \left[1, \frac{[\tilde{M}^i(p^\nu) - p^\nu \cdot x^0]}{p^\nu \cdot (y^0 - x^0)} \right],$$

$$y^\nu = \alpha^\nu y^0 + (1 - \alpha^\nu) x^0.$$

For ν large, α^ν is well defined. y^ν is chosen here so that it fulfills budget constraint and converges to y^0. We have $p^\nu \cdot y^\nu = p^\nu \cdot ((1 - \alpha^\nu)x^0 + \alpha^\nu y^0) \le \tilde{M}^i(p^\nu)$. $\alpha^\nu \to 1$ as ν becomes large. By convexity (CIII), $y^\nu \in X^i \cap \{x \mid |x| \le c\}$. For ν large, $p^\nu \cdot x^0 < p^\nu \cdot y^0$ and $p \cdot y^\nu \le \tilde{M}^i(p^\nu)$. So $y^\nu \in \tilde{B}^i(p^\nu) \cap X^i$ and $y^\nu \to y^0$. Hence the sequence y^ν fulfills the requirements of the sequence needed to demonstrate lower hemicontinuity.

CASE 2 $p^0 \cdot y^0 = 0 < \tilde{M}^i(p^0)$ or

$$p^0 \cdot y^0 = \min_{x \in X^i \cap \{y \mid y \in \mathbf{R}^N, c \ge |y|\}} p^0 \cdot x.$$

Once again we need to construct a sequence y^ν with the required convergence properties. In this case it is trivial. By continuity of the dot product, for large ν, $p^\nu \cdot y^0 < \tilde{M}^i(p^\nu)$. By hypothesis we have $y^0 \in \tilde{B}^i(p^0) \cap X^i$. Thus we can set $y^\nu = y^0$; then for ν large, we have $y^\nu \in \tilde{B}^i(p^\nu) \cap X^i$ and hence $y^\nu \to y^0$ trivially.

Cases 1 and 2 exhaust the possibilities. In each case we have demonstrated the presence of sequence y^ν, so that $y^\nu \in \tilde{B}^i(p^\nu) \cap X^i$ and $y^\nu \to y^0$. This is precisely what lower hemicontinuity of $\tilde{B}^i(p) \cap X^i$ requires. $\qquad$ QED

Theorem 17.2 demonstrates the continuity of the consumer's opportunity set $\tilde{B}^i(p) \cap X^i$ as a function of p. We are not really interested in $\tilde{B}^i(p) \cap X^i$ on its own. Rather, we are interested in the household demand behavior, $\tilde{D}^i(p)$. In order to apply the Kakutani Fixed-Point Theorem and find a general equilibrium we would like $\tilde{D}^i(p)$ to be upper hemicontinuous and convex valued. Upper hemicontinuity follows from Theorem 17.2 and the Maximum Theorem (Theorem 16.3). This is demonstrated in Theorem 17.3.

Theorem 17.3 *Assume P.II, P.III, C.I, C.III, C.V, and C.VIII. Then $\tilde{D}^i(p)$ is an upper hemicontinuous nonnull correspondence for all $p \in P$.*

Proof By Theorem 17.2 above, $\tilde{B}^i(p)$ is continuous with $\tilde{B}^i(p) \cap X^i$ nonempty, compact, continuous for all $p \in P$. By Theorem 5.1, $u^i(\cdot)$ is a continuous real-valued function. $\tilde{D}^i(p)$ is defined as the set of maximizers of $u^i(\cdot)$ on $\tilde{B}^i(p) \cap X^i$. Nonnullness follows since a continuous function achieves its maximum on a compact set. Upper hemicontinuity of $\tilde{D}^i(p)$ follows from the Maximum Theorem (Theorem 16.3). QED

Recall the weak convexity assumption

(C.VI) $x \succsim_i y$ *implies* $((1-\alpha)x + \alpha y) \succsim_i y$, *for* $0 \leq \alpha \leq 1$.

Under C.VI, we have convexity of $\tilde{D}^i(p)$. This is formalized as Theorem 17.4.

Theorem 17.4 *Assume P.II, P.III, C.I, C.III, C.V, C.VI, and C.VIII. Then $\tilde{B}^i(p)$ and $\tilde{D}^i(p)$ are convex valued.*

Proof Exercise 17.3.

Under weak monotonicity (C.IV) we can rely on households spending all of their available income subject to constraint. This is the implication of Lemmas 17.4 and 17.5 below.

Lemma 17.4 *Under C.IV, C.V, and C.VI, $x \in D^i(p)$ implies $p \cdot x = M^i(p)$.*

Proof Exercise 17.4.

Lemma 17.5 *Under C.IV and C.V, $x \in \tilde{D}^i(p)$ implies $p \cdot x \leq \tilde{M}^i(p)$. Further, if $p \cdot x < \tilde{M}^i(p)$, then $|x| = c$.*

Proof Exercise 17.5. The proof follows from weak monotonicity, C.IV. (See proof of Theorem 6.2.)

Lemma 17.6 *Assume C.I–C.VI, $i \in H$. Let $x' \succ_i x$, $0 < \alpha < 1$. Then $\alpha x' + (1-\alpha)x \succ_i x$.*

Proof By C.VI we have $\alpha x' + (1-\alpha)x \succsim_i x$ (weak preference). We must show that strict preference holds as well. By continuity (C.V) and monotonicity (C.IV), there is x'' so that $x''_k < x'_k$ for all $k = 1, 2, \ldots, N$, and $x'' \sim_i x$. Then we have $\alpha x'' + (1-\alpha)x \succsim_i x$. By convexity (C.VI) and by monotonicity (C.IV), $\alpha x' + (1-\alpha)x \succ_i \alpha x'' + (1-\alpha)x$ for all α in the specified range. But then, by transitivity, $\alpha x' + (1-\alpha)x \succ_i x$, as required. QED

Lemma 17.7 *Under P.II, P.III, C.I–C.VI, and C.VIII, $\tilde{D}^i(p)$ is upper hemicontinuous, convex, nonnull, and compact for all $p \in P$. If $x \in \tilde{D}^i(p)$ and x is attainable then $x \in D^i(p)$.*

Proof Upper hemicontinuity follows from Theorem 16.2. Convexity of $\tilde{D}^i(p)$ follows from weak convexity of preferences (C.VI) and convexity of $\tilde{B}^i(p)$ (Theorem 17.4).

If $x \in \tilde{D}^i(p)$ and x is attainable then $|x| < c$. We now wish to show that $x \in D^i(p)$. Suppose not. Then there is $x' \in B^i(p)$ so that $x' \succ_i x$. But then by Lemma 17.6, for all α, $0 < \alpha < 1$, $\alpha x + (1 - \alpha)x' \succ_i x$. For α sufficiently small, then $\alpha x + (1 - \alpha)x' \in \tilde{B}^i(p)$, but this is a contradiction since x is the optimizer of $\succsim_i$ in $\tilde{B}^i(p)$.   QED

17.4 The market economy

We now bring the two sides, households and firms, of the set-valued economic model together. The demand correspondence of the unrestricted model is defined as

$$D(p) = \sum_{i \in H} D^i(p).$$

For the artificially restricted model, the demand side is characterized as

$$\tilde{D}(p) = \sum_{i \in H} \tilde{D}^i(p).$$

The economy's resource endowment is

$$r = \sum_{i \in H} r^i.$$

The supply side of the unrestricted economy is characterized as

$$S(p) = \sum_{j \in F} S^j(p),$$

and for the artificially restricted economy we have

$$\tilde{S}(p) = \sum_{j \in F} \tilde{S}^j(p).$$

We can now summarize supply, demand, and endowment as an excess demand correspondence.

Definition *The excess demand correspondence at prices $p \in P$ is*
$$Z(p) = D(p) - S(p) - \{r\}.$$

The excess demand correspondence of the artificially restricted model is
$$\tilde{Z}(p) = \tilde{D}(p) - \tilde{S}(p) - \{r\}.$$

Having defined excess demand, we can now state and prove the Walras' Law, first for the unrestricted economy and then for the artificially restricted economy.

Theorem 17.5 (Walras' Law) *Assume C.IV and C.V. Suppose $Z(p)$ is well defined and let $z \in Z(p)$. Then $p \cdot z = 0$.*

Proof Let $z \in Z(p)$. Substituting into the definition of $Z(p)$, we have
$$p \cdot z = p \cdot \sum_{i \in H} x^i - p \cdot \sum_{j \in F} y^j - p \cdot \sum_{i \in H} r^i$$
$$\text{for some } x^i \in D^i(p), \; y^j \in S^j(p).$$

For each $i \in H$, by Lemma 17.4,
$$p \cdot x^i = M^i(p) = p \cdot r^i + \sum_{j \in F} \alpha^{ij} \pi^j(p)$$
$$= p \cdot r^i + \sum_{j \in F} \alpha^{ij} p \cdot y^j.$$

Now summing over $i \in H$, we get
$$\sum_{i \in H} p \cdot x^i = \sum_{i \in H} p \cdot r^i + \sum_{i \in H} \sum_{j \in F} \alpha^{ij} (p \cdot y^j).$$

Taking the vector p outside the sums and reversing the order of summation in the last term yields
$$p \cdot \sum_{i \in H} x^i = p \cdot \sum_{i \in H} r^i + p \cdot \sum_{j \in F} \sum_{i \in H} \alpha^{ij} y^j.$$

Recall that $\sum_{i \in H} \alpha^{ij} = 1$ for each j, and that $r = \sum_{i \in H} r^i$. We have then
$$p \cdot \sum_{i \in H} x^i = p \cdot r + p \cdot \sum_{j \in F} y^j.$$

That is, the value at market prices p of aggregate demand equals the value of endowment plus aggregate supply. Transposing the right-hand side to the left and recalling that $z = \sum_{i \in H} x^i - \sum_{j \in F} y^j - r$, we obtain
$$p \cdot \left[\sum_{i \in H} x^i - \sum_{j \in F} y^j - r \right] = p \cdot z = 0. \qquad \text{QED}$$

The Walras' Law tells us that at prices where supply, demand, profits, and income are well defined, planned aggregate expenditure equals planned income from profits and sales of endowment. Hence, the value of planned purchases equals the value of planned sales and the net value at market prices of excess demand is nil. Unfortunately, $Z(p)$ is not always well defined. This arises because Y^j and $B^i(p)$ may be unbounded and hence may not include well-defined maxima of $\pi^j(\cdot)$ or $u^i(\cdot)$, respectively. This shifts our focus to $\tilde{Z}(p)$, which we know to be well defined for all $p \in P$. We now establish the counterpart of the Walras' Law for $\tilde{Z}(p)$.

Theorem 17.6 (Weak Walras' Law) *Assume C.IV and C.V. Let* $z \in \tilde{Z}(p)$. *Then* $p \cdot z \le 0$. *Further, if* $p \cdot z < 0$ *then there is* $k = 1, 2, 3, \ldots, N$ *so that* $z_k > 0$.

Proof $p \cdot z = p \cdot \sum_{i \in H} x^i - p \cdot \sum_{j \in F} y^j - p \cdot \sum_{i \in H} r^i$, where $x^i \in \tilde{D}^i(p)$, $y^j \in \tilde{S}^j(p)$. For each $i \in H$,

$$p \cdot x^i \le \tilde{M}^i(p) = p \cdot r^i + \sum_{j \in F} \alpha^{ij} \tilde{\pi}^j(p)$$

$$= p \cdot r^i + \sum_{j \in F} \alpha^{ij}(p \cdot y^j),$$

and

$$\sum_{i \in H} p \cdot x^i \le \sum_{i \in H} p \cdot r^i + \sum_{i \in H} \sum_{j \in F} \alpha^{ij}(p \cdot y^j)$$

$$p \cdot \sum_{i \in H} x^i \le p \cdot \sum_{i \in H} r^i + p \cdot \sum_{j \in F} \sum_{i \in H} \alpha^{ij} y^j.$$

Note the changed order of summation in the last term. Recall that $\sum_{i \in H} \alpha^{ij} = 1$ for each j and that $r = \sum_{i \in H} r^i$. We have then

$$p \cdot \sum_{i \in H} x^i \le p \cdot r + p \cdot \sum_{j \in F} y^j.$$

Transposing the right-hand side to the left and recalling that $z = \sum_{i \in H} x^i - \sum_{j \in F} y^j - r$, we get

$$p \cdot \left[\sum_{i \in H} x^i - \sum_{j \in F} y^j - r \right] = p \cdot z \le 0.$$

The left-hand side in this expression is

$$\sum_{i \in H} [p \cdot x^i] - \sum_{i \in H} [\tilde{M}^i(p)].$$

If $p \cdot z < 0$ then for some $i \in H$, $p \cdot x^i < \tilde{M}^i(p)$. In that case, by Lemma 17.5, $|x^i| = c$ and hence x^i is not attainable. Unattainability implies $z_k > 0$ for some $k = 1, 2, \ldots, N$.   QED

Lemma 17.8 *Assume C.I–C.VI, C.VIII, and P.I–P.III. The range of $\tilde{Z}(p)$ is bounded. $\tilde{Z}(p)$ is upper hemicontinuous and convex valued.*

Proof $\tilde{Z}(p) = \sum_{i \in H} \tilde{D}^i(p) - \sum_{j \in F} \tilde{S}^j(p) - \{\sum_{i \in H} r^i\}$ is the finite sum of bounded sets and is therefore bounded. It is a finite sum of upper hemicontinuous convex correspondences and is hence convex and upper hemicontinuous.   QED

As an artificial construct to allow us to prove the existence of equilibrium in the market economy, we introduce an artificially restricted economy.

17.5 The artificially restricted economy

We will describe the *artificially restricted* economy by taking the production technology of each firm j to be $\tilde{Y}^j$ rather than Y^j, thus making the supply correspondence $\tilde{S}^j(p)$ rather than $S^j(p)$, and by taking the demand correspondence of each household i to be $\tilde{D}^i(p)$ rather than $D^i(p)$. In this special restricted case we will refer to the excess demand correspondence of the economy as $\tilde{Z}(p)$. By Theorem 17.1 and Lemma 17.8, the artificially restricted excess demand correspondence is well defined for all $p \in P$:

$$\tilde{Z} : P \to \mathbf{R}^N.$$

We use the artificially restricted economy above as a mathematical construct, which is convenient because supply, demand, and excess demand are everywhere well defined. The *unrestricted* economy is defined by Y^j, D^i, and Z. As demonstrated in Theorem 17.1 and Lemma 17.7, $Z(p)$ and $\tilde{Z}(p)$ will coincide for elements of $Z(p)$ corresponding to attainable points in $\tilde{S}^j(p)$ and $\tilde{D}^i(p)$. The set $\tilde{Z}(p)$ is nonempty for all $p \in P$, whereas $Z(p)$ may not be well defined (nonempty) for some elements of $p \in P$.

Recall the following properties of $\tilde{Z}(p)$:

(1) Weak Walras' Law (Theorem 17.6): Assuming C.IV and C.VI, we have $z \in \tilde{Z}(p)$ implies $p \cdot z \leq 0$. Further, if $p \cdot z < 0$ then there is $k = 1, 2, 3, \ldots, N$, so that $z_k > 0$.
(2) $\tilde{Z}(p)$ is well defined for all $p \in P$ and is everywhere upper hemicontinuous and convex valued, assuming C.I–C.VI and P.I–P.IV. This is Theorems 17.1 and 17.3 and Lemma 17.8.

We will use these properties to prove the existence of market clearing prices in the artificially restricted economy. We will then use Theorems 17.1 and 17.6 and Lemma 17.6 to show that the equilibrium of the artificially restricted economy is also an equilibrium of the unrestricted economy. To start the process of establishing the existence of an equilibrium for the artificially restricted economy, we need a price adjustment function. We plan to use the Kakutani Fixed-Point Theorem, and thus we hope to construct an upper hemicontinuous, convex-valued price adjustment correspondence.

Let $\rho(z) \equiv \{p^* \mid p^* \in P, p^* \cdot z$ maximizes $p \cdot z$ for all $p \in P\}$. $\rho(z)$ is the price adjustment correspondence. For each excess demand vector z, ρ chooses a price vector based on increasing the prices of goods in excess demand while reducing the prices of goods in excess supply. Choose positive real C so that $|\tilde{Z}(p)| < C$ for all $p \in P$. We know that C exists (by Lemma 17.8) since $\#F$ and $\#H$ are finite and each of the $\tilde{D}^i(p)$, $\tilde{S}^j(p)$ is chosen from a bounded set (the set of attainable allocations is bounded by Theorem 8.2). Then let $\Delta = \{x \mid x \in \mathbf{R}^N, |x| \leq C\}$. Note that Δ is compact and convex:

$$\rho : \Delta \to P$$

$$\tilde{Z} : P \to \Delta.$$

Lemma 17.9 $\rho(z)$ *is upper hemicontinuous for all* $z \in \Delta$; $\rho(z)$ *is convex and nonnull for all* $z \in \Delta$.

Proof Exercise 17.6.

17.6 Existence of competitive equilibrium

We are now ready to establish existence of competitive general equilibrium. We focus first on the artificially restricted economy and then extend our results to the unrestricted economy.

Definition $p^0 \in P$ *is said to be a competitive equilibrium price vector (of the unrestricted market economy) if there is* $z^0 \in Z(p^0)$ *so that* $z^0 \leq 0$ *(coordinatewise) and* $p_k^0 = 0$ *for k so that* $z_k^0 < 0$.

Theorem 17.7 *Let the economy fulfill C.I–C.VI, C.VIII, and P.I–P.IV. Then there is a competitive equilibrium* p^0 *for the economy.*

The strategy of proof is to create a grand upper hemicontinuous convex-valued mapping, $\Phi(\cdot)$, from $\Delta \times P$, the Cartesian product of (artificially restricted) excess demand space, Δ, with price space, P, into itself. The mapping takes prices and maps them into the corresponding excess demands and takes excess demands and maps them into corresponding prices. The mapping Φ will have a fixed point by (the corollary to) the Kakutani Fixed-Point Theorem. The fixed point of the price adjustment correspondence, $\rho(\cdot)$, will take place at a market equilibrium of the artificially restricted economy. We will then use Theorems 17.1 and 17.6 and Lemma 17.7 to show that the equilibrium of the artificially restricted economy is also an equilibrium of the original (unrestricted) economy. This follows because the equilibrium of the artificially restricted economy is attainable. Hence, at the artificially restricted economy's equilibrium prices, artificially restricted and unrestricted demands and supplies coincide.

Proof Let $(p, z) \in P \times \Delta$, $\Phi(p, z) \equiv \{(\bar{p}, \bar{z}) \mid \bar{p} \in \rho(z), \bar{z} \in \tilde{Z}(p)\}$. Then $\Phi : P \times \Delta \to P \times \Delta$. Φ is nonnull, upper hemicontinuous, and convex valued. $P \times \Delta$ is compact and convex. Then by Corollary 16.1 to the Kakutani Fixed-Point Theorem there is $(p^0, z^0) \in P \times \Delta$ so that (p^0, z^0) is a fixed point of Φ:

$$(p^0, z^0) \in \Phi(p^0, z^0),$$

$$p^0 \in \rho(z^0),$$

$$z^0 \in \tilde{Z}(p^0).$$

We will now demonstrate that (p^0, z^0) represents an equilibrium of the artificially restricted economy. For each $i \in H$, and for each $j \in F$, there is $x^{0i} \in \tilde{D}^i(p^0)$, $y^{0j} \in \tilde{S}^j(p^0)$, so that $x^0 = \sum_i x^{0i}$, $y^0 = \sum_j y^{0j}$, with $z^0 = x^0 - y^0 - r$, and by the Weak Walras' Law, $p^0 \cdot z^0 \leq 0$. But p^0 maximizes $p \cdot z^0$ for $p \in P$. This implies $z^0 \leq 0$, since if there were any positive coordinate in z^0 then the maximum value of $p \cdot z^0$ would be positive. Moreover, we have either (Case 1) $p^0 \cdot z^0 = 0$ (in which case it follows that $z^0 = 0$ or $z_k^0 < 0$ implies $p_k^0 = 0$) or (Case 2) $p^0 \cdot z^0 < 0$ (in which case the Weak Walras' Law implies $z_k^0 > 0$ some k). But in Case 2, max $p \cdot z^0$ would then be positive, which is a contradiction. Hence Case 2 cannot arise and we have $p^0 \cdot z^0 = 0$, with either $z^0 = 0$ or if for some k, $z_k^0 < 0$, then $p_k^0 = 0$. This establishes (p^0, z^0) as an equilibrium for the artificially restricted economy. Now we must demonstrate that it is an equilibrium for the unrestricted economy as well. We have

$$z^0 = x^0 - y^0 - r$$

or

$$x^0 - z^0 = y^0 + r.$$

Since $z^0 \leq 0$, $x^0 - z^0 \geq x^0 \geq 0$. Thus $y^0 + r \geq 0$. Therefore, y^0 is attainable; this implies, by Theorem 17.1, that $y^{0j} \in S^j(p^0)$ for all $j \in F$. Furthermore, since $y^0 + r \geq x^0$, x^0 is attainable. Hence, by Lemma 17.7, $x^{0i} \in D^i(p^0)$ for all $i \in H$. Thus we have $p^0 \in P$, $y^{0j} \in S^j(p^0)$, and $x^{0i} \in D^i(p^0)$, so that $\sum_{i \in H} x^{0i} - \sum_{j \in F} y^{0j} - \sum_{i \in H} r^i \leq 0$, with $p_k = 0$ for all k such that $z_k^0 < 0$. Hence (p^0, z^0) is an equilibrium for the unrestricted economy.   QED

Theorem 17.7 completes the treatment of the existence of equilibrium with set-valued demand and supply behavior. We have demonstrated that all of the results on continuity of demand and supply and existence of equilibrium demonstrated for continuous point-valued demand and supply have counterparts in upper hemicontinuous convex-valued demand and supply. The essential elements that carry over are continuity and convexity in both settings. Note that because the efficiency results of Chapter 12 nowhere depend on point valuedness of demand or supply they are immediately applicable to the correspondence-valued demand and supply behavior studied here in Chapter 17.

17.7 Bibliographic note

The use of set-valued supplies and demands in a general equilibrium model, allowing for flat segments in preferences and technologies, first appears in Arrow and Debreu (1954). It is thoroughly expounded in Debreu (1959).

Exercises

17.1   Prove Lemma 17.3 (homogeneity of degree 0): Assume P.I–P.IV. Let $\lambda > 0$, $p \in \mathbf{R}^N_+$. Then $\tilde{S}^j(\lambda p) = \tilde{S}^j(p)$ and $S^j(\lambda p) = S^j(p)$.

17.2   Prove part of Theorem 17.2: Assume P.II, P.III, C.I, C.III, and C.VIII. Then $\tilde{B}^i(p) \cap X^i$ is upper hemicontinuous for all $p \in P$.

17.3   Prove Theorem 17.4: Assume P.II, P.III, C.I, C.III, C.V, C.VI, and C.VIII. Then $\tilde{B}^i(p)$ and $\tilde{D}^i(p)$ are convex valued.

17.4   Prove Lemma 17.4: Under C.IV and C.V, $x \in D^i(p)$ implies $p \cdot x = M^i(p)$.

17.5   Prove Lemma 17.5: Under C.IV and C.V, if $x \in \tilde{D}^i(p)$ and $p \cdot x < \tilde{M}^i(p)$, then $|x| = c$. This result follows from weak monotonicity (C.IV). See the proof of Theorem 6.2.

17.6   Prove Lemma 17.9: $\rho(\cdot)$ is upper hemicontinuous throughout Δ; $\rho(z)$ is convex and nonnull for any $z \in \Delta$.

17.7   The Arrow Corner is a failure of lower hemicontinuity of the budget correspondence and of upper hemicontinuity of the demand correspondence. It occurs when some prices are zero and when income is just sufficient to achieve the boundary of the consumption set X^i (in a typical example, this will occur at a zero income where X^i is the nonnegative orthant). Consider the following example. Let $N = 2$, $X^i = \mathbf{R}^2_+$, and

$$p^\nu = (1 - 1/\nu, 1/\nu), \quad \nu = 1, 2, 3, \ldots.$$

Then we have $p^\nu \to p^0 = (1, 0)$. Let c (the bound on the size of the demand vector) be chosen so that $100 < c < \infty$. Let household i's endowment vector r^i equal $(0, 100)$, with sale of r^i being i's sole source of income. Then we have

$$\tilde{B}^i(p) = \{x \mid x = (x_1, x_2), |x| \le c, p \cdot x \le p \cdot r^i\}.$$

Let i's utility function be $u^i(x_1, x_2) = x_1 + x_2$ so that $\tilde{D}^i(p) = \{x' \mid x' \in \tilde{B}^i(p) \cap \mathbf{R}_+^2, x'$ maximizes $u^i(x)$ for all $x \in \tilde{B}^i(p) \cap \mathbf{R}_+^2\}$. Demonstrate the following points:

(i) Show that $(0, c) \in \tilde{B}^i(p^0)$.

(ii) Show that $x \in \tilde{B}^i(p^v)$, $x = (x_1, x_2)$, implies $x_2 \le 100$.

(iii) Show that $\tilde{D}^i(p^0) = \{(0, c)\}$

(iv) Show that $\tilde{B}^i(p)$ is not lower hemicontinuous at $p = p^0$.

(v) Show that $\tilde{D}^i(p)$ is not upper hemicontinuous at $p = p^0$.

Discuss this example with regard to the Maximum Theorem (Theorem 16.2).

Part H
Conclusion

We have covered a classic array of topics in this volume: formulation of the general equilibrium model, existence of general equilibrium, efficiency of general equilibrium, the core of a market economy, and futures and contingent commodity markets. It is time to take stock of the inquiries undertaken and results developed.

18

Summary and conclusion

18.1 Overview and summary

The ideas treated in this volume have focused on a single unifying idea as a framework for analyzing economic activity: the general equilibrium of a competitive market. General equilibrium – treating all markets and their interactions simultaneously – is thought here to be the appropriate model to decide whether there are well-defined solutions to the economic decision-making mechanism and whether they have efficiency properties making them desirable. This class of questions goes back well over two hundred years in scientific economics. The way we answer them here is the Arrow-Debreu version of the Walrasian economic model (Arrow and Debreu (1954), Arrow (1951)).

We have come to several principal conclusions:

(i) The models have well-defined solutions; equilibria exist. Sufficient conditions for this result are scarcity, continuity, and convexity on both the consumer and producer sides. This is true both in settings where demand and supply are characterized as point-valued functions and optimizing behavior is uniquely well defined (Existence of General Equilibrium Theorems 1.2, 7.1, and 11.1) and where they are characterized as set-valued mappings (Theorem 17.7) recognizing the multiplicity of equally profitable production plans a firm may have or the variety of equally satisfactory affordable consumption plans households may consider.

(ii) The Brouwer Fixed-Point Theorem, Kakutani Fixed-Point Theorem, or their equivalent are necessary to establish the existence of equilibrium result (Uzawa Equivalence Theorem 11.2).

(iii) General equilibrium allocations are Pareto efficient (First Fundamental Theorem of Welfare Economics, Theorem 12.1). The market ensures against the waste of scarce resources. This is a surprisingly robust result, depending on scarcity and continuity, but not requiring convexity.

(iv) Assuming convexity of tastes and technology, arbitrary Pareto efficient allo-

237

cations can be supported by prices; efficient allocations will be sustained as competitive equilibria subject to an initial redistribution of endowment (wealth). The market can provide the incentives for production and for the desired distribution of any technically feasible output if the income to support it is appropriately distributed (Second Fundamental Theorem of Welfare Economics, Theorem 12.2 and Corollary 12.1).

(v) In a large economy, the core, which constitutes the outcome of strategic bargaining, is a competitive equilibrium – the long-standing focus on competitive behavior as typical of large economies is sound (Core Convergence Theorem, Theorem 14.2).

(vi) We can interpret this family of results as applying across time and under uncertainty, subject to the availability of well-articulated markets for allocation over time and across uncertain events.

There it is in modern mathematical form – just what Adam Smith (1776) would have said. The competitive market can work to effectively decentralize efficient allocation decisions.

18.2 Bibliographic note

For a comment on the scope and interpretation of mathematical models see Debreu (1986). The surveys by Geanakoplos (1989) and McKenzie (1981) provide useful summaries and evaluations of the Arrow-Debreu general equilibrium model. There are excellent bibliographies in Debreu (1982) and Ellickson (1993).

Exercises

18.1   The style of analysis we have been using is known as "axiomatic," involving precisely stated assumptions, detailed modeling, and logically derived conclusions. What are the strengths and weaknesses of this approach?

18.2   External effects (e.g., air pollution, water pollution, annoyance due to neighboring noise, traffic congestion) occur in economic analysis when one firm or household's actions affect the tastes or technology of another through nonmarket means. That is, in an external effect, the interaction between two firms does not take the form of supply of output or demand for input going through the market (and hence showing up in price). It would be characterized rather as the shape of one firm's available technology set depending on the output or input level of another firm. Or it might be characterized as one firm's inputs (like clean air at a tourist resort) being nonmarketed but their availability being affected by the production decisions of another firm.

　　　　Does the Arrow-Debreu general equilibrium model (as presented in this volume) treat external effects? Explain your answer. How does the treatment of externalities (or lack of treatment) show up in the specification of the model?

18.3   Describe the significance of the following results:

(a) The Uzawa Equivalence Theorem, Theorem 11.2 of this volume. Does it have an implication for the importance of mathematics in economics?

(b) The Existence of General Equilibrium, Theorems 1.2, 7.1, 11.1, or 17.7.

(c) The First Fundamental Theorem of Welfare Economics, Theorem 12.1.

(d) The Second Fundamental Theorem of Welfare Economics, Theorem 12.2 and Corollary 12.1.

Bibliography

Anderson, R. (1978). "An elementary core equivalence theorem." *Econometrica*, **46**, 1483–1487.

Arrow, K. J. (1951). "An extension of the basic theorems of classical welfare economics." In *Proceedings of the Second Berkeley Symposium on Mathematical Statistics and Probability*, ed. J. Neyman, pp. 507–532. Berkeley: University of California Press.

Arrow, K. J. (1953). "Le role des valeurs boursieres pour la repartition la meilleure des risques." *Econometrie*, pp. 41–48. Paris: Centre National de la recherche scientifique.

Arrow, K. J. (1962). "Lectures on the theory of competitive equilibrium." Unpublished notes of lectures presented at Northwestern University.

Arrow, K. J. (1964). "The role of securities in the optimal allocation of risk-bearing." *Review of Economic Studies*, **31**, 91–96. English translation of Arrow (1953). [reprinted in Arrow (1970), pp. 121–133]

Arrow, K. J. (1965). *Aspects of the Theory of Risk-Bearing*. Helsinki: Academic Bookstore. Reprinted in Arrow (1970).

Arrow, K. J. (1968). "Economic equilibrium." In *International Encyclopedia of the Social Sciences*, **4**, 376–386. New York: Macmillan and the Free Press.

Arrow, K. J. (1970). *Essays in the Theory of Risk-Bearing*. Chicago: Markham; London: North-Holland.

Arrow, K. J. (1971). "The firm in general equilibrium theory." In *The Corporate Economy: Growth, Competition, and Innovative Potential*, ed. R. Marris and A. Wood, pp. 68–110. London: Macmillan; Cambridge, Mass.: Harvard University Press.

Arrow, K. J. (1974). "General economic equilibrium: purpose, analytic techniques, collective choice." *American Economic Review*, LXIV, **3**, 253–272.

Arrow, K. J. (1989). "Von Neumann and the existence theorem for general equilibrium." In *John von Neumann and Modern Economics*, ed. M. Dore, S. Chakravarty, and R. Goodwin. Oxford: Oxford University Press.

Arrow, K. J., H. D. Block, and L. Hurwicz (1959). "On the stability of the competitive equilibrium II." *Econometrica*, **27**, 82–109.

Arrow, K. J. and G. Debreu (1954). "Existence of equilibrium for a competitive economy." *Econometrica*, **22**, 265–290.

Arrow, K. J. and F. H. Hahn (1971). *General Competitive Analysis*. San Francisco and New York: Holden-Day.

Arrow, K. J. and L. Hurwicz (1958). "On the stability of the competitive equilibrium I." *Econometrica*, **26**, 522–552.

Arrow, K. J. and M. Intriligator, eds. (1981). *Handbook of Mathematical Economics*. New York: North-Holland.

Aumann, R. J. (1964). "Markets with a continuum of traders." *Econometrica*, **32**, 39–50.

Aumann, R. J. (1966). "Existence of competitive equilibria in markets with a continuum of traders." *Econometrica*, **34**, 1–17.

Balasko, Y. (1986). *Foundations of the Theory of General Equilibrium*. New York: Academic Press.

Bartle, R. G. (1976). *Elements of Real Analysis*, 2nd ed. New York: Wiley.

Bartle, R. G., and D. R. Sherbert (1992). *Introduction to Real Analysis*, 2nd ed. New York: Wiley.

Beckenbach, E. F., ed. (1964). *Applied Combinatorial Mathematics*. New York: Wiley.

Berge, C. (1959). *Espaces Topologiques*. Paris: Dunod. Translated as *Topological Spaces* (1963). New York: Macmillan.

Blaug, M. (1968). *Economic Theory in Retrospect*. Homewood, Ill.: Irwin.

Brown, D., G. Heal, M. Ali Khan, and R. Vohra, (1986). "On a general existence theorem for marginal cost pricing equilibria." *Journal of Economic Theory*, **38**, 111–19.

Burger, E. (1963), *Introduction to the Theory of Games*. Englewood Cliffs, N.J.: Prentice-Hall.

Cornwall, R. R. (1979). *Introduction to the Use of General Equilibrium Analysis*. London: North-Holland.

Cournot, A. A. (1838). *Recherches sur les principes mathematiques de la theorie des richesses*. Paris: Librairie des sciences politiques et sociales, M. Riviere & cie. Translated by Nathaniel T. Bacon (1897). *Researches into the Mathematical Principles of the Theory of Wealth*. New York: Macmillan.

Debreu, G. (1952). "A social equilibrium existence theorem." *Proceedings of the National Academy of Sciences*, **38**, 886–893.

Debreu, G. (1954a). "Representation of a preference ordering by a numerical function." In *Decision Processes*, ed. R. M. Thrall, C. H. Coombs, and R. L. Davis, Chap. XI, pp. 159–166. New York: Wiley; London: Chapman & Hall.

Debreu, G. (1954b). "Valuation equilibrium and Pareto optimum." *Proceedings of the National Academy of Sciences of the USA*, **40(7)**, 588–92.

Debreu, G. (1956). "Market equilibrium." *Proceedings of the National Academy of Sciences of the USA*, **42**, 876–878.

Debreu, G. (1959). *Theory of Value*. New York: Wiley.

Debreu, G. (1962). "New concepts and techniques for equilibrium analysis." *International Economic Review*, **3**, 257–273.

Debreu, G. (1970). "Economies with a finite set of equilibria." *Econometrica*, **38**, 387–392.

Debreu, G. (1974). "Excess demand functions." *Journal of Mathematical Economics*, **1**, 15–21.

Debreu, G. (1982). "Existence of competitive equilibrium." In Arrow and Intriligator (1981), **2**, pp. 697–743.

Debreu, G. (1983). *Mathematical Economics: Twenty Papers of Gerard Debreu*. Cambridge: Cambridge University Press.

Debreu, G. (1986). "Theoretic models: mathematical form and economic content." *Econometrica*, **54**, 1259–1270.

Debreu, G., ed. (1996). *General Equilibrium Theory*; series title: *International Library of Critical Writings in Economics*. Cheltenhann, UK and Brook Field, VT: Edward Elgar.

Debreu, G. and H. Scarf (1963). "A limit theorem on the core of an economy." *International Economic Review*, **4**, 235–246.

Dierker, E. (1974). *Topological Methods in Walrasian Economics*. Berlin, New York: Springer-Verlag.

Eatwell, J., M. Milgate, and P. Newman, eds. (1989). *The New Palgrave: General Equilibrium*. New York: Macmillan.

Edgeworth, F. Y. (1881). *Mathematical Psychics*. London: C. Kegan Paul.

Ellickson, B. (1993). *Competitive Equilibrium: Theory and Applications*. New York: Cambridge University Press.

Fenchel, W. (1950). *Convex Cones, Sets, and Functions*. Princeton University (hectographed).

Gale, D. (1955). "The law of supply and demand." *Mathematica Scandinavica*, **3**, 155–69.

Geanakoplos, J. (1989). "Arrow-Debreu model of general equilibrium." In Eatwell et al. (1989), pp. 43–61.

Geanakoplos, J. (1990). "An introduction to general equilibrium with incomplete asset markets." *Journal of Mathematical Economics*, **19**, 1–38.

Gillies, D. B. (1953). *Some theorems on n-person games*. Ph.D. thesis, Princeton University.

Green J. and W. P. Heller (1981). "Mathematical analysis and convexity." In Arrow and Intriligator (1981), **1**, pp. 15–52.

Grossman, S. and Hart, O. (1979). "A theory of competitive equilibrium in stock market economies." *Econometrica*, **47**, 293–329.

Guesnerie, R. (1975). "Pareto optimality in non-convex economies." *Econometrica*, **43**, 1–29.

Hahn, F. H. (1958). "Gross substitutes and the dynamic stability of general equilibrium." *Econometrica*, **26**, 169–170.

Hahn, F. H. (1961). Review of *Theory of Value. Journal of Political Economy*, **LXIX**, 204–205.

Hahn, F. H. (1962). "On the stability of pure exchange equilibrium." *International Economic Review*, **3**, 206–213.

Hahn, F. H. (1971). "Equilibrium with transaction costs," *Econometrica*, **39**, 417–439.

Hart, O. (1975). "On the optimality of equilibrium when the market structure is incomplete." *Journal of Economic Theory*, **11(3)**, 418–33.

Hicks, J. R. (1939). *Value and Capital*. Oxford: Clarendon Press.

Hildenbrand, W. (1970). "On economies with many agents." *Journal of Economic Theory*, **2**, 161–188.

Hildenbrand, W. (1974). *Core and Equilibria of a Large Economy*. Princeton: Princeton University Press.

Hildenbrand, W. (1989). "Cores." In Eatwell et al. (1989), **1**, pp. 666–670.

Hildenbrand, W. and A. Kirman (1976). *Introduction to Equilibrium Analysis*. New York: American Elsevier.

Hildenbrand, W. and A. Kirman (1988). *Equilibrium Analysis*. New York: North-Holland.

Hurwicz, L. (1959). "Optimality and informational efficiency in resource allocation processes." In *Mathematical Methods in the Social Sciences*, ed. K. J. Arrow, S. Karlin, and P. Suppes (1959). pp. 27–46. Stanford: Stanford University Press.

Ichiishi, T. (1983). *Game Theory for Economic Analysis*. New York: Academic Press.

Kakutani, S. (1941). "A generalization of Brouwer's fixed point theorem." *Duke Mathematical Journal*, **8**, 457–459.

Koopmans, T. C. (1957). *Three Essays on the State of Economic Science*. New York: McGraw-Hill.

Kuhn, H. and A. Tucker (1951). "Nonlinear programming." In *Proceedings of the Second Berkeley Symposium on Mathematical Statistics and Probability*, ed. J. Neyman, pp. 481–492. Berkeley: University of Califomia Press.

Lerner, A. (1944). *The Economics of Control*. New York: Macmillan.

Magill, M. and W. Shafer (1991). "Incomplete markets." In *Handbook of Mathematical Economics*, **IV**, ed. W. Hildenbrand and H. Sonnenschein, 1523–1614.

Marshall, A. (1890). *Principles of Economics*. London and New York: Macmillan.

Mas-Colell, A. (1985). *The Theory of General Economic Equilibrium: A Differential Approach*. Cambridge: Cambridge University Press.

Mas-Colell, A., M. Whinston, and J. Green (1995). *Microeconomic Theory*. New York: Oxford University Press.

McKenzie, L. W. (1954). "On equilibrium in Graham's model of world trade and other competitive systems." *Econometrica*, **22**, 147–61.

McKenzie, L. W. (1959). "On the existence of general equilibrium for a competitive market." *Econometrica*, **27**, 54–71.

McKenzie, L. W. (1981). "The classical theorem on existence of competitive equilibrium." *Econometrica*, **49**, 819–841.

Newman, P. (1965). *Theory of Exchange*. Englewood Cliffs, N.J.: Prentice Hall.

Newman, P., ed. (1968). *Readings in Mathematical Economics*. Baltimore: Johns Hopkins University Press.

Nicholson, W. (1995). *Microeconomic Theory: Basic Principles and Extensions*, 6th ed. Fort Worth: Dryden.

Nikaido, H. (1968). *Convex Structures and Economic Theory*. New York: Academic Press.

Radner, R. (1968). "Competitive equilibrium under uncertainty." *Econometrica*, **36**, 31–58.

Radner, R. (1989). "Uncertainty and general equilibrium." In Eatwell et al. (1989), pp. 305–323.

Rudin, W. (1976). *Principles of Mathematical Analysis*, 3rd ed. New York: McGraw-Hill.

Scarf, H. and T. Hansen (1973). *The Computation of Economic Equilibria*. New Haven: Yale University Press.

Schlesinger, K. (1933–34). "Uber die Produktionsgleichungen der oekonomischen Wertlehre," *Ergebnisse eines mathematischen Kolloquiums*, **6**, 10–11.

Shubik, M. (1959). "Edgeworth market games." In *Contributions to the Theory of Games,* IV, ed. A. W. Tucker and R. D. Luce, pp. 267–278. Princeton: Princeton University Press.

Smith, A. (1776). *An Inquiry into the Nature and Causes of the Wealth of Nations*. 2 vols, ed. R. H. Campbell, A. S. Skinner and W. B. Todd. Oxford: Clarendon Press, 1976.

Starr, R. M. (1969). "Quasi-equilibria in markets with non-convex preferences." *Econometrica*, **37**, 25–38.

Tompkins, C. B. (1964). "Sperner's Lemma and some extensions." In *Applied Combinatorial Mathematics*, ed. E. F. Beckenbach, Chap. 15. New York: Wiley. [Reprinted in *Readings in Mathematical Economics*, Vol. 1, ed. P. Newman, (1968).]

Uzawa, H. (1962). Walras' Existence Theorem and Brouwer's Fixed Point Theorem. *Economic Studies Quarterly*, **8**, 59–62.

Varian, H. (1992). *Microeconomic Analysis*, 3rd ed. New York: W. W. Norton.

von Neumann, J. (1937). "Uber ein Oekonomisches Gleichungssystem und eine Verallgemeinerung des Brouwerschen Fixpunktsatzes." *Ergebnisse eines Mathematischen Kolloquiums*, **8**, 73–83.

von Neumann, J. (1945). "A model of general economic equilibrium." *Review of Economic Studies*, **13**, 1–9. English translation of von Neumann (1937).

von Neumann, J. and O. Morgenstern (1944). *Theory of Games and Economic Behavior*. Princeton, N.J.: Princeton University Press.

Wald, A. (1934–35). "Uber die Produktionsgleichungen der Oekonomischen Wertlehre." *Ergebnisse eines Mathematischen Kolloquiums*, **7**, 1–6.

Wald, A. (1936). "Uber einige Gleichungssystem der mathematischen Okonomie." *Zeitschrift fiir Nationaloekonomie*, **7**, 637–70. Transl. by Otto Eckstein as "On some systems of equations of mathematical economics." *Econometrica*, **19(4)**, 368–403.

Wald, A. (1951). "On some systems of equations of mathematical economics." *Econometrica*, **19**, 368–403. English translation of Wald (1936).

Walras, L. (1874). *Elements d'Economie Politique Pure*. Lausanne: L. Corbaz. Transl. by William Jaffe as *Elements of Pure Economics*, Homewood, Ill.: Richard D. Irwin (1954).

Weintraub, E. R. (1983). "On the existence of competitive equilibrium: 1930–1954." *Journal of Economic Literature*, **XXI**, 1–39.

Index

Allais, Maurice, 8*n*
Anderson, R., 169
Arrow, Kenneth, 8–9, 38, 79, 88*n*, 92, 93, 95, 99, 104, 118, 125, 129, 138, 151, 169, 194, 232, 237
Arrow-Debreu contingent commodity markets, 185–190
Arrow securities markets, 190–193
Artificially bounded supply function, 115–118
Artificially restricted economy, 132, 215, 229–230
Attainable production plans, 78

Bargaining (*see* Core)
Bartle, R.G., 65
Berge, C., 213
Binary relation, 44–45
Blaug, M., 38
Blocking, 158–159, 163–164
Boiteux, Marcel, 8*n*
Bolzano-Weierstrass Theorem, 52, 53
Boundedness of attainable set, 112–115
Bounded production technology, 71–108
    and firms, 73–79
        attainable production plans, 78
        form of production technology, 74–75
        strictly convex production technology, 75–78
    and households, 80–95
        choice and boundedness of budget sets, 87–90
        construction of continuous utility function, 84–87
        demand behavior under strict convexity, 90–92
        structure of consumption sets and preferences, 80–84
    and market economy, 96–99
Bounded sets, 51
Bounding Hyperplane Theorem, 1, 63–65, 165, 166
Brouwer Fixed-Point Theorem, 1, 34, 35, 53, 57–63, 66, 101, 133, 135–138, 198, 209, 211, 212, 237
Budget sets:
    choice and boundedness, 87–90
    choice and unboundedness, 120–122
Burger, E., 58*n*, 66

Cardinality, 81
Cartels, 168–169
Cartesian product, 43–44, 207
Centralized allocation, 11–13
Chicago Board of Trade, 179, 181
Chicago Mercantile Exchange, 179
Closed sets, 50–51
Cluster (accumulation) point, 49–50
Coalitions, 158, 163–164
Commodities, 179–180, 185–186
Compact sets, 52
Comparability, 81
Competitive price-taking equilibrium (*see* Core)
Complementation (set subtraction), 43
Complete relations, 45
Connectedness, 52
Consumption decision, 11, 13
Consumption sets and preferences, 80–84
Contingent commodity markets, 175, 185–193
Continuity, assumption of, 82–83
Continuous functions, mathematical, 53–55
Continuous utility function, construction of, 84–87
Contract curve, 25–26, 29, 155, 157, 159
Convexity, 55–56
    of preferences, 83–84, 123
    strict, 75–78, 84, 90–92, 122–125, 197, 215
Core:
    of large economy, convergence of
        equal treatment, 163–165
        exercises, 170–173
        interpreting result, 168–169
        principal result, 165–168
        replication, 162–163
    of market economy
        bargaining and competition, 157–158
        competitive equilibrium in, 160–161
        exercises, 161
    of pure exchange economy, 158–160
Core Convergence Theorem, 238
Cornwall, R.R., 38, 169
Correspondences, 197, 201
    Cartesian product of, 207
    continuous, 206–207

247

Counter-cartels, 169
Cournot, Augustin, 7

Debreu, Gerard, 8–9, 65, 70, 79, 92, 93, 99, 104, 118,
    125, 129, 138, 151, 158, 161, 166, 169, 194,
    213, 232, 237, 238
Decentralization, 4, 6, 9
Decentralized allocation, 11, 13–20

Edgeworth, F.Y., 8, 20, 38, 159, 161
Edgeworth box, 1, 20–31, 143, 155
*Elements of Pure Economics (Elements d'Economie
    Politique Pure)* (Walras), 7
Elements of set, 42
Ellickson, B., 238
Equal treatment property, 163–165
Equation-counting approach, 7
Event tree, 185–187, 190
Excess demand, 31–37, 97–108, 127–129, (*see also*
    Market economy)
Exercises:
    concept and history of general equilibrium theory,
        38–40
    futures markets, 194–195
    general equilibrium of market economy, with
        excess demand function, 104–108, 232–233
    households, 93–95
    large economy, core convergence of, 170–173
    market economy, 99
        core, 161
    mathematics, 66–68, 213–214
    prices and commodities, 70
    production with bounded firm technology, 79
    unbounded production technology
        general equilibrium of market economy, 138–140
        households, 125
        market economy, 129–130
        theory of production, 119
    welfare economics, 151–154

Firms, 71–72
    and bounded production technology, 73–79
        attainable production plans, 78
        form of production technology, 74–75
        strictly convex production technology, 75–78
    and unbounded production technology, 111–119
        artificially bounded supply function, 115–118
        boundedness of attainable set, 112–115
First Fundamental Theorem of Welfare Economics,
    141, 144–146, 160, 237
Functions, mathematical, 45–46
Futures markets, 69, 175, 177, 193
    exercises, 194–195
    sequence economy model, 184
    time, 178–184

Geanakoplos, J., 238
General equilibrium theory:
    development of field, 3–6
    Edgeworth box, 1, 20–31
    excess demand function and, 31–37

exercises, 38–40
history of, 7–9
of market economy, with excess demand
    artificially restricted economy, 229–230
    exercises, 104–108, 232–233
    existence of competitive equilibrium, 230–232
    existence of equilibrium, 100–104
    households, 220–226
    production with convex production technology,
        216–220
    set-valued supply and demand, 215–216
of market economy, with unbounded production
    technology, 131–140
    artificially restricted economy, 132
    general equilibrium of unrestricted economy,
        133–135
    Uzawa Equivalence Theorem, 135–138
Robinson Crusoe economy, 1, 4, 9–20, 29–31
role of mathematics, 6–7
Gillies, D.B., 161
Green, J., 65

Hahn, F.H., 38, 88*n*, 93, 95, 169
Hansen, T., 66
Heller, W.P., 65
Hicks, J.R., 9, 70, 194
Hildenbrand, W., 65, 211
Households, 71–72
    and bounded production technology, 80–95
        choice and boundedness of budget sets, 87–90
        construction of continuous utility function, 84–87
        demand behavior under strict convexity, 90–92
        structure of consumption sets and preferences,
            80–84
    and contingent commodity markets, 188–190
    futures markets, 181–183
    set-valued supply and demand, 220–226
    and unbounded production technology, 120–125
        choice in unbounded budget set, 120–122
        demand behavior under strict convexity, 122–125

Ichiishi, T., 169
Indifference curves, 13, 21–23, 25, 29, 45
Intermediate Value Theorem, 18–19
Invisible hand, 7, 141, 146
Isoprofit line, 15–17

Jevons, W.S., 7
Jin-lung Lin, 138*n*

Kakutani, S., 213
Kakutani Fixed-Point Theorem, 198, 200, 209–213,
    215, 224, 230, 231, 237
Kirman, A., 65, 211
Knaster-Kuratowski-Mazurkeiwicz (KKM) Theorem,
    58, 62–63
Koopmans, T.C., 151

Lagrange, technique of, 25
Laissez-faire doctrine, 194
Large economy, core convergence of, 162–179

equal treatment, 163–165
exercises, 170–173
interpreting result, 168–169
principal result, 165–168
replication, 162–163
Lexicographic preferences, 82–83
Li Li, 101*n*, 133*n*
Logical inference, 41
Lower hemicontinuity (lower semicontinuity),
    204–206

Marginal rate of substitution, 22, 23, 25, 29–31, 33–34
Market economy:
    and bounded production technology, 96–99
    core
        bargaining and competition, 157–158
        competitive equilibrium in, 160–161
        exercises, 161
        of pure exchange economy, 158–160
    general equilibrium of, with excess demand
        artificially restricted economy, 229–230
        exercises, 104–108, 232–233
        existence of competitive equilibrium, 230–232
        existence of equilibrium, 100–104
        households, 220–226
        production with convex production technology,
            216–220
        set-valued supply and demand, 215–216
    general equilibrium of, with unbounded production
            technology, 131–140
        artificially restricted economy, 132
        general equilibrium of unrestricted economy,
            133–135
        Uzawa Equivalence Theorem, 135–138
    and unbounded production technology
        excess demand and Walras' Law, 127–129
        firms and households, 126
        household income, 127
        profits, 126–127
Market equilibrium, defined, 19
Marshall, Alfred, 7
Marx, Karl, 7
Mathematical induction, principle of, 59
Mathematical Psychics (Edgeworth), 8
Mathematics, 41–68
    Brouwer Fixed-Point Theorem, 1, 34, 35, 57–63, 66
    continuous functions, 53–55
    convexity, 55–56
    functions, 45–46
    point-to-set mappings, 201–214
        Cartesian product of correspondences, 207
        continuous correspondence, 206–207
        correspondences, 201
        exercises, 213–214
        Kakutani Fixed-Point Theorem, 198, 200,
            209–213
        lower hemicontinuity (lower semicontinuity),
            204–206
        Maximum Theorem, 207–209
        upper hemicontinuity (upper semicontinuity),
            198–204

quasi-orderings, 44–45
real *N*-dimensional Euclidean space, 46–53
role of, 6–7
separation theorems, 63–65
set theory, 41–44
Maximum Theorem, 207–209, 213, 224, 225
McKenzie, L.W., 8, 104, 238
Menger, Karl, 8
Mill, John Stuart, 7

Nested Intervals Theorem, 52–53
New York Commodities Exchange, 179
Newman, P., 38
Nikaido, H., 66
Nonatomic measure theory, 162
Nonnegativity of prices, 76*n*

Occupational choice, 88*n*
Open sets, 50, 51
Ordered pairs, 43

Pareto, Vilfredo, 12
Pareto efficiency, 12, 13, 17, 20, 24–26, 29, 31, 141,
    159, 189, 237
    and competitive equilibrium, 143–154
Partial equilibrium, 3–5, 7
Point-to-set mappings, 201–214
    Cartesian product of correspondences, 207
    continuous correspondence, 206–207
    correspondences, 201
    Kakutani Fixed-Point Theorem, 198, 200, 209–213
    lower hemicontinuity (lower semicontinuity),
        204–206
    Maximum Theorem, 207–209
    upper hemicontinuity (upper semicontinuity),
        198–204
Positivity of income, 89–90
Prices, 69–70
Price-taking, 10, 15, 16
Production decision, 11–13, 15
Production technology (*see* Bounded production
        technology; Unbounded production
        technology)
Pure exchange economy, core of, 158–160

Quasi-orderings, 44–45

Real analysis, 41
Real *n*-dimensional Euclidean space, 46–53
Reflexivity, 44, 81
Relative prices, 32
Replication in large economy, 162–163
Ricardo, David, 7
Robinson Crusoe economy, 1, 4, 9–20, 29–31, 78,
    143, 147
Roemer, John, 35*n*, 101*n*, 133*n*
Rudin, W., 65

Scarcity, 109, 112, 144
Scarf, H., 9, 66, 158, 161, 166, 169
Schlesinger, Karl, 8

Second Fundamental Theorem of Welfare Economics, 141, 146–151, 238
Separating Hyperplane Theorem, 1, 63, 65, 146–148
Separation theorems, 1, 63–65
Sequence economy model, 184
Set equality, 42
Set intersection, 42
Set theory, 41–44
Set union, 42
Set-valued supply and demand, 215–216, 220–226
Shapley-Folkman Theorem, 169
Sherbert, D.R., 65
Shubik, M., 161
Smith, Adam, 7, 141, 146, 151, 169, 238
Sperner's Lemma, 58–61
Starr, R.M., 169
State of the world, 185, 189, 190, 193
Strict convexity, 75–78, 84, 90–92, 122–125, 197, 215
Subsets, 42
Supply and demand functions (*see* Bounded production technology; Unbounded production technology)

Time, futures markets, 178–184
Tompkins, C.B., 58*n*, 66
Transitivity, 45, 81

Unbounded production technology, 109–140
  and firms, 111–119
    artificially bounded supply function, 115–118
    boundedness of attainable set, 112–115
  and households, 120–125
    choice in unbounded budget set, 120–122
    demand behavior under strict convexity, 122–125
  and market economy
    excess demand and Walras' Law, 127–129

firms and households, 126
household income, 127
profits, 126–127
Uncertainty, 175, 178, 179
  Arrow–Debreu contingent commodity markets, 185–190
  Arrow securities markets, 190–193
Unit simplex, 32–35
Unrestricted economy, general equilibrium of, 133–135
Upper bound of quasi-ordering, 45
Upper hemicontinuity (upper semicontinuity), 198–204, 216–218
Utility function, construction of continuous, 84–87
Uzawa, Hirofumi, 136*n*, 138
Uzawa Equivalence Theorem, 135–138, 237

Varian, H., 104

Wald, Abraham, 8
Walras, Leon, 7, 18*n*, 38, 101, 138
Walrasian Existence of Equilibrium Proposition (WEEP), 136–138
Walras' Law, 18, 19, 33–37, 71, 96–99, 103, 127–129, 178, 198, 227–228
Weak convexity, 215–226
Weak monotonicity, 81–82, 92
Weak Walras' Law, 98–99, 100–102, 132, 134–135, 228, 229, 231
Weintraub, E.R., 38
Welfare economics, 141–154
  exercises, 151–154
  First Fundamental Theorem of Welfare Economics, 141, 144–146
  Pareto efficiency, 143–144
  Second Fundamental Theorem of Welfare Economics, 141, 146–151